VOICES FOR LIFE

BOOKS BY DOM MORAES

PROSE:

Gone Away (1960)
My Son's Father (1968)
The Tempest Within (1970)
The People Time Forgot (1972)
A Matter of People (1974)

POETRY:

A Beginning (1957)
Poems (1960)
Collected Poems, 1955–1965 (1966)
John Nobody (1968)

TRANSLATION:

The Brass Serpent (translated from Hebrew, 1964)

VOICES FOR LIFE

Reflections on the Human Condition

EDITED BY

DOM MORAES

Published in Cooperation with the
United Nations Fund for Population Activities

PRAEGER PUBLISHERS
New York

The views expressed in this book are those of the contributors and do not necessarily reflect the policies or directions of the United Nations or any of its member states.

301.32
M827v
c.2

Published in the United States of America 1975
by Praeger Publishers
111 Fourth Avenue, New York, N.Y. 10003

Library of Congress Cataloging in Publication Data

Moraes, Dom F   1938-   comp.
  Voices for life.

  1.   Population—Addresses, essays, lectures.
  2.   Social values—Addresses, essays, lectures.
  I. Title.
  HB851.M765   1975   301.32   73-21452
  ISBN 0-275-19940-1
  ISBN 0-275-63470-1 (pbk.)

Printed in the United States of America

PREFACE

I am delighted to write the preface to this collection of essays from so many eminent hands. The contributors come from different countries and disparate disciplines, but they have in common with one another and with the United Nations Fund for Population Activities, a deep concern for the improvement of the human condition in our time.

To bring about this essential improvement is perhaps the most difficult of our tasks today. It is nevertheless possible, provided that we are conscious of all the factors involved. The problem, in the face of increasing populations, particularly in the Third World, is the mobilization and proper use of our resources in order to provide for increased numbers of people.

This problem, we know, is not confined to one country or one region. There are massive disparities in the quantity and value of the resources available in different parts of the world, as well as within individual countries. Some years ago development experts in their optimism looked forward to a future in which the resources of the world would supply a standard of living for most of its people on a level equal to that in the richer countries. Better knowledge of the extent of our resources, and, perhaps more important, of the effects of their exploitation on our environment, has brought about a change in our thinking. We now know that there must be a limit to the production and processing of raw materials, and consequently much more attention is being paid to the ways in which resources are used.

At present the greater part of the world's production goes to the benefit of a handful of countries in the industrialized world. In the future, however, the peoples of the less-developed nations may ask for a bigger share of the world's wealth, and eventually many of those people who now consume the bulk of the world's resources will have to learn to limit their demands according to a more just sense of priorities.

How is this minority to learn to limit their wants? One of the most important elements, I believe, is a restored sense of values. In their pursuit of the satisfactions that wealth can provide, some of the industrialized countries seem to have lost sight of the goal that impelled them to seek wealth in the first place. There is a growing sense that something is missing from a life that includes many of the things that the earth can provide but has lost the deeper satisfactions arising from a fundamentally sound relationship with the rest of nature.

So far, international assistance has been largely one way, in the form of transfers of technology, skills, and financial resources from the industrialized to the developing countries. The time has come for a mutually respectful and mutually advantageous two-way relationship.

People who live under conditions of scarcity in a limited but unspoiled environment are nevertheless rich in human values. For the sake of survival each man has to recognize that his fate is bound up with the fate of every other member of the community. In such circumstances sharing goes deeper than material things; there is an empathy, a deep sense of what is essential in the life of another. Despite, or perhaps because of, its material poverty the Third World continues to be wealthy in this dimension of human existence. Can the peoples of the industrialized countries relearn this sense of interdependence?

We live in a time when there is considerable uncertainty about the future shape of the international community, but all our efforts to correct the distortions of wealth among nations, contain population growth, and survive in a threatened biosphere will be meaningless if we cannot learn to overcome our acquisitiveness by reassessing our system of values. A limitation of material desires but an unlimited capacity to share human fulfillment is imperative, especially as we move into an era when no nation or group will be able to command a massive share of the world's resources as if by right.

It is fortunate for us that some voices, in developed as well as developing countries, are constantly reminding us of the basic values. A few of these voices are collected here. I feel that this book, conceived as part of the attempt in World Population Year to take stock of the human condition, will play an important part in conveying to the masses of people everywhere, as well as to the privileged, the dimensions of the questions that face us and the urgency of finding some answers. The opinions represented are not concerned exclusively with population issues but with individual views of human problems to which solutions must be found. The collection is not comprehensive, but it is wide enough, I believe, to stimulate others who think now about the future.

RAFAEL M. SALAS
Executive Director
U.N. Fund for
Population Activities

New York City
August 1974

ACKNOWLEDGMENTS

I would like to thank Rafael M. Salas, Executive Director of the U.N. Fund for Population Activities, and Tarzie V. Vittachi, Executive Secretary of World Population Year, for making this book possible. I would also like to thank my wife, Leela, for her assistance, which she has always given in many ways, and my secretary, Sabina Wenzel, for trying to keep my untidy mind and office tidy. Apart from all this, I would like to thank the various contributors for their work, time, and patience in writing these essays or being interviewed.

DOM MORAES

CONTENTS

Contents

DOM MORAES
An Introduction

Today we have come to a new point in time, to a day of dilemma.
This globe of metals and fire has whirled on its own axis, for
millions of years, in a wilderness of space. It has survived the
explosions of suns and swum away from the flying debris of the
stars. Under its own private sun, over chasms of time we cannot
start to fathom, the bacteria in its swampy seas turned into fish,
the fish crept ashore and turned to carnivorous apes, and the
carnivorous apes turned into men.

Earth must have seemed immense to our first ancestors, immense and inhospitable and unknown, with colossal imponderables
afloat in the cloudy canyons of the sky overhead, and fearful
enemies below. It cannot be an accident that the earliest religious
rituals we know of were concerned with the placation or appease-
ment of shadows and skydwelling beasts and stones. Their cele-
brants lived in times of perpetual anxiety and occasional terror.
But if the space overhead seemed infinite, the rough hide of the
earth, as it became more familiar, turned into a source of comfort. The earth was a full-blooded creature that could be fed
upon forever. Its shield of breathable air sustained life. Its resources seemed limitless, not only in terms of food and water but
of minerals, from which new implements, new weapons, and the
first civilizations came. Slowly the world opened up, empires
towered and shrank away, nations colonized each other, and the
resources and inventions that man was able to utilize increased
century by century. The Industrial Revolution took place in Western Europe, and in the first half of the nineteenth century the

world came to a milestone in its history. Its population reached a billion, a thousand million, for the first time.

Since mankind had been around for some millennia, this is perhaps surprising, but epidemics, famines, wars, and other common features of human life over these years had combined to prevent any very rapid increase in the number of people. The billion mark was reached in 1830, seven years before the accession of Queen Victoria to the British throne. The colonization of the American West was still under way. Hitherto unknown continents were being explored. New species of flora and fauna were being discovered. The world was charted now, and its limits known, but it seemed a huge world still and its resources illimitable.

A hundred years later, in 1930, the world had shrunk a little, as travel turned from a necessity into an industry designed to provide recreation. It had also shrunk a little because the population had doubled to 2 billion. But nobody, as yet, had any fears for the future, apart from the perennially human threat of war. The expected war came and went, and in 1960 the population of the earth stood at 3 billion. The last billion had only taken thirty years to arrive. Improved nutrition and medical techniques, some experts said, had increased the expectancy of life the world over, decreased infant mortality, and stopped epidemic diseases, thus contributing to the rise in population, but there was nothing to fear, the earth's resources were limitless, and man would soon be on his way to the moon.

Man has since been to the moon, and in 1975 the world population will touch the 4 billion mark. A thousand million people will have been added to the population in the last fifteen years. By the year 2100 there will be nearly 8 billion people alive. How alive they will be is the question that should now most concern us. As I said earlier, we have come to a new point in time. We cannot now think of the world as a large planet with infinite resources. It has proved to be a small planet, and its resources have proved to be finite. We have, concomitant with and relevant to the population crisis, other new crises: a food crisis, an energy crisis, a pollution crisis, indeed a crisis of everything. The crisis of conscience we have suffered from since 1945 has now been doubled in intensity, for it seems that we may yet destroy the world as we know it even without the assistance of politicians and nuclear physicists, and that the earth may become once more what it was for our remote ancestors: an area of fear.

Part of the fear, as some essays in this book suggest, is that some nations are terrified to share new wealth with others: the fear of *us* to help *them,* a fear that has been a condition of humanity always. I think it peculiar that today we confess we all share remote and barbaric ancestors with horrid habits, but we all think of each other as different races, and each race thinks that the other has horrid habits. Why is each nation *us*—why is every other nation *them?* Given the acceptance of our shared ancestors, why should we differentiate between *us* and our unfriends of other colors and cultures?

Unlike our remote ancestors whose viciousness toward each other was somehow natural and innocent, we could, if we wanted to, understand what has already happened to us, what is happening, and what may happen. The fact is that not many people find this possible. In the undeveloped nations the bulk of the population is too poor, underfed, and deprived to think of more than immediate necessities. In the developed nations a tradition of material prosperity has deprived the bulk of the population of the desire to think, or at least the desire to think of unpleasant facts. The politicians of the world now seem to believe that their duties are purely political. They appoint committees to deal with matters considered to be outside the realm of politics, such as the future of our children. Even the mass media are largely unconcerned. They look for material that is instantly communicable, the material of a day rather than the material of years, for the issues of the future are complex, and these issues are not hard news.

But despite all this voices still exist on our small planet that are voices for life. It was my purpose to collect the messages of some of these voices between the covers of this book, in the hope and trust that they would have their echoes for some years into the future.

The final contributions to this book did not fall neatly into personal and impersonal approaches. Mostly, they crossed and overlapped both. The landscape of the book opened up further with every new contribution. Eventually, it opened up to include interviews as well as essays. Certain people had not the time to write or wished to speak rather than to write. The spoken word and the written word differ, so the interviews ensured changes of angle and pace as well as approach.

I do not want to try to categorize or define the contributors to this book, who come from so many different disciplines and countries. There are some, mostly professional, writers, who are intensely personal in their approach. What these writers actually describe are minute areas of experience, refracted from those mirrors, their lives, which they always face. But, thus refracted, the light from these small areas is intensified till in some respects it illuminates the way in which not only one person, but all people, live.

Of the others—musicians and administrators, scientists, sociologists, architects, anthropologists, heads of state—some write from a viewpoint that is professional with personal overtones, or vice versa. Others write as pure professionals about the experience they have derived from the work that is their life.

But each contributor is essential to the book for a specific reason. Some of them have opinions in common. Mostly they differ from each other. What they share is a care for humanity, a care uncommon among most people in the world today, a delicate, a particular, a necessary care.

VOICES FOR LIFE

ARNOLD TOYNBEE

ARNOLD TOYNBEE, world-famous historian, born in 1889 in England, is himself part of history. Since 1955 he has been Professor Emeritus of International History at the University of London. Some of the best-known of his over fifty books includes: *The New Europe* (1916), *The Western Question in Greece and Turkey* (1922), *Greek Historical Thought* (1924), the 10-volume *A Study of History* (1934–61), *A Historian's Approach to Religion* (1956), *One World and India* (1960), *Some Problems of Greek History* (1969), *Surviving the Future* (1971).

Since man is one of the social species of living creatures, the quality of life depends partly on the conduct and the standards of each individual human being and partly on those of the society of which he is a member by birth or by adoption. Does my own performance satisfy me? Does my society's performance live up to my aspirations? Is my own performance and my society's performance satisfactory to me in the judgment of my conscience? These questions are intrinsic to the human condition, but for many human beings, for much of an individual's lifetime, these fundamental questions are latent. In 1974 the questions are presenting themselves importunately throughout the world.

Today, unhappily, mankind is as sharply divided as it has ever been: the poor from the rich, the "developing" from the "developed," adherents of "true faiths," old and new, from "unbelievers", fellow countrymen from foreigners. But transcending all these insulating differences—some ancient, some recent—there is a common concern with the problem of the quality of life. For those of us, a minority, who have been brought up in the Christian tradition, this concern finds expression in the words: "What shall

3

it profit a man if he shall gain the whole world and lose his own soul?" The Christian may have become an agnostic (my own case), but the traditional words still make their impact—and this with a force proportionate to the acuteness of this crisis in which all of us are now involved.

The gospel text comes home with especial force to a citizen of one of the ex-Christian developed countries. About four-fifths of the peoples of these rich countries—still only a minority of mankind—have now "gained the whole world." They have extricated themselves temporarily from the poverty that, till recently, has been almost universal, but they have purchased this ephemeral material gain at a high spiritual price. White-collar work at the computer, as well as blue-collar work in the assembly line, is not satisfying either our personal aspirations or our social conscience. We are trying to compensate for the unsatisfactoriness of the nature of modern work by exacting higher and higher payments. In fact, we are demanding a bit more than "the whole world"; we are demanding payment that exceeds the material value of the product of our work. Since there cannot be anything more than the whole, the attempt to obtain real value from this overdraft is doomed to disappointment. The payment of our excessive demands is being canceled inevitably by the depreciation of the purchasing power of the money with which we are insisting on being overpaid. A constant rise in wages, offset by a constant rise in prices, is frustrating and exasperating.

Moreover, the unjustly arbitrary redistribution of shares in the gross national product, which is one of the many evils of inflation, is causing bitter conflicts over the division of the cake. Every individual, and every set of individuals organized in cartels, trade unions, and other quasi-military formations for the furtherance of sectional interests, is now obsessed by the chronic struggle to maximize his or its own slice. But even the winners who succeed, for the moment, in increasing their real (as distinct from their merely monetary) incomes at their neighbors' expense do not find themselves satisfied by this dearly bought and invidious material success. "Man shall not live by bread alone." This gospel pronouncement may make a militant materialist bridle, but he will not be immune from feeling its power. He will not be, because his own daily experience will be demonstrating the cogency of these traditional words.

I am being asked what qualities in life, what factors in life, I myself, at the age of twenty, felt to be necessary for human beings in order to enable them to live a properly human life. At that age I shared my parents' feelings on these questions, and I admired their conduct. They practiced what they preached. At my present age—eighty-five—I still adhere to the standards that were transmitted to me by my parents and were adopted by me, as my own, when I was a child. I was twenty in 1909; my mother was born in 1859 and my father in 1861, so their standards were expressed in Victorian language that now "dates." But the standards themselves do not "date," so it seems to me: I believe that these standards still hold good; I believe that they are the right standards for human beings at all times and places. Some of my parents' prescriptions for applying these standards in practice are no longer practicable in 1974. At the age of twenty-five I was overtaken by World War I, and the changes in the human situation since August 1914 have been continuous. They are still increasing at an ever faster tempo, and, cumulatively, they are already enormous. But, for me, my inherited standards have not been submerged by the deluge.

The conditions that are needed for living a properly human life consist partly of obligations that the individual feels to be incumbent on himself and partly of requirements that he feels to be incumbent on society.

The first obligation in my inherited ethical code is that a human being who has the normal capacity for working must not be a parasite. As soon as a boy has completed his education, he must begin to earn his living. If and when he marries, he must earn a living for his family, including the provision for educating his children; meanwhile, he must save as much as he can to provide in advance for the support of himself and his wife, if and when they eventually reach an age at which they will no longer be capable of working. I was taught by my parents to disapprove of drones, both "idle rich" and "work-shy poor."

I believed, and I still believe, that a grown-up man who is not physically or mentally incapacitated ought to pay his way, but the second obligation that was impressed upon me by my parents was that money-making (money, in pounds sterling, was then still hard coin) ought not to be the paramount consideration in choosing one's profession. One ought to choose work that is intrinsically valuable for society and for the worker himself. If one chose to work primarily for filthy lucre, one would forfeit one's self-respect. One must choose a liberal profession—for instance, social work (my father was employed in that), or medicine (my grandfather had been a doctor), or teaching (my mother had earned her living by teaching before marriage had made her work as a housewife). Other professions that passed muster were the church, the law, the civil service, and the army (sappers or gunners only) and navy (before August 1914 people were insensitive to the criminality of the ancient institution of war). The diplomatic service and the infantry and cavalry were ruled out, because for officers, these were liberal professions that required the possession of private means. The other liberal professions in the foregoing list were poorly paid by comparison with business. But one must acquiesce in earning a comparatively low income, and one could be proud of this, if it was the deliberately accepted price of earning one's living by work that was intrinsically worthy.

"A gentleman does not go into business"—and business meant any profession in which the money that one could make by it was one's paramount reason for choosing it. An example of the kind of business that a gentleman ought to eschew was stockbroking. I smile at myself in 1974 for still taking some snobbish pleasure in the fact that only one of my ancestors was a businessman. My maternal grandfather had been a manufacturer of railway rolling stock, but my maternal grandmother had been a farmer's daughter and my paternal great-grandfather had been a farmer. How and when did my family become gentlefolk? Farmers did not rank as gentlemen, but they were considered to be respectable, and this with good reason, for farming has never been an entirely mercenary occupation. Of course, a farmer has to earn his living, like everyone else who is unwilling or unable to be a parasite, but farming was originally a religious service besides being an economic activity, and, though it is the source of bread, it is not incompatible with the precept that "thou shalt not live by bread alone." Farming still retains, from its origin in the Neolithic Age, an aura of liberality, in the sense of the disinterested pursuit of a profession for the sake of its intrinsic value.

The obligation to do work that has intrinsic value, even if this does not pay financially, was impressed on me by my knowledge of my father's career. He was a salaried employee of a philan- thropic institution, the Charity Organization Society, and workers in philanthropic undertakings are seldom highly paid, whether their employers are private subscribers or public authorities. This relatively low-paid work had not been my father's original pro- fession. My grandfather, the doctor, had died prematurely and unexpectedly, and, to meet the consequent family crisis, my father had been taken away from school and had been put into a business that dealt in tea. In this job he had been miserable. He could not bear the prospect of spending the rest of his working life on work that, in his eyes, had no intrinsic value, so that he would be working simply for the sake of the money that he was earning. One of his elder brothers had been a famous philanthropist, and his father, the doctor, though he had made money by his profes- sion, had worked for love on the urgently needed improvement of the provision for public health in Victorian Britain's mushroom growth of industrial cities. So my father had broken away from the marketing of tea and had dedicated himself to charity organ- ization. For me, this was a parental lesson driven home by my father's own example. The impression made on me by this lesson has been indelible.

Obligations imply reciprocal requirements. When I was twenty I felt the obligation that I still feel, to do work of intrinsic value and to treat the remuneration of my work as a necessary but sub- ordinate consideration. In return for this, I demanded rationality and justice from the social dispensation under which I should be living and working. Besides making this demand on society, I ex- pected that my demand would duly be honored, because I con- sidered that it was reasonable. I expected that, if I were well be- haved and hard working, I should be able to find work that would have value both for myself and for society—work of the standard that had been set for me by my father's example. I expected that my range of choice would be in accordance with my ability, whatever this might turn out to be. I also expected that, when I made provision for my old age, society would not cheat me. For instance, in 1913 I took out a life insurance policy, and at that date I did not suspect—and probably the insurance company, too, did not—that the pound sterling would not retain its 1913 value sixty-one years later. I also did not expect that, if I had invested my savings in consols or debentures, I should be cheated by society over this. In my parents' opinion investment in ordinary shares (euphemistically called equities nowadays) was anathema. It was a discreditable form of gambling. Invest in securities yielding a low fixed interest. Be content with this, and keep yourself free from the financial speculator's time-consuming sordid cares. Before August 1914 consols and debentures were "as safe as houses." In 1909 I did not suspect that houses would ever be bombed from the air. (Aviation was then still in its infancy.) And I did not expect that the purchasing power of fixed interest, and of the sum that would be payable to my executors from my life insurance policy, would dwindle, meanwhile, toward zero.

Nor did I expect that in 1915–16 about half the number of my contemporaries—not only my own compatriots and schoolfellows but young men of the same age in most other European countries, too—were going to be slaughtered in a world war and that I myself was going to survive only through the accident of being physically unfit for active military service. I did not expect that, while some men were being killed, other men would be profiteering from the munitions industry or that, while some people were being ruined by inflation, other people would be profiteering from that. In fact, I did not foresee that the apparently rational, just, and civilized world in which I had grown up was going to turn into the irrationally unjust, savage, and incalculable world that I have lived on to see and to suffer in 1974.

What is the explanation of this enormous disparity between the world of 1914–74 and the world of 1859–1913, that is to say, the Victorian world in which first my parents and then I myself grew up and that created for us our picture both of what life ought to be and what life actually was? Since August 1914 there have been two world wars and a number of local wars, and the distinction between combatant soldiers and noncombatant civilians has been abolished by the practice of bombing from the air. There have been several cases of cold-blooded genocide, and there is now a rising tide of robbery under arms and of kidnapping and hijacking. The motive for these private acts of violence has been maniacally political in some cases; in other cases it has been sordidly economic. I see around me inflation, profiteering, a decline in the standards of honesty and workmanship and industriousness. Worse still, I see not so much the righting of wrongs as the turning of tables. Yesterday's victim has become today's victimizer. The Jews, formerly oppressed in Europe, have become oppressors in the Middle East. Asian and African peoples, liberated from European colonial rule, are imposing their own rule on local fellow subjects of theirs who are weaker than they are. Trade unions that were created as defenses against social injustice are being used, where the balance of economic and political power has changed in their favor, as weapons in a capitalist-style cutthroat economic warfare. So long as these industrial workers were the weaker party, they condemned the barbaric regime of free economic enterprise; today they are as ardent advocates of it as the stockbrokers, the landlords, and the speculators in real estate.

What, then, is the explanation of all this? The answer, I now realize, is that the world of my childhood was a tiny oasis in the midst of a vast desert. Since 1914 the desert has swallowed the oasis up. I grew up in a small privileged class—the middle class—in a smaller privileged region—the northwestern fringe of Europe —during a short spell of peace that was not characteristic of Europe's bellicose history. My parents were poor, if their economic position was measured by the average standard of living of the English middle class of their generation, but they were rich by comparison with the least indigent of the contemporary British industrial or agricultural laborers, and they were still richer by comparison with all but an insignificant minority of Asians, Africans, Russians, and Latin Americans.

My father's profession ought to have given me an inkling of the poverty of the British industrial working class before 1906, when the liberals started to lay the foundations of the welfare state in Britain. The objective of the Charity Organization Society, which was my father's employer, was to rationalize the administration of the limited fund of private charity. Applications to the COS for aid were carefully examined with an eye to making sure that they were deserving cases, and, if it was found that an applicant did deserve help, care was also taken that he should not be aided in any way that might weaken his self-reliance. The contributors to the revenue of the COS were well-to-do, middle-class people, some of whom, no doubt, were living, at least partly, on unearned income. I suppose it did not occur to them that this might weaken their own self-reliance. They were public-spirited, and they had a social conscience, but for the COS it was axiomatic that the Poor Law Act of 1834 had set a permanent limit to the provision of relief for poverty out of public funds. A radical redistribution of wealth through the provision of social services gratis and through increases in income tax and in estate duty would probably have seemed to them not only impracticable but unethical. Unearned income, if transferred from the rich to the poor, would have been expected by the COS to have a demoralizing effect.

The Liberals disagreed. They held that the provision of social services such as sick pay and old-age pensions would ease the hardship and would diminish the injustice that had been suffered by the poor without weakening their self-reliance or taking the edge off their industriousness. I myself became a Liberal and have continued to be one, but in 1974 it looks to me as if experience indicates that the harsh COS doctrine that was challenged by the Liberals in 1906 was more realistic than the expectations of the makers of the welfare state. Self-reliance is truly valuable, and to get something for nothing may really have a demoralizing effect. My parents applied the COS doctrine to themselves. They would have lost their self-respect if they had not earned their living so long as they were capable of earning it and if, meanwhile, they had not made savings to provide for their old age. Not to do this would have seemed to them irresponsible and unworthy—excusable for children, but not for grown-up people.

I ought, by the time I was twenty years old, to have had more idea of the pros and cons of both laissez-faire and paternalism. I ought to have perceived the weak points in both policies and the difficulty of finding a golden mean between them. I ought also not to have been taken aback by the outbreak of a world war in August 1914. This had had a local overture in the Balkan wars of 1912–13, and, though there had been no war in Europe between 1878 and 1912, I was old enough to have been aware of five wars, outside Europe, between 1894 and 1904–05. In two of these five my own country had been a belligerent, but I had not realized, at the time, that Britain's role in the Boer War had been discreditable.

The carnage and devastation caused by war, and the wickedness of an institution that inflicted these evils, were obscured, for boys of my generation, by our passion for playing with toy soldiers. We were avid collectors of these brightly painted figurines and enjoyed setting them up in orderly formations. This turned war into a nursery game for boys of that generation. It hindered us from recognizing what war is like in reality.

I was not unaware of genocide. At least one refugee from the massacre of Armenians in Turkey in 1896 reached London and applied to the COS for relief, but genocide, like war, was not yet a reality for me.

Thus, I already had evidence, in my childhood, that there were blemishes in the Victorian middle-class oasis in which I was growing up and that there were still worse blemishes in the vast desert beyond this oasis's narrow bounds in space and time. I do still adhere to my parents' vision of what life ought to be. I also now recognize the extent of the disparity between the human situation today and my parents' ideals. This disparity existed already, without my having yet perceived it, in my parents' relatively fortunate generation—and this in the Victorian, British, middle-class oasis, as well as in the great desert in which British industrial workers and Asian and African natives were marooned. Has the disparity between ideals and reality grown greater in the course of the last sixty-five years? Can anything be done to reduce this distressing disparity? If it is remediable, who can provide and apply the cure?

The present evils will be difficult to cure, because they have a long past history. They can be traced back to the outbreak of the Industrial Revolution in Britain two centuries ago. This was not only a technological revolution, it was an ethical one too, and the ethical revolution is, so it seems to me, the principal cause of the world's present troubles.

The technological revolution gave temporary wealth to a minority of mankind at the cost of threatening all mankind with permanent future poverty. Modern technology, applied to industry and to transportation, has consumed the planet's irreplaceable natural resources on a scale and at a rate that are unprecedented. We can now foresee that some of those irreplaceable resources on which we have become most dependent are going to be exhausted within the lifetime of people who are already alive. Modern technology, applied to medicine, has reduced the rate of premature deaths drastically, and this beneficent achievement has caused a population explosion in countries in which the people have not yet limited their birth rate to match. A world with an exploding human population and a dwindling reserve of irreplaceable yet indispensable natural resources is heading for a catastrophe. If the present generation does not voluntarily reduce both its birth rate and its expectation of a constantly rising standard of living, measured in terms of material wealth, nature will intervene to bring man back into equilibrium with herself by means of famine, pestilence, and fratricidal war.

The politicians can help the people by telling them the disagreeable truth and by prescribing the unpalatable remedies for mankind's present plight. But a doctrine that was propounded at the time of the eighteenth-century technological revolution is going to make the politicians' task very difficult. This doctrine is that the pursuit of private interests, both individual and collective, is the best recipe for public welfare. The falsity of this doctrine has now been demonstrated by two centuries of history, but people are clinging to it, and they will be reluctant to abandon it, because it whitewashes greed, and greed is innate in every living creature.

If mankind is to salvage itself, it must try to return to the state of relative innocence in which it was living before the outbreak of the eighteenth-century ethical and technological revolution in the West. In order to execute this difficult maneuver, it will have to look for inspiration, guidance, and example either in the preindustrial West or in some non-Western region in which the preindustrial way of life is still a going concern. For a Western leader we must look farther back in time than Adam Smith's generation, to John Wesley, or farther back still, to Saint Francis of Assisi. If we want a leader who is nearer to ourselves in date, we must call up Gandhi from India or Mao from China.

In what parts of the world today are people least dissatisfied with the quality of the life that they are leading? In both India and China the majority of the population still consists of peasants who are living and working in much the same way as their ancestors in the Neolithic Age. Present-day Indian peasants are as poor as Saint Franc's was, and their poverty, unlike his, is not voluntary. But most Indian peasants seem not to be acquisitive-minded, so it is probable that they are happier than their richer Western and Japanese and Russian contemporaries who are earning much larger real incomes as miners or locomotive drivers or factory workers. However, the Indian peasant's resignation to his age-old poverty is a passive form of contentment. The Chinese form seems to be more active and more positive. Under the present regime the Chinese people seem to be finding satisfaction in the quality of their way of life. They seem to be feeling something like what my father felt when he broke away from his job in the tea-selling business in England and took service with the Charity Organization Society.

The Chinese people's present exhilaration would be precarious if it depended solely on the prospects of China's present regime. This regime is still in its early days; within a quarter of a century it has been subjected to changes that are bewildering to non-Chinese observers. Its moving spirit, Chairman Mao, cannot now be far from the end of his active career, and the outlook for Maoism without Mao is unpredictable. Chinese history, however, did not begin with Mao's coming into power, and the Chinese people's spirit, which has apparently been so responsive to Chairman Mao's lead, has been formed by indigenous Chinese philosophies that are far older than Mao's Sinified version of Marxism. Under the present regime Confucius is in disgrace; he is condemned for having preached an authoritarian doctrine. It is true that the way of life that Confucius commended was hierarchical, not egalitarian, but, on his hierarchical lines, he did stand for the sanctity of social obligations, and he called upon his fellow human beings to shoulder these obligations, not reluctantly, but with a pious zeal. For more than twenty-one centuries Confucianism was China's official philosophy; in the course of that eon the Confucian attitude to life became the Chinese people's spiritual heritage, and, though the present regime has repudiated Confucius, Mao owes to Confucius the alacrity with which the Chinese people have responded to Mao's appeal.

The Confucian inculcation of the duty of sociality is, in fact, the antithesis of the paradoxical eighteenth-century Western doctrine that selfishness is socially beneficial, and the Confucian antidote is what is needed in a world in which Adam Smith's philosophy has worked such havoc. Moreover, Confucianism has a complement in Taoism, the other major philosophy that took shape in China in the last millennium B.C. Taoism reinforces Confucianism in standing for moderation, but it redresses Confucianism's bias toward discipline by laying emphasis on the virtue of spontaneity. It deprecates acquisitiveness—the industrialized people's characteristic vice—with an Indian-like sincerity. This twofold Chinese spiritual heritage gives good grounds for hoping that China may recapture for mankind the quality of life that has been lost in countries that have undergone the Industrial Revolution.

China still has a freedom of maneuver that the fully industrialized countries have lost. The economic basis of China's life is still agriculture—an activity in which man remains in harmony with Mother Earth. It is open to China to supplement her own traditional way of life, which is also the traditional way of the rest of mankind, by grafting on it selected elements of the civilization of the modern West. China is free to pick and choose. She need not burden herself with those elements of industrialism that have made life in the industrialized countries lose its savor.

Countries that have plunged into industrialization up to the neck have a less promising future. Evidently, it is going to be more difficult to de-industrialize a country than to refrain from putting it through the industrial mill. We may guess that, in the new chapter of mankind's history that is now opening, the intensively industrialized countries—the United States, Japan, Europe, the Soviet Union—will be preoccupied with agonizing domestic problems and that they may have little attention and energy to spare for attempting to maintain their recent ascendancy over the rest of the world. This might be painful for these countries, but it would not be a tragedy for mankind. What mankind needs is a restoration of the quality of life that the industrialized countries have forfeited. If the Chinese people can perform this service for their fellow human beings, China, which led Eastern Asia, that is to say, nearly half the world, from Confucius's generation until the Anglo-Chinese Opium War of 1839–42, is likely to be accepted by the world as its leader in a postindustrial age of restabilization.

JIDDU KRISHNAMURTI

An Interview

JIDDU KRISHNAMURTI, philosopher, was born in South India in 1895 and educated in England. Hailed early in life as a great spiritual leader, he rejected that adulation and instead devoted himself to counseling and lecturing throughout Europe, Asia, and the United States. Among his publications are: *Education and the Significance of Life* (1953), *Think on These Things* (1964), *Commentaries on Living* (1965), *Life Ahead* (1967), *First and Last Freedom* (1968), *The Awakening of Intelligence* (1973).

MORAES: The poet W. H. Auden once said we must love one another or die. What do you think of that as a statement?

KRISHNAMURTI: It sounds right, but actually love cannot exist in that sense because there are nationalistic groups, religious groups, sectarian groups, class divisions that obviously prevent affection, a sense of unity, a sense of human relationship. Unless these things work, I don't see how we can really love one another.

MORAES: Auden said we must love one another or *die*. Do you agree with the second part of his line?

KRISHNAMURTI: Well, obviously we are destroying ourselves. We have nearly destroyed nature now; we have destroyed certain species of animals; we are destroying the earth with pollution. We are dying.

MORAES: Why do you think we are dying? Because we did not love one another?

KRISHNAMURTI: Not only that, I think there are much deeper reasons. First of all, we are colossally selfish. We are dying because, especially in the East, tradition throttles people. They are everlastingly quoting the authorities, the authority of the Zen, the authority of the Upanishads and the Gita, or accepting various scriptures—Christian, Hindu, Moslem, etc. None of these traditions opens the door; they block it rather. And Western countries, not having such deep traditions as these, want to create their own. They feel they must have traditions—especially the United States.

Tradition is really a betrayal. You must know the semantic meaning of the word, which also means betrayal. So we are dying because of tradition, and we are dying because people accept authority—religious authority, the psychological authority of philosophers and psychologists, or any local authority—a priest, a guru, and so on. That's one of the reasons. The authority makes you conform, makes you imitate others, so human beings are becoming, if I may say so, secondhand people. Obviously, the division of nationalities and all that is creating the causes of death —the degeneration and the decay of the human mind.

MORAES: Sir, in the West now there are large number of young people who are going to the East to find an example. What do you think of this?

KRISHNAMURTI: I have seen strange sights in India when hippies go there—extraordinary sights. I think they are going there perhaps firstly because it is cheaper to live there, then for romantic reasons. Then there is the idea that you will find enlightenment there; also because there is more freedom. You can put on rags and you are respected; you are not kicked around; you are welcomed; various temples feed you. I have met thousands of young hippies. They come to my discussions. They are in the traffic of drugs. I have seen a girl—the daughter of a very famous author. Now she has become a Tibetan nun. She had a son. She left her husband and took the son with her. When I met her next I asked, "Where is he?" And she said very casually, "I left him with some of the hippies in the North." I said, "What!" She said, "In perfect hands." Then I saw her again last year and asked her where he was, and she said, "He has become a Tibetan Lama." A boy of seven! I said, "Is it not rather terrible what you are doing?"

She said, "No. This is what we want." I have seen all this. They want a kind of life that is not the Western life. Some I have noticed have become gurus. As your father * used to say, he was allergic to gurus.

MORAES: Are *you*?

KRISHNAMURTI: I am very much opposed to the whole system of gurus and all that, because I think they are part of this dreadful degenerating process of tradition—carrying on and on and on, repeating the Gita, repeating the Upanishads—not understanding what it all means.

MORAES: In order to stop this process of degeneration or whatever, how many of the old values do you think we should retain? How many do you think we should discard? Do you think we should completely discard all values and start from scratch?

KRISHNAMURTI: Values in terms of quality or quantity?

MORAES: Quality.

KRISHNAMURTI: Quality—personally, I have not read the Gita and the Upanishads or any of the ancient scriptures of India or Europe or the Arab world, because somehow they bore me. I have read the Bible for its language, which is very simple. I like that very much. I have not read the others, though being a Brahmin one is brought up in tradition always. But tradition has never entered my consciousness; it has never conditioned me. If we understand the meaning of the word "tradition," it is handing down betrayal and all the symbolic process that goes on semantically in that word. The rituals of religion have no meaning really either in Sanskrit or Latin or Italian or Greek; they have really no meaning. They might have had when they began, but now they have no meaning at all. If you take all their symbols, which need interpretation and examining, if you take certain mantras from Hindu scripture when they are made common, the gurus paralyze the meaning—at thirty-five dollars a mantra. Everybody meditates, as they call it now, in this absurd kind of meditation that is

* The late Frank Moraes, a famous Indian newspaper editor.

going on in this country. And if we mean by tradition the continuation of knowledge, as scientific knowledge, as biological knowledge, it is usually based on facts and accumulated by the mind that is capable of examining facts. You can't remove knowledge from the whole world, but when knowledge is used as a tradition, as an authority to make people obey, conform, I think that is why the human mind is becoming so mechanical.

MORAES: But, sir, is this not what the young people of the West are trying to do? In a sense, are they not rebelling against their traditions?

KRISHNAMURTI: It is not action but reaction; it is rebellion without meaning, without depth. In California, in England, wherever I go, I don't know why, but I seem to attract dozens and dozens not only of the fairly intelligent, the fairly obvious audience, but also of the drugged people, the neurotics, all kinds of people. This is a reaction, this is a romantic idealization of man caught in a prison. I think one reason is that in the West the good life—*i.e.,* money, plenty of entertainment, the pursuit of sensation, the pursuit of pleasure, drink, sex—though intellectually people may be bright and clever, is a very shallow life. I think a great many of the people in the world, in the United States, in India, too, are brilliant intellectually; you get the professors, the writers, the intellectuals living this kind of life. I am not condemning them. But it is a superficial life, and because it is a superficial life many Westerners are rushing to the East, to various gurus in India, to find depth.

MORAES: You mean they are rushing from one superficial life to another?

KRISHNAMURTI: To another superficial life.

MORAES: Sir, when you were a child in what way did you perceive human beings as living—both externally and internally, within themselves?

KRISHNAMURTI: I don't remember. I was much too vague. When the Theosophists picked us [he and his brother Nitya] up, Dr. [Annie] Besant considered that I was very ill, very thin, emaciated. They thought I was not going to pull through. So, in my childhood there was a certain vacancy, a certain sense of absence. Much later did people found a big organization around me, and I went through all that. Then, only much later I began to see outwardly and inwardly. Probably in my childhood I did not articulate as clearly as now, if I can articulate even now, that is. I felt we were all caught in a trap—the trap of civilized man, the trap of sophisticated man, the so-called religious trap, the economic trap—and there was no way out through thought. Thought was not going to help man or free man from sorrow or free man from his egotism, free man from his idiocies. All the rituals and all the religious thought were not the way out. Thought has created the outside horrors.

MORAES: In what way do you think thought has created circumstances, the physical circumstances?

KRISHNAMURTI: Physical, outer in the sense of the political, religious, the whole environmental structure, nature—thought creates an opposition to that. The inner, the me, and the not me. Me and they: this division cannot be transcended or broken up or finished through any movement of thought, however clever, however intelligent, however rational, however logical.

MORAES: Do you think that people develop as they grow older, or do you think their minds remain the same, only receiving different impressions?

KRISHNAMURTI: Don't you think most minds develop up to the age of thirty? Because up to the age of thirty, or perhaps a little more, they are enthusiastic, inquisitive, they are eager to find out, they are not frightened too much of society or of themselves. They are not too concerned with their own security till marriage and all that begins. Up to that age they are more pliable, more uncertain, somewhat more discontented, more unhappy, and looking. After that they seem to settle down.

MORAES: How about the mass of human beings? Do you think they can develop as people toward being something different from what they are?

KRISHNAMURTI: I wonder what you mean by the word "mass"?

MORAES: I mean everybody who lives in the world.

KRISHNAMURTI: They are made up of individuals, too. So, is the individual different from the mass? I am just asking, not saying.

MORAES: I suppose every individual is different from every other.

KRISHNAMURTI: Again we have to find out what we mean by the word "individual."

MORAES: One man in his own body.

KRISHNAMURTI: He may think he is an individual. I might think I am different from you, from somebody else, but actually am I different? I have my problems, as you have. I have my idiocies, my idiosyncracies, my battles, my sorrows as ten thousand people have. Only the mind is slightly varied, varied slightly, colored slightly, more slightly or less—but it is a universal misery. I think I am different because I have a different name, a different nose, a different approach, my appetites might be strong or less strong. Yet am I really an individual at all? Or is it a cultural, social, educational thing that has created my need? What individual really means, doesn't it, is one who is not divided in himself individually? But human beings are *so* frightened they are not interested in that. Therefore, each one is like a million people everywhere else.

MORAES: Now, at this moment, everything is coming to us in terms of crises—fuel crisis, energy crisis, food crisis, population crisis. Everything is a crisis. Why do you think this has happened, and what do you think is going to happen about it?

KRISHNAMURTI: What is a crisis? A challenge.

MORAES: A crisis is a challenge, but surely a crisis is also when a point of despair is reached.

KRISHNAMURTI: What does that mean? There is an energy crisis, a population crisis, a pollution crisis, a starvation crisis, the haves and have-nots, you know, all that business. So what is a crisis? Is it the result of our stupidity—national, religious, economic stupidity—or is it self-generated?

MORAES: Self-generated by the individual?

KRISHNAMURTI: By the mass, by the greed of people. I do not know if you saw the other day on the television a baby seal being killed. A man comes along and kills it with a cudgel. Do you not feel that—*a baby seal?* That is what is going on all through the world. I think this crisis, the multiplication of crises, is our product and not a product of divinity or of some mysterious chance. We have made it ourselves, and it will continue all the time till we say, "For God's sake, let us stop it"—that is the way we are living.

MORAES: Sir, it has frequently crossed my mind that people have always needed some idea of omnipotence, of God or something, and in place of God, they have substituted governments.

KRISHNAMURTI: You were asking about government as a substitute for God. What an idea! Ha, ha! I think it was Lenin or the communists who talked of the withering away of the state. This withering can only exist when man is *really* moral, is *really* responsible in the deep sense of that word, is *really concerned* with his neighbor, whether he is next door or ten thousand miles away. As long as that does not exist, governments must go on whether they become the substitute for God or not. It is a lovely idea. Probably they will, because man is becoming more and more so-called rational, more and more "humanistic," more and more mechanistic in his mind. Probably the idea of God will gradually disappear because nobody believes in it anymore. From the ancient times, before the Egyptians, the Sumerians and so on, people all looked to something beyond this world. The modern world may be very mechanistic, but people must ask something, they must say, "Is this all?" And if they question "Is this all?" therefore, there must be something else, and if there is something else, is it the image, the picture, the ideal, the God with the beard or no beard or whatever it is? Religion in a sense *is* a factor in life, whether you like it or not. The intellectuals spin on that word, but it is a fact that the religions that now exist are just propaganda, irrational, superstitious—whether Christian superstition or Indian superstition. It is all just projected by men and worshiped because it is their image.

MORAES: If instead of worshiping a religion you start worshiping a government—is that necessarily better?

KRISHNAMURTI: No, probably not. But it *may* be better. Then you look after the government, how well behaved it is, whether it is corrupt, whether it is sane, whether it is run by decent politicians and so on.

MORAES: But do you really think that people have control over their governments?

KRISHNAMURTI: Not necessarily.

MORAES: Do you think anywhere in the world people have control over their governments?

KRISHNAMURTI: No, I am afraid not. They do talk a great deal about democracy and all the rest of it in India, and over here in the West. But rich people control life; you know, the whole business.

MORAES: Sir, Marx said that man was born free but is everywhere in chains. Would you agree with this?

KRISHNAMURTI: I wonder what he meant by freedom?

MORAES: Well, I think the original concept of democracy is that every man was born equal.

KRISHNAMURTI: I wonder if it is so. Take a Brahmin Indian or a good cultured, educated, intelligent European or American. They are not born free, they are conditioned. I would say all human beings are conditioned. That is a fact.

MORAES: Would you then say the opposite of what Marx said: that all human beings are born in chains and can be made free.

KRISHNAMURTI: That's right. All human beings are born conditioned and chained. You can see it in certain genes. Through right education we should be able to set human beings free, not to swallow them up, not to destroy them. I think that is the responsibility of education and of society.

MORAES: In what way do you feel that society can improve itself, can pull itself up?

KRISHNAMURTI: Society means relationship. That word "relationship"—what does it mean to be related?

MORAES: It means to have a connection, a contact, a communication.

KRISHNAMURTI: A contact, a communication, a feeling of companionship, a feeling of affection, of care, all that is involved in that word "relationship," which creates the society. If our relationship is greedy, or all our human relationships are greedy, we will create a structure or a society that will help us to be greedy. If we are violent, we will create a violent society, which is what we are doing. Whether it is the communist world or any other does not matter. So society can only change mutually, in our relationships. And in our relationships we are antagonistic; we are divided. The husband thinks about himself, the woman about herself. So in a relationship, the real contact, the physical contact, does not exist; ideologically it may exist, but actually it does not exist.

I am not being cynical but just pointing out that unless human beings, collectively and individually as human beings, change, how can you change society? The dictatorships like Hitler's, Mussolini's, the communists' tried to change man according to the pattern of what they thought society should be, which is still a superficial society in the sense we are talking about. To escape from it then people go off to churches, as they are doing in Russia; it is being encouraged now. Maoists are cursing Confucius because they are afraid to go back, but yet their insistence is on the superficial. Man cannot live on superficiality, so he will escape to something: drink, sex, whatever it is.

MORAES: This gets us back to the original question about Auden's line, "We must love one another or die." You don't think it is possible for one man to love another in the present state of affairs?

KRISHNAMURTI: Again, what does that word "love" mean? That word is so spoiled, it has become a dirty word. To care. To care for my son. What does that mean? For him to have the right education, not to be sent off to war to be killed, or not to destroy himself through perpetual entertainment, not to give all his life to the office, to the factory. Education also needs leisure. And now leisure means, gosh! drugs, or no drugs and swimming, you follow—*amusement,* so when we use the word "love," I think it has quite a different meaning.

MORAES: What meaning?

KRISHNAMURTI: One thinks of love of God, love of your country, love of your ideal. I love my book, I love my food. I think love means something entirely different. It is a real communication without word, without gesture, without demand, without dependence. That requires a tremendous sense of nonattachment, which means you can stand alone and not depend and be corrupted.

MORAES: I see.

KRISHNAMURTI: If that is what Mr. Auden means, that is what I feel. If that can be brought about, we can then forget all the governments and all the rest of it.

MORAES: Yet at the moment the world's population is 3.8 billion, and whatever anybody does there is nothing to prevent its doubling in thirty-five years, so by the year 2000 or a little later it will be 7.6 billion . . .

KRISHNAMURTI: The earth will sink!

MORAES: . . . and now, I don't know if you agree, but many of the antagonisms you were speaking of—the bad relationships, the lack of care between people—I think have been created in recent years by the fact of crowding of national boundaries. If in thirty-five years there are going to be twice as many people, the antagonisms will be increased. Can you see anything to stop it?

KRISHNAMURTI: You can see what is happening in New York, when you are living in crowded places like this, everybody on top of each other, no space. When there is no space you must be violent. Somebody was telling me the other day they had experimented putting a lot of rats in a cell. They destroyed themselves; they were disoriented, and they killed their own children. The husband killed the wife and so on. But, you see, religions are partly responsible for what happens to people—the so-called religions, not the real thing.

MORAES: What do you call the real thing?

KRISHNAMURTI: The real thing, if you are interested, is total negation of everything man has put together about reality, his philosophies, his gods, his rituals, his beliefs, his behavior, everything denied totally, denied because you see its absurdity, because it is irrational, it is insane, it is idiotic. Therefore, because you understand it, you deny it—that is the first basis. The foundation of the religious mind is this freedom from belief and how you treat it.

Meditation is implied in what I call religion, which is not a self-projective vision, not doing miracles (that is fairly easy; that is too childish). You know there is the film called *The Exorcist*. It is not a new concept. I will tell you something that happened to me. In India somebody came to see me and said, "My wife is possessed." He didn't use psychoanalytic terms; he said, "My wife is possessed." He said, "Please come." I don't know anything about exorcism or possession, but I went there, and I saw the woman—she must have been about thirty—standing on her head, shouting, speaking in Telugu, or some South Indian language, I think, and saying crazy things. She was shouting hysterically but at the same time was very bright. You know, the sharp look at you, without hysterical outbursts, bright, clear-eyed, watching, but there was slight insanity in that stare, and as I entered the room she screamed at me. I sat down, and I didn't say or do a thing. I didn't exorcise her. Presently she finished, empty, completely empty, and she became quiet, and she came to me afterward and said, "Thank you very much." She prostrated in the Indian fashion and said, "You have done me good, it will never happen again."

MORAES: Sir, what do you mean by meditation?

KRISHNAMURTI: You know anything about meditation at all?

MORAES: I only know that sometimes I sit by myself and think a great deal.

KRISHNAMURTI: Yes, the ordinary meditation is to control thought. That is generally accepted. Control thought or follow a system that will quieten you. Follow a practice that will help you to meditate. The meaning of yoga, I believe, is that, any system, any method that helps you to meditate. There is Zen and dozens of schools in India about meditation, and now that has spread all over the West. To me that is not meditation, because practicing a method is mechanistic and practicing a sound, mantra, which some of these yogis are advocating in this country and making a lot of money out of it, is not meditation, because you can mesmerize yourself. One must go into it with a mind that has space not occupied with thought, with enlightenment, with sex, with money, a mind that is totally unoccupied, empty, which means space and also means a nondirective mind. Therefore, no action of will enters the mind. Out of that comes real silence, not the silence that one fabricates, the silence of noise and so on. All that is meditation and more, because after that something you cannot describe, something that you cannot put into words, happens. But there must be no fear. That is very important.

MORAES: And you feel people don't do this? People are incapable of doing this?

KRISHNAMURTI: No, I think they are capable of doing this, but they are being led astray. By gurus, by all the repetition. You must be free of all that. You must understand yourself, not react.

HEINRICH BÖLL *

HEINRICH BÖLL is a German novelist renowned for his dry wit. He was born in 1917. His *Gruppenbild mit Dame* (*Group Portrait With Lady*, 1971) won the 1972 Nobel Prize for Literature. Some of his other well-known works include: *Wo warst du, Adam* (*Adam*, 1951), *Haus ohne Hüter* (*Tomorrow and Yesterday*, 1954), *Billard um Halbzehn* (*Billiards at Half Past Nine*, 1959), *Ansichten eines Clowns* (*The Clown*, 1963), *Entfernung von der Truppe* (*Absent Without Leave*, 1964).

For a long time now there have been cans for sale at the Station Zoo in Berlin that, according to the label, contain Berlin air, a little something, I suppose, to take with you when you leave Berlin or to give to those who have left. This clever idea from the souvenir industry could soon develop into a serious selling line, and the label need not even say "Berlin air," but simply "air." Not oxygen, not what iron lungs dispense, but perfectly ordinary air for breathing. You would give your children a few cans to take with them to school, take some yourself to the factory or office, and take a few gulps of fresh air at breakfast or in the lunch break in between mouthfuls of bread, milk, or coffee. Sometimes, when I put my car in a garage or car park, I would be really glad for a can of fresh air. Since you can already buy water (not mineral water but perfectly ordinary spring water), the idea of air in cans seems to me to be in no way a satirical exaggeration. In such a production- and efficiency-oriented world as ours, where we constantly increase profits and turnover, there will be (for us Europeans at any rate) enough bread, wine, and

* Translated by Jenny Lines.

schnapps, even milk, butter, and beer, but no water and no more air. If we efficient, modern people in this modern industrial society are looking for a new myth, there is really only one that comes to mind: the legend of King Midas, for whom everything he touched or came into contact with turned to gold. If you substitute for gold, productivity, efficiency, profit, gain, growth, then this myth could easily fit our situation.

All the fruits and pleasures of this world will be there for us to enjoy, only water will be scarce and air rare. In the middle of our marvelous supercities where we are building subterranean parking to create more space for cars, an archetypal, oriental-looking figure will probably emerge once more, the water merchant, and standing next to him will be a completely new category of merchant, the air seller. He, too, will have a big tank on wheels and for a few pennies will just briefly hold his air pipe to our mouths. Perfectly ordinary air for breathing will be treated as a valuable commodity, and we will drive for miles out into the country to some place or other where there is still said to be genuine, perfectly normal drinking water. We will take some of the water home with us from these weekend excursions in bottles, flasks, and skins, because we have found out for ourselves that it tastes better than that which our water merchant supplies every day or every week.

From the beginnings of mankind people have pondered the exploitation of man by man, but concern for exploitation of his natural surroundings is more recent. With a blind, profit-greedy optimism, industrialization has been carried on for over a century and a half with an attitude of "Let's get on with it, as long as the cash holds out." It has held out, up to a point, but now it seems that not only are man and his natural surroundings being exploited but that even the elements are being poisoned or driven away.

Plenty of architects, sociologists, psychologists, and now and then even a few theologians have warned and scolded, but nothing much has happened as yet. And if we wonder why that section of humanity, so difficult to define, that we call youth, is so apathetic or even pessimistic, we should ask ourselves: What kind of future have we prepared? What kind of future do we hold in readiness for them? What kind of quality of life? The water seller and the air merchant will not be able to reconcile them to this suicidal civilization.

By the year 1985, so we are informed by the United Nations, 9,000 billion marks will have been spent on armaments, in bald figures 9,000,000,000,000 marks—that is surely an almost mystical cipher, because the zeros can only be manipulated laboriously and the figures only laboriously translated into words—and in order to prevent a catastrophic water shortage 234 billion marks will have to be raised by the year 2,000, the equivalent of ten West German army budgets. In order, therefore, to prevent all the possible catastrophes, too many to list here, we must have open space regulation, urban planning, transportation planning, health services, educational reforms, and environmental protection. We must work toward a completely new conception of values that will clash, of course, with the existing ones—profit, productivity, increased turnover—and the priority in planning for all these various, complicated problems is time, because it is high time, and time passes quickly. And any politician who believes that all this can be planned without tax increases is deceiving himself or others.

It no longer looks like mere nonsense, but like suicidal cynicism if, considering the problems only touched upon here, a word like "plan" is denounced by a party such as the Christian Democratic Union, whose aim is to solve domestic and foreign political problems. Just how are these problems to be solved if nothing is planned? The opposite of plan need not be freedom, it can also be lack of planning, and the results of planless, reckless industrialization are what we see now.

Air for breathing and drinking water must not be allowed to become the property of a privileged class who can afford to drive out into the country to a second home where, moreover, they have at their disposal the other two elements that have become scarce for city dwellers: fire in the grate and earth in the park or garden. The new phrase "quality of life" is not a meaningless one; it stands for something very old, the stuff of life that we take for granted: air, water, fire, and earth. And something else that is not included in the classical count must be added as becoming the property of the privileged: peace and quiet. The number of people driven away by noise grows daily, not to mention the number of those who cannot afford to flee from unbearable noise because they have to fear for their jobs.

Like the air merchant there could soon be a man who sells people peace and quiet—in other words, someone who discovers a system of holding a little bit of peace or quiet to the ears of these poor, wretched, crazy, hunted followers of Midas. And, of course, the water, air, and peace merchants will only be retailers. Wholesale dealers and combines will develop to buy up water, air, and peace, hoard them, and sell them to the retailers at a profit. Considering the development that is no longer just foreseeable but has already begun, it is surely inconceivable that words like "plan" are denounced. Plans are constantly made; after all, advertising programs are planned, and in vocabulary drawn from the province of war, they are called campaigns.

States and communities are not alone in having budgets, the earth has one too. It has, among others, an oxygen and a nitrogen budget, and we have long since been living on credit. In the blind reconstruction phase of the Federal Republic of Germany, exploitation and sellouts directed only toward profit were carried on in a state of reckless euphoria, and the rest of the world marveled at this reconstruction and saw it as a kind of miracle. Behind this miracle lay not only hard work but also a blindness common to all the parties concerned. "Let's get on with it." The cash held out, partly in the pay packet and partly in the price share index. Great times, to be sure.

But the second miracle will be harder to bring about: National planning is not enough; the problems have long since been international, as the Soviet scientist Andrei Sakharov proclaimed years ago when he wrote about ecological problems, in other words about the budget of the earth.

JAMES CAMERON

JAMES CAMERON, perhaps the greatest English journalist of his time, was born in 1911 in Scotland. As a foreign correspondent, he traveled widely throughout the world and produced a number of TV films, including his travel series "Cameron Country," which was seen on the BBC. In *Who's Who* he lists his recreations as "Private life, public houses." Among his books are: *Touch of the Sun* (1950), *Mandarin Red* (1955), *1914* (1959), *The African Revolution* (1961), *1916* (1962), *Here Is Your Enemy* (1966), *Witness* (1966), *Point of Departure* (1967), *What a Way To Run the Tribe* (1968).

I have to present some tedious preliminaries in this context to give myself any relevance at all.

By definition an essay is, I suppose, an attempt, a trip into the tentative; I must say this is no great change for me. I have come to the age, which I believe grows younger each generation, when contemplation bores me, memory exasperates me, and speculation terrifies me. Just when this state of affairs takes charge tends to vary. I could say that I am about thirty years younger than Bertrand Russell or Winston Churchill would now have been, assuming such a macabre consideration, and thirty years older than, say, Keats. Anyone with a small Japanese pocket calculator can therefore work out that I grew to man's estate (the only estate I ever inhabited) smack in the middle of what we shall shortly call the first, or dress rehearsal, World Depression—not only that, but in the deepest valley of the shadow of that Depression, in a Scottish industrial ghost town with 48 per cent unemployment at one end and Victorian-Gothic opulence at the other. In consequence, it occurred to me—slowly, for I was a dull

32

lad—that there was probably something illogical about a society in which one lot got rickets and the other got gout. I believe I was more struck by its folly than its wickedness. I came to realize later that it was far from foolish and extremely wicked, but that took time.

I arrived at this situation singularly ill equipped to understand it, having lived thereto a sheltered life, that is, if you can define shelter as an erratic scramble from one umbrella to the next. It was once the custom of intelligent but indigent Scottish families to send their more ordinary sons to school in France; it was partly a relic of the old alliance and partly frugality, for Europe in those days was, oddly enough, cheaper than Britain. My father was a changeable man and could never make up his mind where I should be, with the result that I was bounced around from one infantile seat of learning to another, discovering how to count up to seven but no more, since each move sent me back to square one. The years have not improved me.

I thus left school at sixteen virtually illiterate in two languages at once. This determined the nature of my subsequent career, since in what trade could a youth of absolutely no educational qualification find employment other than journalism?

This rootless characteristic was hard to shake off, and for a surprising number of years I managed indeed to make a living out of it. It was surprising in the sense that I seemed to be perpetually at odds with an endless succession of employers and patrons, and for many years my staple nourishment was taking bites out of the hands that fed me. I do not recommend it as a recipe for tranquillity, but it keeps the weight down. Moreover, the energy involved in keeping at least one jump ahead of the bourgeoisie—not to mention the bailiffs—took me by and by to every country in the world, bar one, large numbers of which did not even exist when I first encountered them. This is a paradox easily worked out, since it concerns the gestation and birth of what is known as the Third World.

All this has to be said in order to establish that my disenchantment with the global scene is not derived from a study of the works of Enoch Powell nor yet the late Karl Marx, nor even from remote observation of the antics on the Washington merry-go-round, and much elsewhere, but quite a deal of personal involvement, one way and another. I came in for the last act of the British Empire, not only unregretful but offering little parting shoves and nudges where I could. The colonial Empire evaporated in the usual abrasive way, channeling every potential Prime Minister through the accepted routine of opprobrium and jail: thus, Nehru, Nkrumah, Makarios, Kenyatta—all graduating through prison to the inevitable ritual cuppa tea at Windsor Castle. When the process stopped, the point was still not made: We never learned, we just ran out of colonies.

We bequeathed them our parliamentary democracy and our speakers' wigs and maces and God knows what of the archaic symbolic nonsenses that the British value so much, patted them on the head, and handed over a set of electoral principles that they simply could not wait to abandon, with the result that there is not one single social democracy left in all former British Africa and but one in the Caribbean. The South African Government, which argues that it is against God and nature for black men to run their own show, now looks northward and feels not only justified but vindicated, as well it might, given the boneheaded reasoning of the Afrikander.

There is India, which I have known for thirty years, and to which beguiling and tragic country I am now bound by marriage— I never set foot there but I wonder why I came; I never go but I leave half of me behind. When independence came in 1947 and Jawaharlal Nehru's thin voice broke the midnight with his "tryst with destiny," I felt exalted as never before, so long had this especial liberation been my life. I now see the dream collapsing almost daily, the tryst with destiny eluded, the helplessness betrayed by vain and corrupt time-servers, a mysterious and wonderful country surviving only through a flagging historical momentum.

By now it may be detected that my trade has involved much chasing about the planet in pursuit of one manifestation of human perversity after another, frequently revealed in the most preposterous and uncomfortable situations, like wars. It was enough to make a cynic out of St. Francis. It so happened that I had no instruction in the supernatural, and it is my experience that only card-carrying Christians can be cynical; I cannot rid myself of the habit of sentimental heresy, if there is such a thing. That is to say, I believe that mankind, the lot of it, is, in fact, blundering into an enormous booby trap of its own contriving (or more properly, the contriving of its handful of anointed eggheads), but that in spite of every jot of rational evidence a solution can be found, and that it will come about through social democracy of some kind or another, even if it has to be a kind that has yet to be invented. What interests me, as one given to useless self-examination every hour on the hour, is how on earth I still manage to believe this.

I quote myself from something written years ago, in an even bluer age:

> When it comes to prophecy, the remote and imponderable is easy; only the near things are hard to see. It is impossible to foretell the behaviour of a lover, commonplace to predict that of a planet. The astronomer incapable of prophesying the result of this afternoon's football game can infallibly announce the precise moment years ahead when the moon will obscure the sun. The mathematician who knows the exact transition of a Satellite does not know if he will have his coronary tomorrow. It is only the small things, like life and death, that cloud the crystal ball. All else is written.
>
> We occupy a world whose functions are eminently predictable, in which only extremely holy people could ever be genuinely surprised. Its aberrations must necessarily breed their like. Despite the historians, history insists on repeating itself, since the imbecilities of today are the in-things of tomorrow. When we plod about our silly occasions protesting that life has got out of hand and that it is idle to plan in such a mess of guesswork we kid ourselves, and like it. Thus nobody has ever to decide anything for what is known in the trade as "the foreseeable future."
>
> Most things are foreseeable, and most are bloody awful. However, to say a thing is predictable is not technically to say it is inevitable. Now here one is up against a really copper-bottomed dilemma discovered centuries ago when Prophets genuinely were in business. If the seer can foresee the future, and dislikes what he has foreseen, and takes steps to avert what he has foreseen, and in fact is successful in so doing—then he has by his own initiative proved himself no prophet, and sold himself out of the market, since the undesirable future he presaged has been dodged.

This is what G. K. Chesterton called the old game of Cheat The Prophet, ducked by almost everyone except weather-forecasters and diplomatic correspondents. Still, so far from invalidating prophecy it enhances it. Nothing whatever in the world would have changed, no star skip its course, but for the pressure of all the non-prophets, especially those with voting rights, who from time to time get up and put a stop to the inevitable.

Allowing for a certain callow glibness, I think I would let that stand today but probably just as an act of faith. All those famous nonprophets with voting rights would not today, I fear, rush to put up their banners and hasten to the barricades—or even, alas, the polling booths. My obstinate belief in the principle of democratic socialism is not the easiest thing in the world to sustain in the face of even greater obstinacies, in both the national (or local) sense and the international (or simply human) sense.

The world was probably never fuller than now of what the Quakers call "concern," that is to say, a sort of mild anguish about the human condition and an intermittent impulse to do something about it. This is informed by a very decent belief that the world's democratic leaders, properly stimulated, could somehow or another come to the rescue of a deprived mankind without disturbing the equanimity of its several freedoms. It is argued that within a comparatively short space of time, world poverty (which is simply to say hunger) will be quite insoluble without truly massive transfers of resources from the rich societies to the poor ones, and that this can be achieved by a form of logical persuasion —*i.e.,* democratically. We talk in cosmic terms of World Population Years and "decades of decision" and arbitrary eras of this and that, the reform of industrial society, and a new appraisal of education and so on; we are shouting into a deaf world, and we know it in our hearts. All democratic governments without exception are composed of individuals obsessed with issues like getting re-elected or, in many cases, survival. Being intelligent men they are aware of the natural resources crisis and the coming doubling of the global population of people; they know that already a fifth of mankind is desperately undernourished, and they know damn well that the hungry ones are mostly black or blackish.

They must be aware that these desperate masses cannot be relied on to sit on their skinny fannies forever repining their misfortunes, not now that they can watch the opulent vulgarities of the other half on the communal village telly. They will encourage Oxfam and other aid programs. But not one single constituency vote will it catch them, because . . . because why, I wonder?

I suppose that in honesty I can talk only of the political environment in which I now live, which is that of Britain, and of the kind of people I mostly know, who are the well-intentioned working class and their hangers-on, the theorists. We clung to social democracy as a relief from revolution, because the heroics had been kicked out of it; it was something built on the realizable hopes of people as they are rather than as they ought to be; it did not have to create ruins on which it could be founded; and, though manifestly it would be a long job, it was an attainable thing. So we thought. (As I say, I still do, having no other alternative.) We identified with, for example, the British Labour Party; its obvious imperfections could be accepted because its achievements were occasionally real: a National Health Service, at least an embryo welfare state. One day, it was clear, the People would catch on to what was good for them. That was, of course, some time ago.

It took us about twenty-five years to appreciate what everyone else had apparently always known: that the People, whoever they may be, are in fact people, whose interests are notably different, having in most cases very little to do with doctrine and a great deal to do with mortgages and the payments on the family car. Professional social democrats in Europe, and especially in Britain, have got to come to terms with the fact that while as individuals and local tribunes they may be respected and even wanted by their constituents, their theories are not. Labour Party members of the English Parliament are there because of the inanity of the opposition and because the trade union vote has nowhere else to go, not because their party nationalized steel and created a health service that is a model to the world. The welfare state no longer excites enthusiasm among those for whom, and largely by whom, it was made; it is now time to complain about the taxes that sustain it. In a word, an electorate begins to reject what social democracy must, by its own mythology, regard as the people's achievement. And if that is so for the simplicities of local affairs, what price the fellowship of global man?

For that matter, what price for an even smaller abstraction, the European man? I would suggest that he was, to all intents and purposes, virtually stillborn, which, considering the travail of his delivery, was hardly surprising. It was evident from the outset that the Common Market had everything to do with market and little enough to do with commonalty. It may not be the total capitalist conspiracy of some Little Englanders' dreams, but it most palpably is the instrument of the multinational industrial corporation and Big Business *in excelsis* and as such offended many of our social democratic sensibilities. More of these sensibilities, however, were outraged by the discovery that certain of the Common Market countries had higher wages than we did, tougher trade unions, higher pensions, all of which had been somehow or other produced without any reference to formal socialism, so that left some of our ideologues up a bit of a dialectical gum tree.

Nevertheless, it is probably true to say that the great debate about entry into Europe aroused rather less popular interest in England than a disputed cup tie goal. The votes won or lost on the issue would not have elected a Puddlecombe Parish Council. In Britain, at least, it is axiomatic in all candidates' manuals that no one ever filled a schoolroom meeting, let alone a ballot on a matter of foreign affairs. Why this should be so in a nation that historically poked its nose into more foreign affairs than anyone, even to the extent of dominating a third of the world for a couple of centuries, can be explained only by the theory that if you let a consumer society have its head and promote its avarice on every billboard and every TV screen, then you must accept that politicians must similarly promote themselves exactly like cornflakes, which inevitably they will daily more closely resemble. This is becoming blindingly true not just of Britain but of every consumer society in the world, which is to say that the only people who could do something about the miseries of the other world not only do very little about it but are rarely told how they could even try.

Hence the hundreds of thousands of pounds' worth of material aid sent in a rush of sentiment to Bengal after the catastrophic ty-

phoons hanging about for months on the Calcutta wharves because
of the bureaucratic imbecility of Indian customs officers; hence the
red tape that held up ambulances until the duty had been paid
on them. You drop your five dollars into the collecting box; only
after a while do you realize that for all the good it does to the
unknown and faraway victims you might as well have spent it on
a bottle of Scotch.

Right now we have a tremendous tragedy building up in West
Africa, revealed from time to time in the Sunday newspaper sup-
plements with appropriate Oxfam illustrations of skeletal children.
A wide climatic zone called the Sahel, two thousand miles across
with millions of people, is just becoming uninhabitable for
human beings. No one seems to know exactly how the drought
came about, whether it is just hapless mismanagement of the
ecosystem or a long-term natural shift that no human agency can
prevent. Whatever it is, it involves four landlocked republics—
Mali, Upper Volta, Chad, and Niger—all less than fifteen years
old and without economic resources of any kind, in which, according to the Carnegie Endowment report, more than 100,000
people died last year from hunger or famine-related diseases, and
where precisely the same thing or worse is going to happen again.
These new countries, according to a *Times* newspaper I read today,
"are reduced to so many isolated bureaucracies sitting in air-con-
ditioned oases in the midst of the desert, inefficiently administering
an inadequate charity to an unemployed and starving population."

According to Dr. Waldheim's requirements for his special fund,
about £10 million must be found to save lives immediately. It is
a pitiably small sum of money, about a fiftieth of what the broke
and bewildered British Government offers its own building societies to keep the local mortgages down, about one two-hundredth
part of what it squanders on the preposterous technology of "defense." It would not make much of a hole in the budget of
Monaco. It will doubtless be found somehow or other, but whether
it will ever get to the right place at the right time is another
matter. And supposing some cruelty of nature has decided that
the West African Sahel can no longer support human life, what
then? An entire population will have to be resettled, something
only possible with international finance. That too is perfectly con-

ceivable—but only if these little states concerned accept some kind of federation or union with their southern neighbors along the Guinea Gulf. Nothing in the world would be more sensible, since it would reverse the process of balkanization initiated by the Europeans in the "scramble for Africa" during the last century. But could these proud little principalities agree? And will those who have it in their power to help ever care enough, or even know enough, to explain?

There is no moral nor even a deduction from this, except that while the Sahel emergency may not be the most sensational or mind-blowing catastrophe in the world it is surely far from the least, and that a realistic and not merely symbolic program of help is perfectly easily within the well-fed world's power and pocket. Yet Britain has just had a major election campaign in which *not one word* was breathed about this or any related foreign misfortune. In the presidential elections in France nothing, you may be certain, was said about world population or world poverty to stir the opaque and oily pool of Élysée politics. The *Land* elections in Germany, rich as Croesus as she is, will contain not one footnote on a hunger problem of which all good Germans know nothing and care less. "I'm all right, Jack" is readily translatable into most European languages.

All this and more has been said a million times before; for fifteen years books and pamphlets have been rolling off the presses into this kind of oblivion or that. It seems pretentious to say it again. From time to time a bitter and well-intentioned film on some tragedy like Bihar or Sahel or Biafra briefly interrupts the moving wallpaper of the television and causes some indrawn breaths of compassion or anger; it is usually followed by peevish protests, as a rule from the government of whatever nation was being exposed.

Twenty-five thousand million dollars a year splashed around the world on ducky little devices for defense, which is to say neat technologies for taking life, a thin buck for saving it. This is the nub of the whole thing. Indeed it *is* the whole thing.

This morning I came upon this in the daily newspaper:

> Those of us who would be hard put to call ourselves Christian, or indeed anything at all, can still respect the Pope's words on

disarmament as human politics of the highest order, despite the three-ring circus from which they were spoken. His call to arrest the lunatic arms-race was specifically and for the first time addressed not solely to Catholics, or even fellow-Christians, but to everyone, including "strangers to the Church" and even those who denounce it [by which he must have meant honest communists]. Thus the Pope emerged from an ostentatious isolation and entered the lists of politically-operational Heads of State.

In that day's *Times* the lead letter was signed by, among others, the Archbishop of Canterbury, the Chief Rabbi, and the moderators of the Church of Scotland and the Free Churches. It had nothing whatever to do with ecumenism or for that matter even faith. Instead, it recalled the preamble of the famous Moscow Atomic Test Ban Treaty, which, as ninety-nine people out of a hundred have forgotten, "urged the speediest possible achievement on general and complete and unequivocal disarmament." These churchmen also recalled that the Pugwash Conference of international scientists insisted that "disarmament—essential for a new society in which poverty could be abolished—is no longer Utopian. If people want it enough." And they said: "We hope that all men irrespective of party or race, will make the utmost and immediate effort to mobilize public opinion and action for these most immediate reforms."

This is doubtless banal enough; what is notable is that both these appeals, from the top men of various faiths, were made to people and not to politicians. They were, in fact, carefully addressed over the heads of the politicians.

So what has happened to the politicians? Today in all the basic aspects of the great ideological dialogue the initiative is surrendered by the statesmen to others. Popes and prelates and so on are important enough individuals, but the responsibility for affairs does not lie with them. Yet almost any statement of political meaning above the level of the international parish pump comes now not from the elected representatives of the people but from sources of no democratic pretensions at all. One can applaud the Pope's final emergence on the right side and the churchmen's sudden discovery that there is a correlation between guns and butter or rockets and rice. Yet how much one wishes that this sort of thing could occasionally be invoked by some of the curious graven images we ourselves put in positions of power.

All this would doubtless be of more relevance had I not glanced at that newspaper and discovered—as so happens in my disordered surroundings—that its date was precisely to a week ten years ago.

They don't make them like that now.

However, I just read in some current document or other that the Peruvian anchovy catch is so great that it could supply the protein deficiency of the whole of South America. Instead, 91 per cent of it goes into cans of North American pet food, since poodles pay better than peons.

Back in those Depression days in Scotland I knew these ironies and cruelties and injustices were a human aberration, to be redeemed one day. The system—everybody said—carried within it the seeds of its inevitable destruction. Even then I'm obliged to say it seemed to me to be carrying the seeds of everyone else's destruction, but I did not argue. I envisaged the image of The System as some sort of old coconut, inside which this famous seed was daily germinating, preparing suddenly to burst forth in a radiant growth of human hope and social justice, rather like a tulip tree. Alas for that; the nut was a good deal harder to crack, and the seed has clearly decided to take it easy and settle down, at least for the time being.

I shall always believe in its existence, however. Is there anything else?

INDIRA GANDHI

INDIRA GANDHI, political leader, born in 1917 in Allahabad, India, once told the editor of this book that she would have liked to be a writer. The daughter of her nation's first Prime Minister, Jawaharlal Nehru, she has since 1966 been Prime Minister in her own right. Some of her publications are: *Selected Speeches* (1971), *India Speaks* (1971), *Indira Speaks on Genocide, War and Bangladesh* (1972), *Aspects of Our Foreign Policy* (1973).

The quality of life has many meanings. In my grandfather's time it consisted of cultivated conversations and gay parties amidst rich materials, beautiful silver, exquisite carpets. By the time I reached the age of appreciation, these were all things of the past.

My father's sensitivity made him abhor all show and ostentation. My mother, too, though for a different reason. She was by nature simple to the verge of austere. I grew up with only one thought: that nothing at all mattered without freedom. There could be no quality under the humiliating conditions of colonialism. This was an obsession that gained wider dimensions after acquaintance with Western liberal thought. An obsession sears, but it can also inspire and strengthen. No one who has not shared the experience can imagine the intensity and all-pervasiveness of feeling.

I was, of course, aware of the evils of our social and economic structure. Our own freedom struggle had generated a great movement for the reform of Indian society—to change the unequal rural structure, to eradicate the monstrous practice of untouchability, to bring about communal harmony, to defend women's rights. It was intolerable that some sections of the people should exploit others, or that a person should be condemned to inferior status by reason of his caste or sex, or that there should be any differentiation on account of religion.

Once we had attained political independence, we were also free to deal with these questions. For freedom would be meaningless for the millions whose lives were overshadowed by poverty, inequality, and superstition.

A certain material well-being is presupposed for any description of quality. The crucial word is "certain." What is the minimum level of material welfare that is absolutely essential?

As we have progressed, material prosperity has gradually seeped downwards. Some sections remain below the poverty line, but many classes and sections are far better off than they were. However, society as a whole has become permeated with acquisitive thinking; the market and advertisements constantly beckon to better, more attractive goods. Demand and dissatisfaction grow together. The affluent, the better off, the better equipped with power, money, organization, or even an aggressive personality get the larger share, leaving less and less for the poorer and the weaker sections.

Hence tensions are bred and explode. Quality suffers. Since taste takes time to build, it also deteriorates in the rush and the competition.

I am not lauding the old society. I have myself rebelled against tradition and meaningless conventions and rites. There can be no quality without freedom of spirit, freedom from fear, and freedom from deprivation, whether of food or of what one needs for mental and spiritual growth. And the old society with its authoritarianism, its built-in inequality, the narrow confines of custom and habit, made all the more oppressive in India by the divisions and taboos of caste, did deny the freedom to think and to develop. There was leisure for only a particular class. Yet the very confines, the accepted norms, gave some sense of belonging and security, and for those who hesitated to think for themselves, a well-settled direction. Industrialization has shaken this security but without strengthening those aspects of personality, without cultivating mental attitudes and abilities to hold one's own and to grapple with the whole new set of challenges and problems that are being thrown up.

Science speaks of light-years, but the human mind seems only to grasp the immediate. The world has changed, but not the proportion of rich to poor. Some societies have abolished hunger, but this cannot be said of the world as a whole. Production grows apace unaccompanied by any machinery or even real desire for equitable distribution. But if people's absorptive and reflective power has not grown, their visual observation has. It is not hard for the poorest and the most unlettered to see the distance between his poverty and the affluence of advanced nations or some sections of his own. Millions now know that their misery is avoidable, that the world has the means to give them a better deal. Indeed, for the first time in history, mankind has the capacity to solve the problems of hunger and want. It is true that there are more mouths to feed today, and the growth of population is a real issue and must be checked. But all of the world's imbalances cannot be visited on this one factor. When it is known that the level of consumption in many affluent countries is twenty times more than that in the poorer countries, it is evident that with a more rational rearrangement of needs and resources the hungry can be fed and the sick tended.

The stumbling block is the assumption that nations that had an earlier start in industrialization have a superior claim to the utilization of resources. The prospector's right is accompanied by greed for quick gains, unconcerned with the long-term perspective. The problems of worldwide poverty and pollution are both products of the unbridled profit motive. What is considered "efficiency" has cast its accompanying shadow in the shape of spiritual disquiet. Increasingly, the question is asked "comfort at what price?"

To me, the good life means the appreciation of quality, no less than quality itself, the effort toward excellence in achievement, pride in work, and a sense of inner harmony. It means the constant expansion of awareness, the stretching of one's ability to observe, to feel, and to comprehend. I do not think this implies complacency or acquiescence, nor does it conflict with any instincts of rebellion.

The quality of life of an individual lies not in what he has but what he is. It can be measured only in his capacity to achieve harmony and resonance with his fellow human beings and with nature, to perceive the meaning of thought, and to experience the beauty of action—in short to find joy in life. This is what will lead human beings to richer, more creative, and fulfilling lives.

Can this vision be achieved? The purpose of life is to believe, to hope, and to strive.

The various movements of the black and brown peoples, women's liberation, and youth power are all different facets of the desire of those who for ages past have been made to feel inferior and helpless to discover and establish their own identities and to make their presence felt, their voices heard in the affairs of their societies, their countries, and the world. This can only be possible in systems of national and international government that give full opportunity for the individual to participate.

There is the simplicity of tribal and rural folk, but there is also a return to simplicity that is consciously achieved, as if coming full circle after traversing many experiences of sophistication. Similarly, I feel that decentralized or local government in a sense wider than that with which the word is today endowed can be effectively possible only after a centralized government has drawn up a broad pattern and laid the main directions. Without such a centralized government, the country would be fragmented. Equally, without working toward decentralization, we could well throttle local and individual initiative. Conditions must be created to enable personalities to grow and flower, but in their turn people must bear their responsibility and play their part in the endeavor and sacrifice to create such a society.

We in India, along with likeminded people the world over, must continue to work for peace and the lessening of tensions, so that the world's thought and energies can be devoted to ensuring equality of opportunity to all peoples and to a fairer distribution of the world's natural resources and material goods and services. We want to create a new society where a person can grow and develop at his own pace and in his own way and be different if he so desires and where each type or skill is given due regard. Human beings cannot be transformed into angels. Evil, envy, and avarice will perhaps always exist. Our endeavor should be to establish norms that discourage and ridicule these tendencies, which make it more difficult for one man or class or group to take advantage of another, and which will urge humanity toward greater understanding, concern, and cooperation, not because of idealism but because of the realization that in working for the common good lies his own and his children's future happiness.

Much has to be changed, but much has also to be conserved: the beauty and purity of nature and wild life as well as the architectural and art treasures of our past. Cooperation and collaboration in these larger objectives are as important and urgent as those in economic, technical, or cultural fields.

I wish for my people not riches or power but their basic necessities, so that they can have the opportunity to be human and to experience the fullness of life, not to be afraid of hardship or sorrow or danger but to meet them face to face as part of life. All hopes cannot be fulfilled nor all aspirations attained. It would be unrealistic to expect to overcome all our frailties, but we can try, and if we succeed even in some small measure, it will be worthwhile.

CARLOS FUENTES
An Interview

CARLOS FUENTES, novelist, was born in 1928 in Mexico City, Mexico. At present he is a Fellow at the Woodrow Wilson International Center for Scholars in Washington, D.C., where he is working on a new novel. Some of his already published works include: *Los Dias enmascarados* (1954), *La Region mas transparente (Where the Air Is Clear*, 1958), *Aura* (1962), *La Muerte de Artemio Cruz (The Death of Artemio Cruz*, 1962), *Cantar de ciegos* (1964), *Zona sagrada (Holy Place,* 1967), *Cambio de piel (Change of Skin,* 1967), *La Nueva Novela Hispanoamericana* (1969), *Todos los Gatos son pardos* (1970), *Cuerpos y ofrendas* (1972).

MORAES: I suppose one defines the human condition as the way in which people live, both physically and inside themselves. When you were a child, in what way did you conceive that people lived?

FUENTES: I think my earliest consciousness of being in the world was immediately related to the fact that I was a Mexican and to the fact that I was not alone. I believe I had my first vision of values, of true values, when I realized I was living in a world and that there were other people in it. So whatever the value of my values, they were useless unless confronted with the values of the experience of the world outside myself. What gave me the idea of values as a child? Two things, I think. First, simply seeing newsreels and seeing other children. I was a child of the '30s and early '40s: simply seeing a picture of a Chinese child in a bombed-out station in Nanking or newsreels of the British children being taken to the countryside because of the "blitz," or Jewish children being herded along in Warsaw. Second, my sense of conflict, because I do think that conflict and values are always twins and always come in pairs, came as a child in this city where we are now, in Washington. My father was the Counsellor in the Mexican Embassy at the time. I went to a public school. I was well liked. I participated in the community. Suddenly, the President of Mexico at the time, Lázaro Cárdenas, expropriated the foreign oil holdings. There were screaming headlines in the American press. Overnight, from being a well-liked child in my school, I became a leper, an outcast, a communist. This threw me back on the values to which I felt I had to belong in some way, which were the values of my nation. I came to see them first as very definite international political values: the principles of non-intervention and of self-determination. But as time went on, I realized these were defensive, negative values and that behind them one had to give content to a positive order of values. The possibility of giving cultural content to our national identity was a first step. Very early as a child I was reading. I had wanted to be a writer since I was a child. I realized that there was a universal culture. But at the same time I believed that we would not accede to this culture without first creating a viable national community. And to this day I believe that the value of interdependence depends on the value of independence, that you can only be interdependent if you are first independent, that the interdependency of dependence would only be a cloak for hegemony. So I think first the way we live inside ourselves and we live with others must be established within the radius of a given national community. Then perhaps we can give something to a world civilization, and through the acceptance of a plurality of cultures we can achieve a rich and fecund polycivilization instead of a dry uniform monocivilization, which I think is close behind the present drive toward interdependence. But as I said, the interdependence of the dependents is not independence.

MORAES: But don't you feel that the worst world disasters have been basically the consequence of a feeling of nationalism?

FUENTES: I think there is a nationalism of the mighty and there is a nationalism of the weak. I belong to a weak society, and this weak society is trying to work along with other weak societies in the Third World to achieve particular effects, not as a negation of others but as a contribution to this polycivilization I am talking about. I think the danger today in the world is that one single model of co-existence, of progress, of welfare, should impose itself with no regard to the national aspirations and to the concrete experience of peoples in cultural contexts totally alien to the general model of development proposed by the industrial states. By this term I mean both the capitalist and the highly industrialized communist countries. I think it will be all to the good—and very positive—if Mexico, Argentina, Nigeria, Egypt, India, Indonesia, Japan, China, etc., contributed their own models of progress to a universal model integrated by plural contributions, not by one or two contributions imposed from above on us. This has nothing to do with our real inner or related life, nothing whatsoever. This has to be worked out in local terms.

MORAES: Since it is not very possible that the developed countries will accept any such concept or model from the Third World, will this not tend to cut the Third World off from the developed countries even more than it is today?

FUENTES: I wonder if a certain degree of distance from the highly developed countries will not be all to the good for the countries of the Third World. I cannot visualize any future for my own country, for Mexico, unless we recapture in our country the totality of our past. I think you cannot have a present or a viable future if you do not have a past, and in Mexico and in many countries of Latin America the great problem of our whole structure of values is to recapture what has been mutilated, what has been killed in the past and give it a chance, a second opportunity to really integrate the totality of our values. In the case of Mexico this is very clear, and I would generalize it in talking of Latin America. Since we achieved independence from Spain, between 1810 and 1820, we immediately proposed to ourselves as a model for happiness, as a model for the future, the kind of progress protagonized by Great Britain, France, and the United States. We came out of the long night of three centuries of Spanish colonialism totally sealed off from the modern world. Instead of looking back and by a really human, intellectual effort trying to reintegrate this colonial past and the Indian past, we plunged acritically into formal imitations of the West. We simply superimposed the masks of Adam Smith and John Locke on the masks of Philip II and Moctezuma. The result was a total divorce between *le pays réel* and *le pays légal*. Today in Latin America we have in certain aspects on certain levels reached that stage we have been searching for since independence. But we have reached it at the same time that this model is being shown as bankrupt in the very nations where it was once a success. Given the failure of the positivist model and of its correlative concepts of lineal time, unbounded progress, future orientation, all in crisis today, we ask ourselves if it is worthwhile to continue on that path or if we should rather stop, take a hard look at these values, and look inside ourselves and try to restore and integrate the values of a society based on harmony and not on progress as conceived by the Western industrialized nations.

MORAES: Will this not be an extremely drastic kind of switch? Having pursued this path so long can you afford suddenly to stop and turn around?

FUENTES: We pursued it only for 150 years. Behind that we have three hundred years of colonialism and behind that, in the case of Mexico, we have thousands of years of the indigenous life of the plural Indian cultures. These cultures are alive today. What I insist upon is that we will not be orphaned if we suddenly cut off, or critically re-examine, the present model for progress, and then look inside ourselves to integrate another model with a variety of wells from which we can drink. Frankly, many of these wells are full of water. They are there; they are alive: the Indian cultures of Mexico. As we grow disillusioned, and more and more the intelligentsia and the ruling class of Mexico are becoming disillusioned with the Western model for progress, we find an alternate value in the Indian sense of community; in the Indian sense of time, which is not the linear time of the West but a memorious cyclical time; in the idea, which is the basic utopian idea, very much alive in the Indian communities in Mexico, that the community has a greater value than the authority, that the authority is there to serve the community and not vice versa; in the idea of gentle pantheism in which all things are sacred because all things are related and all things are related because all things are shared; in the value given to the body, to the idea that the culture of the man is not in his possessions but in the way he walks, in the way he eats, in the way he says hello, in the way he gazes at the sky and the value given to objects because they are singular and beautiful—no object produced by an Indian in Mexico resembles another object. We have these things from which to draw, and we have many other historical factors that were mutilated in the past and that I think we should resurrect critically to see how they can help us—we also have the great utopian tradition, for instance, in the founding of the New World, which was sacrificed and corrupted by the epic of conquest and colonization of Spanish America, along with the libertarian traditions of Erasmus and Bruno. There are many values I think we could go into.

MORAES: Do you think it is *practically* possible, making Mexico go back to a system that has not been actually implemented for many years?

FUENTES: I don't mean going back, I mean going forward. If we are able intellectually and critically to employ these plural factors in our cultures to elaborate a new model for progress, it will not be a resurrection of the Aztec model. It will not be an actual translation of the utopian ideas that came into the New World with many of the friars, which were actual implementations at the moment of the thought of St. Thomas More and Campanella. I mean that what we today, as men of the twentieth century, see that these ideas can give us, will be one of many factors that will come to create a new model for progress, neither a return to the sacrificial pyramid of the Aztecs nor a blind plunge into the fog of ecocide, loneliness, or the production of garbage. What I propose is a revaluation of traditions that are also ours: Utopia means community above power; Bruno means metamorphosis against fixity; Erasmus means the ironical praise of folly against the ironclad sufficiency of egotistic reason. Because, you see, what we have been through is the whole experience of development within underdevelopment, actually the development of underdevelopment, guided by the reductionist traditions of Machiavelli, Cartesian reason, Lockean property, and the Enlightenment's unbounded faith in absolute progress in an absolute future. These negative strains are at odds with the positive strains of our original, suffocated, but living Indian and Renaissance heritages.

The idea that you can create a viable capitalistic society in a dependent country by accumulation of wealth at the top, a concentration of wealth with the Hamiltonian idea that this wealth will eventually spill over from the top to the bottom is not true and has never been true. We have gone through this experience of dependent capitalism. In Mexico since 1940, in Venezuela with the Pérez Jiménez regime, in Brazil after the military came to power, in many parts of Latin America, the wealth has stayed at the top; it has created a small group of privileged people; it has completely paralyzed social and cultural progress in our countries. So we have arrived at this stage of crisis of development for development's sake, and we have to look for other ways for a new elaboration.

MORAES: But is it feasible?

FUENTES: I think it is. It depends a great deal on our capacity to create an open forum for discussion and to create new priorities. If the priority for development for development's sake was created in the past, why cannot a new priority, a new set of priorities, be created in the future? Now it seems difficult, but the difficulty is not because the model we have is forceful and there to stay. I think, on the contrary, it is quite weak; it is nothing but a façade; it is cosmetic. The real time and conscience and memory of a country like Mexico is somewhere else, it is not Western at all, and it has been waiting for centuries to really express itself. I think we can achieve this, but it requires in a sense a revolution whereby all the components of this future model can actually speak out and propose their own goals and objectives freely.

MORAES: So far you have been talking mainly about Mexico and Latin America and mainly in terms of ideological change, which may also be a physical practical change. Now, the fact of the matter is that throughout the whole world the population is going to double in thirty-five years. We are already facing crises of food, of energy, of raw materials, and so on. The countries that are going to be affected most are going to be the Third World countries. Life everywhere is going to be difficult for everybody, but in the Third World it may become impossible, unbearable. Therefore, if you are suggesting that the Third World should get farther away from the developed world, will the hardship not be much greater?

FUENTES: I have referred mostly to my own country, because that is what I know best. I have just spoken of the strengthening of the state in Mexico and the creation of a public sector. Now thanks to this creation of a public sector Mexico has become more or less self-sufficient in many matters: petroleum, for example, since we are in the midst of an energy crisis. Mexico did not have to appeal for imports. Thanks to the nationalization of oil in 1938 the resources of the country were protected, were rationally exploited, and today we do not have the problems of the West. We have a sufficiently diversified industrial plant. That it is working at 40 per cent capacity only is due to the fact that the Mexican entrepreneurs, the Mexican bourgeoisie, will not see beyond their own noses. They feel that once the metropolitan, urban markets are saturated, there is no need to go beyond to the other half of the population, to the other Mexico, the peasants and the Indians. We have an internal market among ourselves in Latin America, and we can fight for better terms of trade precisely because of the lack of raw materials in the Western industrialized nations.

I don't see the situation as darkly as you suggest is possible. I do see the future as very dark if we continue along the lines I have condemned before, of development for development's sake. I think we are not going to suffer from the problems you have just indicated, that we are capable of solving all these problems within our own national borders. But I think also that if we just envisage these as frigid, cold, statistical problems we will get nowhere. We have to give them this human content that I have been trying to explain. Our first duty is to put our houses in order.

MORAES: You talked earlier about the interdependence of weak nations. Now, possibly Mexico can solve its own problems within its own borders, but if it is going to be as you suggested, interdependent with other underdeveloped countries, is this not going to take its toll on the Mexican economy and the life of the people?

FUENTES: I don't think so, if it is done with justice in the integration, let's say, of the Latin American countries in the first place. Mexico felt, and I think our government was right in this, that in helping the Allende government in Chile economically it was helping itself. And I think in the future there will be the possibility of cooperating with nationalist and libertarian regimes on the continent to solve precisely the sort of problem that you pointed out in your previous question. No, I am not speaking of sheer autarky. I am against this. I believe we can be interdependent in Latin America, and get better terms of trade, and work out our own problems, and create our own priorities without excessive interference from the industrialized nations.

MORAES: Do you envisage a future time in Latin America in which, since there is that great link of language and so forth all over the continent, the whole continent might make one state?

FUENTES: No, I don't think this is possible. There are very wide differences between a country like Mexico with a basically mixed-blood Indian component and a predominantly white or totally white country like Argentina, a country derived from immigration. The people have a completely different make-up. There is the language link, and there is a cultural link, but I don't think that in the foreseeable future any nation in Latin America would be willing to give up what it considers its national characteristics, its national values. I think that the ideal is a confederation or a greater interdependence among ourselves and a greater unity in our voice when we speak to the powerful countries, to imperialist countries.

MORAES: Now, again, to go beyond Mexico to the world—you already were talking about how the concept of democracy as the West has proclaimed it is breaking down its façade and so forth. How do you see the whole world going? Do you look on it with some despair?

FUENTES: I don't look at it with despair, because I am sure that the people of countries such as the Soviet Union and United

States are themselves in flux. I don't think these are, in spite of appearances, especially in the case of the Soviet Union, rigid societies. The extent of education, the extent of underground change, in the Soviet Union, I believe, must be enormous. In this country [the United States] there is also change. It is boiling over. I think not only the style of life but the model for progress, the ideological model itself, is in a deep, deep crisis. What can the future bring? Well, I think something different. Hopefully, an international order of cooperation without subjection.

You know, Lévi-Strauss says something that really illuminates what we are talking about: The difference between civilizations is not due to their isolation but to their interaction. A creative relationship between cultures supposes a distinction between them; it excludes uniformity. But this, in its turn, presupposes an international order built on respect for the diverse national identities. What I am against is the imposition of a single identity—the North American or the Soviet or the resultant of their condominium of power—on Africa, Asia, Latin America, and Europe. Uniformity will impoverish all. Diversity will enrich all.

MORAES: Do you think the balance of power in the world is going to shift from what are now called the developed nations to underdeveloped nations?

FUENTES: I don't understand the world in terms of balance of power. It smacks too much of Metternichean politics. I think simply that if we achieve the possibility of negotiating from a greater strength than we have had until now—and this seems to be in the offing—we will achieve a more just international order. This is what we are aiming at, not the preponderance of greater strength by one nation, or a group of nations, but actually a better model for international co-existence whereby nobody loses but all give something. Right now there are too many takers and too few givers.

MORAES: Do you think it is actually conceivable that nations will forget their national feelings, what Ardrey calls the territorial imperative, and share with each other?

FUENTES: Well, this is an ideal, of course, I wish it were so. I know the difficulties. We all know them. I think, nevertheless, that many nations have proven, the Arabs very recently, that they can wield a certain power and force the United States or the Soviet Union or any of the big powers to a position that is more just in their relationship with the weaker nations. So I think there is a margin for maneuver, which will with each victory drive us nearer to the ideal of a really interdependent world order on the basis of justice and respect of the sovereignty of states. It is not achieved from one day to another. We have been speaking of the problem of the national state in Latin America and how essential it is to have the national state in order to cope with these problems. Now, the national state did not arise from nothing. It was the product of a long, arduous process. I think Mexico is the country in Latin America that has the most integrated and strongest of all national states. This was not achieved overnight. Certainly it was an inconceivable idea in 1850, when we had been defeated by the United States and half of our territory had been taken by the Americans. But it was precisely the shock of this that made Mexico react, and a very small elite group of the liberal intelligentsia of the country created a political movement, the reform movement, headed by Benito Juárez, that eventually set the basis for the strengthening of the state and the nation. From, as I say, a very limited elitist seed, this sprang to a whole process, which was not achieved overnight, as I think the ideal of international cooperation will not be achieved overnight. It will take a lot of wrangling, it will mean resisting invasions, menaces, pressures, but profiting from whatever margin of maneuver for negotiations we achieve through the international organizations or through national acts of strengthening the state and the social community to win these battles.

This is also true of an initiative such as President Echeverría of Mexico's proposal for an international charter of economic rights and duties of states, now before the United Nations. Some of the developed nations consider it as utopian, but at the same time they are wary of signing it, for a moral obligation can, with time, become a binding legal obligation. After all, law has always had a moral origin: Law had always proposed what *should be* beyond what *is*. Were this not so, we would all be cannibals. I believe that

Nehru was right when he said that the idealism of today is the realism of tomorrow.

MORAES: In many countries in the world, in fact, I would say in most countries in the world, writers and intellectuals generally—if writers are intellectuals—are regarded either as a terrible nuisance or are completely ignored. Would you say that this is the case in Latin America, in Mexico?

FUENTES: I think that through most national histories writers have been ignored, because they are feared. It is a way of trying to neutralize them, through being unaware of them. But the fact is that in a society as closed as Latin America, the power of the written word becomes much more explosive than in societies where the word is common currency and a plurality of social and political forces express themselves through it, criticizing, demanding, and what not.

Sometimes the writer in Latin America has had to play the role of legislator, of union leader, or newspaperman, because of a void, because of the absence of a plurality of social forces capable of taking on these critical tasks. But there is a danger here, of course. That is that the writer feels that in order to get his message through he must sacrifice the aesthetic components of his work. So during a good part of our independent history the writer was very nobly endowed with all these qualities of being the public spokesman for those who had no voice. Then he realized that the lack of aesthetic quality of his work was really a boomerang. The message was not getting through, because the works were in themselves aesthetically perishable. At a given time they were so topical, so limited to very, very strict circumstances, that they could not survive.

I think that, thanks to writers like Pablo Neruda in poetry or Alejo Carpentier in the novel, a revolution came into being in Latin America, a literary revolution, whereby the political, social, and aesthetic components of the work were welded together. It seems to me that the dispute between committed art and art for art's sake is a totally frivolous and formalistic dispute. Any social significance a work might have is totally identified and given power by the strength of the aesthetic form of the work and by the writer's personality. But what we also came to realize very strongly in the past twenty years as writers in Latin America was that, apart from these duties we traditionally felt, we had other, more demanding duties. One was the duty toward language. We came to realize that one of the props of power, and particularly of oppressive power, is language, and that when language is kidnapped or sequestered by power it ceases to be what it is essentially, something that is owned by all, like air.

Language is like air. It belongs to all; it belongs to nobody; it is one way of being human. And when this language is simply a prop for a repressive regime and for a tradition of oppression in sex, family, religion, then it is not our language. We have had to reconquer our language, which is essentially the language of the Spanish counterreformation and its transcendent plan, a language sealed off from whatever was happening in the world outside Spain. We had to break up this language to give it a sense of simultaneity in time and space, a sense of extension of our possibilities, extension of our dreams. We have only been able to do this by realizing that to have the present and to have a future we must have a past. Our past has been a past of silence. Constantly, the voices of love and rebellion and imagination have been silenced throughout Spanish America since the sixteenth century. If we look back on our lives and our history, we hear nothing but silence, a din of silence behind us.

In Mexico there was a very clear case, the case of the nun Juana Inés de la Cruz in the seventeenth century. This woman of powerful imagination, who suddenly began to write about her dreams, her fears, her life, and her death, was promptly silenced by the secular powers and by the Inquisition. Therefore we lost the conscience of our colonial experience, because nobody was writing after Juana Inés de la Cruz had been silenced. There was a void. And we face, therefore, the responsibility of the challenge of filling this void, of giving voice to three centuries of silence, of filling in an immense void of words.

We have all these challenges in Latin America, and that's probably why we have, I believe, one of the most powerful literatures in the world. Many European and North American writers say to me, "We have nothing to talk about. All our topics are being taken over by movies and television and the media. Or by sociologists, or the economists, or the newspapers." This is not, fortunately or unfortunately, our case. I think in Latin America, by writing about the past, you are writing about the present. If you are giving life to what has been silenced, you immediately enhance your own present. I am not saying that one has to write historical novels or poetry about the Indian civilizations. It is more than that. It is, precisely, realizing that one of our marvelous assets is our capacity to make all times simultaneous. If you look at recent productions of Latin American novelists and poets, such as Octavio Paz and Julio Cortázar, what you find is this simultaneity of time and space, which is a negation of the very limited lineal sense of time imposed on us by the West. In the arms of literature we are resurrecting a different concept of civilization and giving it a new shape. From this we will create a new society.

MORAES: In the West, writers quite often are known completely by their work to a literate audience and not known by their particular public actions. In Latin American countries, where sometimes the degree of literacy is not very high, is there not some danger that by becoming involved in public work and public actions, writers will become known to the public more by their actions than by their work, that few people will actually have read them but many will know their names?

FUENTES: Well, I give you a prime example against that danger, which is the case of Pablo Neruda. What he achieved was a total poetry in which the totality of our lives, the totality of our history and our culture, was brought to life. And this was read by millions and millions of people. He even achieved the greatest distinction a writer can achieve. His poetry is quoted and recited by illiterate people who do not even know who wrote the poem.

MORAES: How did they get to the poetry?

FUENTES: It was handed down. Somebody recited it publicly; somebody else learned it. The man who learned it taught it to his child. The child, when it grew up, recited it in turn to somebody else. We have a living literature that is not enclosed exactly within the principles of either Gutenberg or McLuhan. It goes well beyond that. We do have a tremendous old tradition coming down from the Indian civilization for centuries: You go now to an Indian village in Mexico, and you will hear the most marvelous myths spoken and acted by people who do not have a literary tradition.

MORAES: Still, do you believe that writers might be more capable of running a country properly than politicians?

FUENTES: No, no, no. I am very anti-Platonic in this. I think I come back to my central view, which is that a country has to be run by all its citizens, by its writers, and by its farmers, by its workers, by its professional people, and by its politicians, by its civil service. The danger is when only the politicians think they can run a country and reach for the absolute. Then we are in trouble. But if we are capable of creating societies where everybody feels that he is co-governor of the country at his level of work and activity then I think we are heading toward a real democratic ideal.

MORAES: But no society has ever been run so far as I can remember by the whole community. It is always the politicians who have run it.

FUENTES: True, but the politicians only run it to a certain degree. When the society is strong, I think it is only an illusion that the politicians run it. I think, for example, in this country [the United States] the society is very strong. Nixon has not gotten away with all his shenanigans.* Actually in the United States the power of an independent press, an independent judiciary, proves that the society is strong and that the people are to a great extent governing.

As a writer, I believe in the political power of language. Why did the Nazis burn books? Because they were afraid of what Solzhenitsyn calls "the second government." But in the long run, Thomas Mann outlived Hitler, Osip Mandelstam outlived Stalin, Arthur Miller outlived Senator Joe McCarthy, and Pablo Neruda

* This interview took place in Washington some months before the resignation of former President Nixon—D.M.

will outlive the Chilean junta. This is what I mean by another power that constantly wrests absolute power from politicians.

MORÁES: But you said that the Western idea of democracy had not succeeded . . .

FUENTES: No, no, no. Not democracy. I am sorry. I said the *model* for economic progress and industrialization and its imperialist extensions. No, I would not go along with pseudo-Marxist theories, which say that certain rights of man such as the right of free speech and the right of free press, and the right of petition, and the right of protest are simply bourgeois rights to be done away with when the proletariat comes into power. I profoundly disagree with this. I agree that all these values were achieved by the bourgeois revolution, but they are the rights of man. Any revolution that rode over them, a socialist revolution, or whatever you want to call it, would be mutilated, would be condemning itself to death. We cannot sacrifice the conquest of the past to achieve the conquest of the future. We should integrate past, present, and future into a plural model in which many strings will produce a symphony.

I am not proposing any absolute model. I think what would condemn us in Mexico and in Latin America is precisely to choose any absolute model of economic and democratic and human progress. I think we have to take the risk of proposing a model of contradiction and plurality as the only possibility for having really viable, democratic states, not just states that have a higher gross national product and a higher rate of literacy and better hospitals, but total societies. There these chords, which are in the wells of our being, which are waiting for a chance to express themselves, which have been brutally mutilated by history, will be heard. And then we will see what will happen. We will see what the meeting of all these chords in our culture will give us when they actually emerge from underground and meet each other in the air.

ROBERT KWEKU ATTA GARDINER

ROBERT KWEKU ATTA GARDINER, civil servant and international administrator, born in 1914 in Ghana, has been Executive Secretary of the United Nations Economic Commission for Africa since 1963 and, since 1970, chairman of the Commonwealth Foundation as well. His books are: *The Development of Social Administration* (1954, with Helen O. Judd), *A World of Peoples* (1966), *U.N. Regional Commissions in International Economic Cooperation* (1967).

The vast majority of the world's poor live in Africa, Asia, and South America. In Africa approximately 350 million people live in developing countries (1973 estimates) whose average per capita gross domestic product (GDP) is about $200, as compared with an average of more than $3,000 in some of the richer developed countries. However, in making such a comparison, it must be borne in mind that there are still ten African countries with a total of 62 million people whose average per capita GDP is below $100.

Average incomes in individual countries are made up of the high incomes enjoyed by a small proportion of the population and the very low incomes of most of the other inhabitants. Thus, it is likely that in the developing African countries as many as three-quarters of the people (most of whom live in rural areas) have incomes that average out to less than $150. In the poorest of these countries such people have average incomes of $75. When income levels are this low, it is not possible to use the expression "quality of life." The bare existence level at which most African people are still destined to live needs a description of its own. The term "absolute poverty" is probably more realistic.

There are all sorts of measures used for assessing levels of living, and two of these are life expectancy at birth and the proportion of income that is expended on foodstuffs. The life expectancy of a baby born in most of the countries of East, West, and Central Africa is not much more than forty years, which compares with a life expectancy of nearly seventy years in the world's richer countries. Probably about 60 per cent of income is expended on foodstuffs in these same countries, whereas a figure of about 30 per cent is typical in the rich industrial countries. Even the quality and quantity of the food consumed in African countries is often inadequate to supply the food nutrients required. Universal primary education is still only a long-term target for the majority of the countries of Africa, while it is the general rule in the developed world. Illiteracy is widespread and wage-employment levels are very low, leading to wide-scale unemployment or at best underemployment in the rural areas.

Any yardstick used to measure affluence in the developed world, such as food-protein intake, doctors and hospital beds per thousand people, power production, road and rail mileages, can also be used to measure the lack of affluence in the underdeveloped world. The contrasts are startling, and it is probable that the most crucial ones are in food-protein intake and the number of doctors and hospital beds. The difference in life expectancy at birth can probably be directly related to poor nutrient levels, the lack of medical services, and poor environmental hygiene. Poor food and endemic diseases also have their impact on the laborer's ability to perform a hard day's work. It is not surprising that malnutrition, insanitary living conditions, illiteracy, and limited employment opportunities have been used to define absolute poverty.

Even though no two poor countries are alike, we have come to associate certain characteristics with them all, such as bare subsistence in rural areas, beggars in overcrowded urban slums, insufficient government services, low productivity in most, if not all, sectors of production, and poverty of opportunity. These are indeed the outward signs of basic underdevelopment, while lack of roads, railways, and communications reflect the absence of infrastructure. Dependence on a limited number of exports consisting mainly of agricultural, forest, and mineral raw materials, which in some cases are exported to only one or two metropolitan countries, is an indication of a faulty economic structure that creates and perpetuates dependence and poverty. The only practical way in which a better standard of living can be obtained for the people of Africa, thus improving the quality of life, is for the whole development process to be speeded up. The increased income thereby created in the poorer countries would lead to a better level of food consumption, and the higher government revenues could be used for better educational and health facilities and to improve living conditions in general.

An increasing number of poor people in African countries live in an environment that provides very few employment outlets; yet a growing number of persons are becoming aware of their minimum human needs and are no longer able to accept without protest the enforced idleness, despair, and endless frustration that governs their lives. An obvious key to Africa's development is to create more and better job opportunities in agriculture and industry, the one being the major economic sector in Africa, the other being the leading growth sector. It is necessary in this connection not to confine industry to the urban areas but to encourage simple processing activities and the production of simple tools in the rural areas. Unfortunately, the rate at which jobs are created in many countries of the region is at present well below what is needed to cater to the growing number of school-leavers who are increasingly better educated, let alone to have some impact on the existing numbers of unemployed. A clearer perspective can be given to the employment situation, if consideration is also given to the number of rural dwellers who would flock to town if employment opportunities existed. There are obvious exceptions to this rule. For example, there are countries where a high rate of investment expenditure is creating a sufficient number of jobs to absorb virtually all new entrants to the labor force. However, in most African countries, and particularly those classified as least developed, the economy is not growing fast enough.

The rural economy can create wage employment through large-scale projects for sugar, cotton, rubber, and palm production, and an increasing number of such projects are being developed. However, where most people in the rural areas are concerned, there is need for continued emphasis on their own production of consumption crops and, it is hoped, on a steady expansion of commercial crops. There is very little up-to-date information from rural budget surveys as to how families in rural areas make and spend their incomes. The inference is that a family unit will produce most of its own food, selling its surplus food output, commercial crops, and livestock to purchase some of the products of the modern economy. It is difficult to assess how far this view departs from reality. There are obviously families that do very well in a rural environment. Some have large livestock holdings or farmland on which cocoa, coffee, rubber, sugar, groundnuts, cotton, and other crops are grown on a considerable scale. The more typical picture, however, is probably one of a small land holding being farmed by traditional methods from which a barely adequate grain crop is harvested in a good year. Whether there is any production of commercial crops is problematical, but the family may have some livestock grazing on communal land. Unfortunately, this livestock may represent the family capital, and it may not be exploited economically, leading to overgrazing and other ills that droughts tend to accentuate.

Sometimes these hardships led to the conclusion that the answer to them lies in the adoption of population policies in Africa. The doubts that Africans often express are the result of comparing conditions in Africa to those in other parts of the world. In France the population per square mile is estimated at 217, in Great Britain at 573, and in the Netherlands at 884. To take some examples from the developing countries, the density in Pakistan per square mile is 275, in India 364, and in Jamaica 367. Some African density figures are 8 per square mile in Angola, 9 in Algeria, 26 in Tanzania, 53 in Ghana, and 112 in Nigeria. But there is need to emphasize that the well-being of populations is not determined by figures alone. Even the relatively small numbers in Africa are the victims of poor food, endemic diseases, crop failures, the ravages of pests, and the inability to build food reserves to fall back on.

It must not be overlooked that the population under fifteen

in most African countries exceeds 40 per cent, and even where low rates of growth are used, projections indicate that by the end of the century the population of the continent may be in the neighborhood of 800 million. Unless improvements are made in productivity and general living conditions, the population growth will intensify the problems that Africa faces today.

The pressure that exists on the limited cultivable areas or pastures in Africa has recently been illustrated in a tragic way in the countries of the Sahel and in certain provinces of Ethiopia. After years of above-average, normal, or near-normal rainfall, population and livestock numbers were built up in the countries or areas concerned. When rainfall was reduced (as it was, quite drastically, in the last two seasons), grain production was reduced to half of the normal output, and pasturage available was not adequate for the large livestock holdings. As a direct consequence, considerable quantities of grain and foodstuffs had to be imported, but animals still died in substantial numbers, because the transport services could not cope with the large quantities of animal feed required to keep them alive.

Although the memory of similar experiences in the past did not linger long enough for the necessary steps to be taken to prevent the present recurrence of disasters, there are many lessons that can be learned from such an experience: First, water must be stored in good years to help soften the impact of serious droughts in bad years. Second, grain must be stored properly in good years. Third, adequate transport links must be developed. Fourth, livestock holdings must be kept at a level that prevents overgrazing and the emergence of situations such as the present one, with about 16 per cent of the total cattle herd of 22 million in six countries lost in 1973 alone; also, abattoir and meat-processing facilities must be more generally available, so that the herds can be reduced in times of crisis by slaughtering and the meat and meat products obtained can be sold.

Drought and its attendant suffering is one distressing aspect of the reality of Africa today. However, it is possible to give many examples of the progress that is being made in Africa to offset the impression that the Dark Continent may still be dark for most of its people. There is the obvious success of a number of integrated rural development projects in which resources for the production of commercial crops are concentrated in selected areas. The result is a better balance of consumer crops that is increasing the level of farm incomes. These schemes usually provide both health and educational facilities in the areas concerned. There are plans for large-scale dam projects and for an increased number of transport links in the Sahel. As an immediate measure boreholes are being sunk to tap existing underground water resources, and every effort is being made to take remedial action. Food-grain aid is continuing to help the Sahelian countries until the next rains come in the second half of 1974.

In urban areas many industrial projects have been and are being developed. Large office blocks, hotels, schools, and hospitals have been built; the services required for such establishments—water, electricity, transport, sewage—are being continuously expanded. The number of dwelling units is constantly rising, although some of them may not be up to the standard required. The growth rate of the population of the urban areas is probably in excess of 5 per cent a year, compared with an over-all population growth rate of nearly 2.8 per cent a year. The urban population growth rate is close to the growth rate of the GDP for the economy as a whole, which averaged about 4.6 per cent a year for the period 1971–73, *i.e.*, the first three years of the Second Development Decade.

The target growth rate for developing Africa from 1971 to 1975 was 6 per cent a year, but this rate has not been attained to date. If there were two really good agricultural seasons in 1974 and 1975, the average for the five years could approach 6 per cent. However, on the basis of past experience, it is difficult to be confident that the rainfall will be such as to produce the crops and pastures required.

Mineral production in Africa has been developed comparatively rapidly, although in recent years the output of crude petroleum has been reduced in Libya to conserve resources for the future. New deposits of minerals are being discovered continuously, and it is often the case that the development of a new mine leads to the creation of an entirely new urban area. Transport links on the continent are also being constantly expanded, both within individual countries and from country to country. A road map today would show many more and higher-quality roads than one drawn up ten years ago. However, there is still a long way to go before the transport system can be considered to be basically adequate.

Similarly, other services and facilities have been and are being built up as Africa moves slowly toward that better way of life that is still only a promise for most of its people. The extent to which education and health facilities are provided is probably a good indicator of progress insofar as the basic wishes of the people are concerned. There are wide variations in the stage of development of such facilities reached in individual countries. The wealthier countries have probably achieved or nearly achieved universal primary education, whereas the poorer ones may have an enrollment rate as low as 20 to 30 per cent. The provision of health service as measured by the numbers of hospital beds and doctors per thousand people is also related to the level of per capita GDP, better facilities being found in the wealthier countries and, within countries, in areas serving the wealthier members of the community.

Environmental problems in Africa are two-dimensional: In taming nature to make the continent habitable, rational policies for the exploitation of natural resources are needed. Traditional agriculture has been destructive of the soil, indiscriminate felling of trees for timber has led to deforestation, and careless mineral exploitation of resources ruins the countryside. These negative aspects of development are already noticeable, and urgent action is required to reverse a trend that can only add to the hardships of the African countries. There is also an urgent need to ensure the supply of potable water and clean water both for fisheries and agriculture by preventing the destruction of water resources by pollutants from nascent industries. Similarly, the development of transport links must not lead to the destruction of nature's attractions, including its wildlife.

Having touched briefly on the reality of life on the African continent, it may help to express a few ideas on what life should be like in the ideal state for most of Africa's people: First, all Africans must be assured of a reasonably varied diet providing adequate nutrients. Second, clean water supplies must be available in every part of the region in adequate quantities to meet the requirements of both people and animals. Third, water resources must be stored in realistically sized dams and used over the normal weather-cycle period to help produce sufficient food supplies and to prevent famine. Grain should be stored in good years to help meet the shortfall in the bad years. Fourth, educational facilities must be available to all children, so that universal primary education becomes a reality. The secondary and higher-level educational facilities provided should be related to Africa's requirements for middle- and high-level entrants to the labor force. Fifth, health facilities should be gradually expanded so as to provide a reasonable level of health care. They should include clinics in the rural areas, supplemented by rural hospitals, then district hospitals, and finally central or referral hospitals. Sixth, the housing stock available must be expanded and improved to allow more of Africa's people to begin to enjoy the type of amenities that are taken for granted in the developed countries of the world. The seventh point, which is probably of fundamental importance, is that wage-employment opportunities should be available to all persons willing to work. Most countries in the region are nowhere near this happy state at the present time, but continuing economic development should begin to make it an increasing reality. As a corollary of point seven, the social security systems in Africa must be built up so that people who lose their employment, suffer sickness, or reach retirement age can have a reasonable level of income.

Rural development must reach the stage where the differences between the way of life in rural and in urban areas become very minor. This would ensure that the pull of the urban areas as a means to a better life would be eliminated and a more sensible two-way flow between urban and rural areas could result.

As these changes come about, continuous attention will need to be paid to certain other factors that assist in enhancing the quality of life. For example, the emptiness of life that is typical of large agglomerations in the developed countries can be avoided. Large urban areas should develop as clusters of small-sized areas, so that a village atmosphere can be maintained. This would ensure that the loneliness experienced by so many urban inhabitants would be avoided. Travel to and from work should be cut to an absolute minimum. This is possible in medium-sized urban communities but is almost impossible in the larger urban areas.

Within urban areas atmospheric pollution must be kept to a minimum. Industries that create dirt should be kept on the outside of large urban areas, and a maximum effort should be made to remove the dirt and impurities created in industrial processes. Noise levels must be kept to a minimum in the urban areas. The major offenders are some types of motor vehicles, and the noisier type of vehicle should either be absolutely banned or kept outside inhabited areas. One can hope that the move away from the internal combustion engine, which has already started, may solve this problem. The larger urban areas should develop their own entertainment centers, and there should be adequate facilities available for recreation. A capital city would normally be a focus for such amenities as entertainment and cultural events, but a reasonably sized provincial city should also be able to build up such attractions.

Finally, a word should be said about the need for more rapid progress in the development of Africa's resources. From evidence that exists in developed countries, a high standard of living appears to bring with it a reduction in the size of the average family. Resistance to the reduction of the size of families appears to be breaking down in Africa. In the past, when the infant mortality rate was high and only one out of four or five children survived, a large family provided some kind of insurance. Also, up to very recently (and this is still true in some parts), children could act as extra farmhands at a very early age. With the spread of education the period of dependency has been extended, and whereas children used to contribute to the resources of a household, material and financial resources now have to be expended on them during the time they remain unproductive. It is becoming increasingly common for both parents to be educated and working. The reason for this development is that the increased income made by the household helps to meet the needs of children for food, shelter, clothing, and education more adequately. Such changed living conditions and the growing awareness that children should be given a better quality of life are leading African communities to accept the need for national population policies.

I have emphasized the unsatisfactory nature of the situation as it exists now. But the present situation must be changed, and every effort must be directed to the most appropriate ways of bringing about the necessary changes. There is still an urgent need for the African economy to grow at a rate at which it can begin to meet the aspirations of its people for a better way of life. The resources of the continent must be exploited in a way that brings a much fairer distribution of incomes. Whether family limitation will make much of an impact on the typical standard of living over the next decade is problematical, but population planning can focus attention on present realities. It makes sense to reduce the average natural growth rate of the population in Africa, so that the increase in the per capita GDP becomes much more significant year by year. Unless incomes are equitably shared, however, rural families might see little in the way of real improvement in their living standards.

I have also said that the level at which African families subsist is usually so low that it is impossible to talk about quality of life in any meaningful context. The primary necessity at the moment is to create circumstances for the achievement of a basic minimum level at which families are able to eat better, to live in more sanitary conditions, and to benefit from more adequate education and health services. If this were made possible for all people in Africa, then a very important first step would have been taken in the direction of providing quality of life.

ISAAC
BASHEVIS SINGER

ISAAC BASHEVIS SINGER, novelist and short story writer in Yiddish, born 1904 in Poland, is now an American citizen. His short story collection, *A Crown of Feathers,* shared the 1973 National Book Award for fiction. Among his other works are: *Satan in Goray* (1955), *Gimpel the Fool and Other Stories* (1957), *The Spinoza of Market Street and Other Stories* (1961), *The Family Moskat* (1966), *In My Father's Court* (1966).

I know in advance that anything I have to write is either known to you already or available on the shelves of your library. For that reason I have decided to forget modesty and write about myself; on that subject at any rate I am somewhat of an authority. I hope that you will find my case history of some value.

I have in my lifetime lived through a number of epochs in Jewish history. I was brought up in a home where the old Jewish faith burned brightly. Ours was a house of Torah and holy books. Other children had toys; I played with the volumes in my father's library. I began to write before I even knew the alphabet. I took my father's pen, dipped it in ink, and started to scribble. The Sabbath was an ordeal for me, because on that day writing is forbidden.

My father moved to Warsaw when I was still very young, and there a second epoch began for me: the age of the Enlightenment. My brother, I. J. Singer, who later wrote *The Brothers Ashkenazi,* was at that time a rationalist. It was not in his nature to hide his opinions. He spoke frankly to my parents, advancing with great clarity and precision all the arguments that the rationalists—from Spinoza to Max Nordau—had brought against religion. Though I

73

was still a child, I listened attentively. Fortunately, my parents did not lack answers. They replied with as much skill as that with which my brother attacked. I recall my father saying, "Well, who created the world? You? Who made the sky, the stars, the sun, the moon, man, the animals?" My brother's answer was that everything evolved. He mentioned Darwin. "But," my mother wanted to know, "how can a creature with eyes, ears, lungs, and a brain evolve from earth and water?" My father used to say, "You can spatter ink, but it won't write a letter by itself." My brother never had an answer for this. As yet none has been found.

My parents attempted to further strengthen the case for faith by constantly telling stories of imps, ghosts, and dybbuks, and of the miraculous feats of famous rabbis. Some of these events they themselves had witnessed, and I knew that they were not liars. My grandfather, the Rabbi of Bilgoray, had once been visited by an old man, a fortune teller, who had been able to read the text of a closed book; whatever page my grandfather touched with his finger, the fortune teller could recite. I later used this incident in a story of mine, "The Jew of Babylon," which has not yet been translated. My mother knew of a house inhabited by a poltergeist. Indeed, I can truthfully say that by the time I was seven or eight I was already acquainted with all the strange facts that are to be found in the books of Conan Doyle, Sir Oliver Lodge, and others.

In our home the most pressing questions were the eternal ones; there the cosmic riddles were not theoretical but actual. I began to read in *The Guide for the Perplexed* and the *Chazari,* even in the Cabalistic literature, at an early age. But nevertheless, despite my studies, I remained a child and played joyfully with other children. At *cheder* I astounded my fellow students with fantastic stories. I told them once that my father was a king with such convincing detail that they believed me.

When World War I broke out, I experienced all the social evils of the period. I saw the men on our street marching off to war, leaving behind them sobbing women and hungry children. Men from the very house I lived in were taken. In his debates with my brother, my father argued, "You keep on talking about logic. What logic is there to this war? How does it happen that learned men and teachers assist in the manufacture of bombs and guns to destroy innocent people?" Again my brother had no answer. He himself was drafted. During the short time that he was a recruit, he endured every kind of humiliation. The Russian and Polish recruits accused him of murdering Jesus, poisoning wells, using Christian blood for Passover *matzoth,* and of spying for the Germans. In the barracks reason was bankrupt. My high-minded brother fled to Warsaw and hid in the studio of a sculptor. I used to carry food to him there.

No, the world that was revealed to me was not rational. One could as easily question the validity of reason as the existence of God. In my own spirit there was chaos. I suffered from morbid dreams and hallucinations. I had wildly erotic fantasies. Hungry children, filthy beggars, refugees sleeping in the streets, wagons of wounded soldiers did not arouse admiration in me for human or divine reason. The spectacle of a cat pouncing on a mouse made me sick and rebellious. Neither human reason nor God's mercy seemed to be certain. I found both filled with contradictions. My brother still clung to the hope that in the end reason would be victorious. But young though I was, I knew that the worship of reason was as idolatrous as bowing down to a graven image. As yet I had not read the modern philosophers, but I had come to the conclusion by myself that reason leads to antinomies when it deals with time, space, and causality; it could deal no better with these than with the *ultimate problem,* the problem of evil.

In 1917 my mother took me and one of my younger brothers to Bilgoray, which was being occupied by the Austrians. Kerensky's revolution had occurred and was regarded as the victory of reason, but soon after came the October Revolution and the pogroms in the Ukraine. Bilgoray had just endured a cholera epidemic. The town had lost a third of its inhabitants. Some of my relatives had been stricken. The gruesome tales of that pestilence are still fresh in my memory.

In Bilgoray, a village with no railroad and surrounded by forests, the Jewish traditions of a hundred years before were still very much alive. I had already become acquainted with modern Hebrew and Yiddish literature. The writers of both languages were under the influence of the Enlightenment. These authors wanted the Jew to step out of his old-fashioned gabardine and become *European*. Their doctrines were rationalistic, liberal, humanistic. But to me such ideas seemed already obsolete. The overthrowing of one regime and the replacing of it with another did not seem to me to be the crux of the matter. The problem was creation itself. I felt that I must achieve some sort of solution of the puzzle or perish myself.

While in Bilgoray I became acquainted with the literature of other nations. I read in translation Tolstoy, Dostoevsky, Gogol, Heine, Goethe, Flaubert, Maupassant. I read Jack London's *The Call of the Wild* and the stories of Edgar Allan Poe—all in Yiddish. It was at this time also that I first studied Spinoza's *Ethics* in a German translation. I pored over each page as though it were a part of the Talmud; some of the axioms, definitions, and theorems I still remember by heart. I am now able to see the defects and hiatuses in Spinoza's system, but my reading of the *Ethics* had a great effect on me. My story "The Spinoza of Market Street" is rooted in this period. Later I read a history of philosophy and Hume, Kant, Schopenhauer, and Nietzsche. My philosophic pursuits were not undertaken to make me a philosopher. My childish hope was to discover the truth and through the discovery to give sense and substance to my life. But, finally, my conclusion was that the power of philosophy lay in its attack upon reason, not in the building of systems. None of the systems could be taken seriously; they did not help one to manage one's life. The human intellect confronted existence, and existence stubbornly refused to be systematized. I myself was the insulted and shamed human intellect. Many times I contemplated suicide because of my intellectual impotence.

All these storms took place inside me. On the outside I was just a Hassidic boy who studied the Gemara, prayed three times a day, put on phylacteries. But the people of the town were suspicious anyway. They considered me an exotic plant. I saw with grief and sometimes envy how other boys my age made peace somehow with this world and its troubles. I lacked their humility.

At that time I began to write in Hebrew. So perturbed was my spirit that I expected my pen to express, at least partially, my rage. But I saw with shame that nothing issued but banal and thrashed-out phrases, similar to those I read in other books and that I criticized severely. I felt as if a devil or imp held on to my pen and inhibited it. A mysterious power did not let me reveal my inner self. After many trials I decided it was the fault of the Hebrew language. Hebrew was near to me, but it was not my mother language. While writing, I kept on searching in my memory for words and phrases from the Bible, the Mishnah, and later literature; in addition, each Hebrew word dragged after itself a whole chain of associations. I came to the conclusion that writing in Yiddish would be easier. But I soon found that this was not so. I still had not lost my inhibitions. Satan did not allow me to express my individuality. Despite myself, I imitated Knut Hamsun, Turgenev, and even lesser writers. Every creator painfully experiences the chasm between his inner vision and its ultimate expression. This chasm is never completely bridged. We all have the conviction, perhaps illusory, that we have much more to say than appears on the paper. I began an investigation of the techniques of literature. What, I asked myself, makes Tolstoy and Dostoevsky so great? Is it the theme, style, or construction?

My brother, I. J. Singer, had left Poland and gone to Russia. He was residing in Kiev, where he wrote for the Yiddish press and had already published his story "Pearls." One day he showed up in Bilgoray to spend the day. As a writer he had already "arrived." I had sufficient character not to show him my manuscripts. I knew that I had to find my way by myself.

Some time thereafter I went to live in Warsaw, which was then the center of Yiddish culture in Poland. My brother was co-editor of the *Literarishe Bleter,* and I got a job there as a proofreader. It was in the early '20s. I had not yet published anything. At that time my brother was a friend of the famous Peretz Markish who was later liquidated by Stalin. Other members of his literary circle were Melechkatvitch, Uri Zvi Greenberg, today a famous Hebrew poet, and American Yiddish writers like Joseph Opatoshu who came on visits to Warsaw. A spirit of revolution permeated the new Yiddish literature. This coterie preached that classic and academic literature was bankrupt and spoke of a new time, a new period, a new style. Markish wrote in the style of Mayakovsky, and Alexander Blok, the Russian poet, author of the poem "Twelve," was the most beloved writer of that group.

I was afraid to set myself against writers who were all well recognized, although I saw that their art was neither new in spirit nor style. They had merely dressed up the old clichés in red clothing. All they did was juggle words. Even a young boy like me, from the provinces, found the doctrine that the Bolshevik Revolution would do away with all evil incredibly naïve. The Jewish situation in Poland was especially bad. The Polish people—the people themselves, not merely the regime—had never come to terms with the Jews. The Jews had built a separate society in Poland, had their own faith, language, holidays, and even political aspirations. We Jews were both citizens and aliens. My father, for example, could speak no Polish. I myself spoke Polish with an accent. Though my ancestors had lived in Poland for six hundred years, we were still strangers. No revolution could unite these two so profoundly separated communities. Communism and Zionism, the two ideals that split the Jews of Poland, were both completely alien to the Polish people. I do not mean to imply by this that I had remarkable prescience, but I saw clearly that the Jews were living in a volcano. In my bitterness I spoke about the coming catastrophe, but those around me were puffed up with optimism, rationalism, and red dogmatism.

My brother soon freed himself of revolutionary illusions, but he kept his belief in reason. He still thought that through evolution and progress man would slowly see his mistakes and correct them. We had many discussions. In a sense, I had taken over the position of my parents. I tried mercilessly to destroy his humanistic optimism. I regret now that I did this, because what did I have to offer? My parents at least advocated religion. Mine was only a negative philosophy. My brother was always tolerant and deeply sympathetic to me, but I was rebellious and often insolent.

A new *Weltanschauung,* which I find difficult to characterize, began to develop in me. It was a kind of religious skepticism: There is a God, but He never reveals himself; no one knows who He is or what is His purpose. There are an infinite number of universes, and even here, on this earth, powers exist of which we have no inkling, both stronger and weaker than man. This system allowed for the possibility of angels, devils, and other beings that are and will remain forever unnamed. I had, in a curious way combined the Ten Commandments, Humian philosophy, and the Cabalistic writing of Rabbi Moshe from Cordova and of the holy Isaac Luria, as well as the occultism of Flammarion, Sir Oliver Lodge, Sir William Crooks. This was, as one can see, a sort of *kasha,* a porridge, of mysticism, deism, and skepticism, well suited to my intellect and temperament. Instead of a concrete universe of facts, I saw a developing universe of potentialities. The thing-in-itself is pure potential. In the beginning was potentiality. What seem to be facts are really potentialities. God is the sum of all possibility. Time is the mechanism through which potentiality achieves sequence. The Cabala teaches that all worlds are created through the combination of letters. My own position was that the universe is a series of countless potentialities and combinations. I had already read Schopenhauer's *The World as Will and Idea* and so knew the Schopenhauerian view that the will is the thing-in-itself, the noumenon behind the phenomenon. But to me, the basic substance of the world was potentially seen as a whole.

I did not conceive of this as a philosophy for others but strictly for myself. Somehow or other it made sense for me, but I didn't have the means or need to systematize it and make it understandable to others. I would say that it was more a philosophy of art than of being.

God was for me an eternal belle lettrist. His main attribute was creativity, and what he created was made of the same stuff as he and shared his desire: to create again. I quoted to myself that passage from the Midrash that says God created and destroyed many worlds before he created this one. Like my brother and myself God threw his unsuccessful works into the wastebasket. The flood, the destruction of Sodom, the wanderings of the Jews in the desert, the wars of Joshua, these were all episodes in a divine novel, full of suspense and adventure. Yes, God was a creator, and that which he created had a passion to create. Each atom, each molecule had creative needs and possibilities. The sun, the planets, the fixed stars, the whole cosmos seethed with creativity and creative fantasies. I could feel this turmoil within myself.

I availed myself of the doctrine of *zimzum,* that wonderful notion which is so important in the Cabala of Rabbi Isaac Luria.

God, Isaac Luria says, is omnipotent but had to diminish himself and his light so that he could create. Such shrinking is the source of creation, not only in man but also in the Godhead. The evil host makes creation possible. God could not have his infinite works without the devil. Out of suffering, creativity is born. The existence of pain in the world can be compared to a writer's suffering as he describes some dreadful scene that he lives through in his imagination. As he writes, the author knows that his work is only fiction produced for his and his reader's enjoyment. Each man, each animal exists only as clay in the hands of a creator and is itself creative. We ourselves are the writer, the book, and the hero. The medieval philosophers expressed a similar idea when they said that God is Himself the knower, the known, and the knowledge.

I am not seeking here to state a new philosophy. All I desire to do is to describe a state of mind. Just as an artist hopes throughout his whole life to create the great and perfect work, so does God yearn throughout all eternity to perfect his creation. God is no static perfection, as Spinoza thought, but a limitless and unsatiated will for perfection. All His worlds are nothing more than stages and experiments in a divine laboratory. When I went to the *cheder* as a boy and studied "Akdamoth," the poem for Pentecost, I was amazed by the verses in the poem that said that if all skies were parchment, all men writers, all blades of grass pens, and all the oceans ink, these would still be insufficient to describe the mysteries of the Torah. That parable became my credo: The skies were indeed parchment, the grasses pens, and all men, in fact, writers. Everything that existed wrote, painted, sculpted, and sought for creative achievement.

Since the purpose of creation was creation, creativity was also the criterion of ethics and even of sociology. There was a place only for those social systems that could advance creativity. Freedom was nothing but the freedom to create. Since creativity required leisure and some degree of wealth, men must create a system that would furnish the requisites necessary to experiment.

Yes, God is a writer, and we are both the heroes and the readers. A novel written by the Lord cannot be only for one short season. As heroes of God's novel we are all immortal. A great writer's work can be understood on many levels, and this implies that our existence has more than one meaning. We exist in body. We exist as symbols, parables, and in many other ways. When the critics praise a writer they say that his hero is three dimensional, but God's heroes have more than three dimensions. Their dimensions are numberless. Good novels are often translated into many languages, and so is the novel called Life. Versions of this work are read on other planets, on other galaxies of the universe.

Apropos of the critics, like all writers, the Almighty has His critics. We know that the angels have nothing but praise. Three times a day they sing: Sublime! Perfect! Great! Excellent! But there must be some angry critics, too. They complain: Your novel, God, is too long, too cruel. Too little love. Too much sex. They advise cutting. How can a novel be good when three fourths of it is water? They find it inconsistent, sensational, antisocial, cryptic, decadent, vulgar, pointless, melodramatic, improvised, repetitious. But about one quality we all agree: God's novel has suspense. One keeps on reading it day and night. The fear of death is nothing but the fear of having to close God's book. We all want to go on with this serial forever. The belief in survival has one explanation: We refuse to have any interruptions in reading. As readers we are burning with a desire to know the events of the next chapter, and the next, and the next. We try to find the formula for God's best seller, but we are always wrong. The heavenly writer is full of surprises. All we can do is pray for a happy ending, but according to the Cabala God's novel will never end. The coming of the Messiah will only be the beginning of a new volume. Resurrection will bring back some characters the reader, but not the writer, has already forgotten. What we call death is but a temporary pause for purely literary reasons.

My way in literature at last became clear to me: to transform inhibition into a method of creativity; to recognize in the inhibition a friendly power instead of a hostile one; in the terms of the Cabala, to lift up the holy sparks that had fallen from the sacred into the impure, from the world of emanations into the unclean host. Even though I realized that this philosophy was nothing but my private concoction, I considered it valid and useful as a basis for my work. In the world of the artist the teaching of Isaac Luria is certainly true: The shadow is often the precursor of the light; the devils and imps are temptations and challenges to further achievement. The purpose of each fall is a new rising. Each occasion for sin can become an occasion for virtue. Each passion, no matter how low, can become a ladder to ascend.

Satan in Goray, which I wrote in 1932, was a product of this state of mind. Writing about the epoch of Sabbatai Zevi was for me a rare opportunity to express these thoughts in a symbolic way. This epoch was for me a lesson in both religion and creativity. One must learn from the inhibition, discover its higher purpose; one must neither ignore it completely nor submit to it. The inhibition in the broadest sense is always an indication of new potentialities. In almost all my later works I try to show man's urge to create, to find what is new, unique, and to overcome the disturbances and barriers in his way.

Creativity is for me a very encompassing idea. I would say that everything that gives a man pleasure is creative, and what causes him pain is an inhibition in his creative desire. Like Spinoza I am a hedonist. Like the Cabalists I believe that the principle of male and female exists not only in the lower worlds but in the higher ones as well. The universal novel of creation, like the novel of an earthly writer, is finally a love story.

The Cabalists compared the unclean host to the female, and this comparison has deep significance. A male can bring out his semen quickly and in abundance, but the female demands time, patience, and a period of ripening. She is, if you want, the inhibition, but she is also the power that transmutes intention into deed. The Cabalists saw in God a division into the masculine and the feminine, which they called the *shechinah.* God himself must have time and space for his work. In His original form He is not perfect but ripens in infinite time; even the universe is expanding. Men can serve him by creating within their narrow worlds, in their small way, conditions that will permit creativity for all—from the bee to man, from the microbe that sours our milk to the artist. The freedom to which we aspire should not be an end in itself. Its ultimate aim must be man's boundless creativity.

God creates continuously, and continuous creation is man's

destiny, too. God, like the artist, is free. Like the artist His work cannot be predetermined. Continual change is their very essence. Beauty is their purpose. God's fantasy is their limit. God, like the artist, never knows how His work will develop. Only the intention is clear: to bring out a masterpiece and to improve it all the time. I once called God a struggling artist. This continual aspiration is what men call suffering. In this system emotions are not passive as in Spinoza's philosophy. God himself is emotion. God thinks and feels. Compassion and beauty are two of his endless attributes. In my novel *The Slave* I have expressed this notion in these words:

> The summer night throbbed with joy; from all sides came music. Warm winds bore the smells of grain, fruit, and pine trees to him. Itself a Cabalistic book, the night was crowded with sacred names and symbols—mystery upon mystery. In the distance where sky and earth merged, lightning flashed, but no thunder followed. The stars looked like letters of the alphabet, vowel points, notes of music. Sparks flickered above the bare furrows. The world was a parchment scrawled with words and song. Every now and then Jacob heard a murmur in his ear as if some unseen being was whispering to him. He was surrounded by powers, some good, some evil, some cruel, some merciful, but each with its own nature and its own task to perform.

EUGÈNE IONESCO*

EUGÈNE IONESCO, playwright, born in 1912 in Rumania, now a French citizen living in Paris, is one of the leading figures of the avant-garde French theater. His plays have formed the major part of the Theater of the Absurd. They include: *Amedée* (1958), *La Cantatrice chauve* (*The Bald Soprano*, 1958), *Le Rhinocéros* (*Rhinoceros*, 1960), *Le Roi se meurt* (*Exit the King*, 1963), *Macbett* (1972).

How should human beings live? What is to be done so that human beings live as they should? What is a truly human existence?

People lived yesterday and live today exactly as they deserve to. In fact, men themselves are responsible for the way in which they live. Since their origin they have been exploiting one another; each one wants to make the other his slave or his tool; they kill one another; they hate one another; they oppress and torture one another. The situation does not appear to be improving. *Homo homini lupus.* We know that animals generally have no desire to destroy other animals of the same species. There are exceptions like the ants, who wage really destructive wars among themselves, or the termites, who, shortly after they are born, massacre the preceding generation. But that does not prevent the survival of the species. People kill each other for reasons that may seem to be ideological, religious, nationalistic, but none of these constitute the true reason, which is not apparent. In fact, with common sense everything could be settled—a redistribution of economic welfare, a rearrangement of available living

* Translated by Leela Moraes

space, etc. Many animals of the same species share their living space. Why can't people share things in a friendly way? Why is it that people do not want to share things in a friendly way? I may be told that I am being simple-minded, that the question has no solution, or one that will never come about, or that we do not want to solve it. But it is from such simple and naïve questions that solutions could emerge. This seems to me obvious. By getting to the basic factors of a problem, one sees the problem more clearly. There is the aim and the means. If one can say that the aim is reasonable, one cannot say that the means are. In the name of religion one tortures, persecutes, builds pyres. In the guise of ideologies one massacres, tortures, and kills. In the name of justice one punishes. In fact, one judges to be able to punish. Every tribunal passes sentences. In the name of love of one's country or of one's race one hates other countries, despises them, massacres them. In the name of equality and brotherhood, there is suppression and torture. There is nothing in common between the end and the means; the means go far beyond the end—so much so that I am convinced that the means actually become the end. Ideologies and religions act as alibis; they are the alibis of the means.

We know that everything is conflict, everything is war: the class struggle, the confrontation of empires, the battles of clans, personal squabbles. If man does not have an enemy at hand to kill or fight, then he is at war with himself, in conflict with himself. He goes to the extent of committing psychological or physical suicide. Actually, it seems to me that the whole world can no longer stand itself. Aggressiveness and aggression are straightforward, plain, of a basic level. What the philosophers, educators, psychologists, and psychoanalysts were hoping for has not come about: Aggressiveness has neither been channeled nor sublimated, nor has it disappeared. All you see are people being killed. What has happened recently over much of the world, where many adults as well as children have been massacred by terrorists representing one cause or another, is extremely revealing. Beyond their immediate targets, they were after children, consciously or not. This slaughtering shocks us, depresses us, makes us despair because it has happened recently, because we have been told about it, because we have no memory. To murder children has been a habit in mankind's history. The Bible tells us about it, and so many others of the innocent have been massacred.

Building houses, inventing waste disposal, being able to have a bath in one's flat, knowing how to protect oneself from the heat or the cold, taking a ride in a car, achieving great strides in medicine, in surgery, climbing on planets, all this is of no use as long as man is the aggressor of man. The most extraordinary invention—the atom bomb—proves very clearly that man begrudges man, that man is after man.

When I was fifteen I had already come to understand that life is only suffering. I had understood that one cannot avoid or cure this suffering, that it was handed out to us, and that, unfortunately, the way people have to live is in suffering. And then I soon understood that people can only live hating, hating one or the other, because "hell is others." I read and was told that men were revolting because man was exploiting man and that those who were exploited were right to revolt, that the rebellious were "good." I was given and I read a great many explanations and justifications for violence. People also wanted me to believe that we lived in a bad society and that a good society would take care of everything. There is no good society.

All societies are bad, if one looks around and analyzes the historical facts that go beyond ideologies. Societies that once seemed as if they could be utopia have been erected; unfortunately, they are worse than others. In countries that are still called socialist tyrants control everything. Free societies are like jungles where people are driven by the ruthless and stupid struggle to acquire. We know, as Albert Camus, among others, reminded us, that the victims can become the tormentors and the tormentors victims. It seems equally clear to me that the victims aspire to become the torturers.

It makes me laugh when we are told that the "evil in oneself" does not exist and is only the product of our society. In fact, when those who have revolted create a new society, it seems that this new society only strengthens the making of a liberal or bourgeois society that had lost its structure, become decadent, let itself go, whose decay spawned anything bad, because a flawed authority allowed one, at least, to "breathe." The new society reinstates authority and dogma. Its rulers, with the pretext of an ideology that has a clear conscience, can commit injustices in the name of justice and crimes in the name of brotherhood, can set up the most rigid hierarchy in the name of equality, can proceed to massacre their people, precisely in the name of their people. All the new societies are like concentration camps. David Rousset showed us that concentration camps were in society's image, in a harsher form. Revolutionaries are bent on turning their new societies into concentration camps. In one of the Latin American countries the regime is, as its rulers themselves call it, "institutionalized revolution." Those who revolt obviously lead us to this sort of thing, and they, consciously or unconsciously, bring up new absolute standards without which societies become decadent. It is only when societies become decadent that the individual can live. That is the paradox. Man is a social animal who cannot stand society. "Institutionalized revolution" as a phrase is a slip of the tongue, but it is extremely revealing that it has been chosen by the government of a great country. Men are fooled by History because History is crafty, as Hegel said. But if men end up in sorrow when they talk to you about happiness, it may mean that their unconscious wants sorrow and tyranny. Hitler claimed he wanted to lead Germany to conquer the whole universe—he destroyed her. The Russians claimed they wanted to set up a paradise on earth—their unconscious chose hell. They have murdered their scientists, their poets, the soul of their people. The criminal is spreading in every country. In totalitarian countries it is those in power who are criminal. What is better? To be afraid of robbers and murderers or to be afraid of the police? The Tibetan civilization, the only metaphysical civilization in the world, has been profoundly altered. The Russians have destroyed a great part of the Orthodox Church and the traditional Jewish culture that sustained itself in Russia and in Poland. The socialists were afraid of religion. A French philosopher recently declared that we have every reason to revolt and that we should revolt. In my opinion one should not revolt against societies, or the Establishment, or against institutions that contain all that man has achieved and wanted. The discontent is not social or political, it has to do with our existence. It is not one's social condition that is inadmissable, it is the condition of our existence.

But perhaps our revolutions have to do with this basic discontent. We get the impression of being the toys of some capricious fate that hides the real aims of its whims and substitutes others that seem obvious but are false. In fact, one can say that the purpose and the meaning of revolts are ambiguous. In demystifying them we find that they are made of a desire to destroy and a desire to rebuild, to restore. The whole of Marxism expresses ideologically what is already included in mythology. The idea of progress is the myth of ascending; the perfect communist society speaks of our tendency, our desire, to find the lost paradise again: the "de-alienated" man is, in reality, man transfigured by his glory or resurrected in a glorious embodiment. The final struggle that is to take place between the old and the new society, this inevitable and catastrophic conflict, is in fact the Apocalypse, after which man will at a point be reintegrated beyond the reach of history, that is to say, in paradise—a paradise where all conflicts will have disappeared—so that he will control his own history. When Christianity started, its adherents talked about the New Man; it is the New Man that the Marxists talk about. The Messiah's second birth has not taken place, and the Kingdom of Heaven keeps us waiting when we thought it was soon to come. After the revolution Marxists were also hoping for a "new Jerusalem soon." But as with Christianity, the Marxists now can see that the perfect society will not come about tomorrow and is also pushed back to some distant and vague future. All utopians harbor Biblical myths.

There is no "human" existence in the natural world. Social and biological existence is not enough for man; historical perspective is not what he wants. All this means that his existence, his life, his condition are tragic. His aspiration is religious or metaphysical. Since this aspiration cannot be satisfied, men go around in circles, as if in some infernal cage, and massacre one another.

Men cannot stand to be born and to be born in this world, to live in it and to die in it. It is a paradox, but it is so: We kill and we kill because we hate death, because we hate our condition.

The "ideal" of the human condition is no longer to be human, to be free of the condition. We clearly see that the fulfillment of material needs is no real satisfaction. Economic benefits and wealth do not cure what is wrong with us. We can eat better, we can eat our fill, but that does not basically change our situation. The unfortunate Hindus who are dying of misery seem to be more resigned. It's obvious that we should share our bread with them. It is imperative that we do. However, the cataclysms that science and futurology foresee threaten us and in a not-so-distant future, a future that is much less distant than all those tomorrows that we glow about. It may be that mankind is aware of its secret goal: its own destruction.

What can governments do to remedy what is wrong in the world? I have said in these pages why they are powerless. Reform, revolutionize, restore? This is little; it is nothing. Often it only compounds matters.

We are born alienated. If governments want to socialize man so that all he turns out to be is a civil servant of society, cutting him off from his metaphysical roots, they will only alienate him a little further. Man cannot be shut in the social cage, he needs another dimension. We have talked enough of freedom and of various types of freedoms that further do away with freedom. Behind every affirmation, behind each person, behind every slogan a bad intention is concealed. The skies fool us, as well as the statesmen, politicians, and revolutionaries. But those who lead us to catastrophies are themselves guided, without their knowing, by pulsings they cannot control.

To soften our fate the least bit, culture must control what is mechanical and not the other way round, as Charles Reich said. Other modern thinkers like A. S. Neill argue that politics cannot change man because politics is based on hatred. Love and contemplation cannot be given to us by governments. What is there to say of the political opposition, like that in France for example, which does not want the government to restore any economic equilibrium and does its best to prevent this, otherwise it would lose its purpose? The politicians' fight has to continue at our expense.

For us to reduce what is wrong with us to a minimum, we need competent administrators who have no ambition, resentment, or doctrines. As for a fair sharing of economic goods, we could suggest that it be left to programmers. But there again, it would not do much to our situation as creatures who will die, or to our tragic existence.

JONAS SALK

JONAS SALK, bacteriologist, born in 1914 in the United States, developed the inactivated poliovirus vaccine whose widespread use after 1955 helped bring under control the dreaded child-crippling disease. Besides an extensive list of scientific publications, his books include: *Infectious Molecules and Human Disease* (1962), *Man Unfolding* (1972), and *The Survival of the Wisest* (1973), from which this article was adapted and excerpted.*

An unprecedented explosion of interest and movements concerned with the survival of the species is now taking place. The idea of the extermination, by Man, of various forms of life on the planet, and the danger to human life, induces a fear that preoccupies increasing numbers of individuals, especially of the generations now maturing. Those who are ecologically oriented and those who are profoundly concerned about the quality of life for the species as well as for the individual appear to stand in opposition to others less aware of such problems, who are more concerned with themselves in their own life spans. The fundamental difference between these two attitudes is that the first expresses concern for *the individual and the species;* the second reveals principally, and perhaps exclusively, an interest in the *individual* and the *particular group* of which he is a part. The more broadly concerned (*i.e., with the species and the individual*) fall into two categories. One consists of those born after such threats came into full evidence; the other, of those born earlier but who, having witnessed the change, are now reacting to previously prophesied dangers which have become realities. Those preoccupied only with their own problems are either unaware or unperturbed in the face of a process in human evolution to which others are sensitive and, if aware, feel frustrated, helpless, or apathetic.

A major threat to the species is attributed to the increasing size of the human population, which, in turn, is ascribed to successes in science and technology. This "explanation" has evoked an attack upon science and the exploitation of its technology, to the development of which are attributed many adverse effects upon the human species and upon other forms of life. "Polluters" who befoul the planet affect the "quality of life" and are regarded as a threat to the present and future equilibrium of the species and of the planet. Those who consider themselves *on the side of* Nature, and therefore of the human species, see others in opposition to both Nature and Man. Hence we are to be concerned not only with Man's relationship to Nature but with Man's relationship to himself.

Viewed in this way we realize how much blindness to Man's true nature actually exists. This may be understandable in the young, who have not lived very long, but it is equally true of those who have lived longer. How we grapple with our blindness is of the greatest importance for the present and the future; it is the central problem of our time.

If human life is to express as much harmony, constructiveness, and creativity as are possible for fulfilling the purpose *of* life, as "required" by Nature, and the purposes *in* life, as "chosen" by Man, an attitude will be needed, not of Man "against" Nature, but of Man "inclusive with" Nature. A more reasonable attitude would be for Man to "serve Nature" in order to serve himself, rather than to "serve himself" without regard for, or at the expense of, Nature and others. By recognizing and respecting the natural "hierarchies of purpose" Man would be better able to gauge his latitude to select and pursue his own "chosen purposes" without coming into conflict with the "purpose of Nature," which appears to be the continuation of life as long as conditions on the planet permit.

As a process, evolution seems to be Nature's way of finding

means for extending the persistence of life on earth. This involves the elaboration of increasingly complex mechanisms for problem-solving and adaptation. The ability of tne human mind to solve the problem of survival is part of this process. In this respect Man has evolved so successfully that he is now to be tested for his capacity to "invent" appropriate means to limit the harmful or lethal excesses of which he is capable. The conflict in the human realm is now between self-expression and self-restraint *within* the individual, as the effect of cultural evolutionary processes has reduced external restraint upon individual expression and increased opportunities for choice.

The fork-in-the-road at which Man *now* stands offers either a path toward the development of ways and means for maximizing self-expression *and* self-restraint, by means of external restraints that are not suppressive or oppressive, or an alternative path of limitless license which would unleash destructive and pathological greed at the expense of constructive and creative individuals. In the latter case, a strong reaction can be expected to develop in response to the sense of order upon which their survival is based. The challenge is to establish an equilibrium between *self-expression with self-restraint* on the one hand and *self-protection with self-restraint* on the other. If Man is to take advantage of opportunities to remedy difficulties that have arisen as a result of his evolution, then he needs to understand his relationship to the evolutionary process which plays with and upon him.

As a logical overture, let us look at the growth of the human population on the face of the earth and the present reasonable projection over the next few decades to the year 2000. It raises vast and complex implications for the character and quality of human life that concern relationships as well as resources for the present and the future. It raises questions as to the means that Man or Nature will invoke to deal with the excesses that have developed and the insufficiencies that persist. Will Man create his own procedures to deal with them or will Nature's simple ways come into play, some of which may prove quite undesirable from Man's point of view? This, in fact, may already be occurring. Before turning our attention to the questions

Voices for Life

and consequences of the rapidly mounting curve of population
increase as drawn in Figure 1, or to the implications of its cur-
tailment or of its continuation, let us look at patterns of growth in
other living systems. For example, Figure 2 shows the growth
curve of a fruit-fly population in a closed system as observed
by Raymond Pearl in 1925.

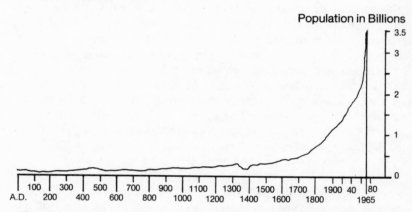

Figure 1. World population estimates, A.D. 0-1965. Adapted from *World
Facts and Trends*, by John McHale.

The S-shaped, or sigmoid, curve that describes the growth of
fruit flies is also seen in curves of growth of micro-organisms
and of cells or molecules. Since the planet earth can be considered a closed system and *since the sigmoid curve reflects the
operation of control and regulatory mechanisms that appear to
be associated with survival of the individual or of the species* it
would seem reasonable to expect that the pattern of future population growth in Man will tend to stabilize at an optimal level
described by an S-shaped curve. It is possible, of course, that
an alternative pattern might resemble that of the lemmings
(Figure 3), in which periodic catastrophe occurs with enormous
loss of life. However, Man's attitude toward human life would
have to alter significantly for such patterns to be endured; he is
more likely to choose *other ways than catastrophe for maintaining
optimal numbers on the face of the earth while remaining within
the limit of available resources.*

As Man has still to complete a cycle of growth on this planet, he has not yet fully revealed the pattern biologically programmed in him, or the way it will be influenced by factors he is responsible for, or by natural forces beyond his control. Therefore we are unable to know the pattern of his trajectory in the short-

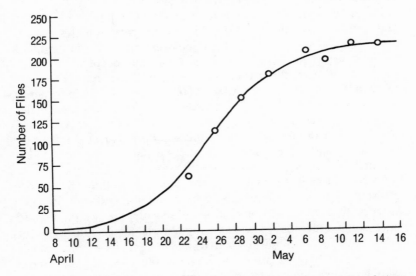

Figure 2. Growth of fruit-fly population. From *The Biology of Population Growth*, by Raymond Pearl. Copyright 1925 by A. A. Knopf, Inc. and renewed 1953 by Maude de Witt Pearl. Reprinted by permission of the publisher.

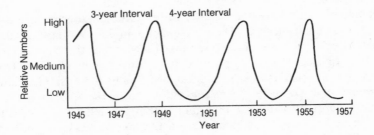

Figure 3. Generalized curve of the three-to-four-year cycle of the brown lemming population. From CRM Books, *Biology: An Appreciation of Life*, © 1972 by Communications Research Machines, Inc.

or longer-term future. The "catastrophists" and harbingers of doom *are in themselves evidence that Man possesses a signaling mechanism for sounding warnings* of danger, sensed more acutely and more clearly by some who alarmingly represent the problem of population increase as shown in Figure 1.

If we assume, however, that Man has the power of choice and can influence the course of his growth curve on this planet, then it is of special interest to look carefully at the sigmoid curve in terms meaningful for him. Since our deeper purpose is to try to discern the nature of order in the human realm in relation to the nature of order in the realm of life in general, it is interesting to explore the possible meaning of the similarities observed in the human population growth curve as manifested thus far, and the first portion of the growth curve of the fruit-fly population and similar curves in the subsystems of other living systems.

Since, through the process of natural selection, living organisms that have survived have revealed their fitness for persistence thus far in the evolutionary scheme, we would like to have some prevision of Man's program. Is he programmed for relatively short-term survival in which his end may come of his own doing? Or is he programmed for a life in which only those who have lost the power to discriminate, or who are otherwise degenerate, will continue to inhabit the planet as long as reproductive activity continues to supply "victims" of life, struggling to preserve itself in the "human" form? And what other alternatives exist?

It is likely that Man's brain has developed as it has, in the course of natural selection, partly in response to exogenous forces active against survival. Does that same brain also possess the capacity to tame and discipline those inner forces that act against long-term survival, in opposition to a life of high quality? The struggle for survival once manifest principally *between Man and Nature now seems to be taking place within the human species itself, between Man and men* and within the individual himself.

My purpose is to elucidate the factors and forces affecting the quality of human life through ideas that emerge while "playing with" the growth curve and reflecting upon the developmental and evolutionary processes of Man in the critical stage in which we seem to be at this point in time.

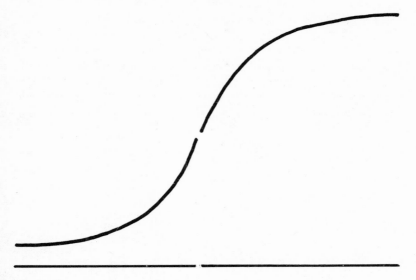

Figure 4.

As we study the curve in Figure 4 consideration of the lower portion only gives the impression of continuous, even explosive expansion, whereas consideration of the upper portion gives the impression of modulation and control of this expansion, so that finally a limit is established. At the junction of the lower and upper portions of the curve is a region of inflection at which there is a change *from progressive acceleration to progressive deceleration* and at which the influence of the controlling processes is cleary visible. The break apparent in this region suggests that a "signaling" mechanism of some kind must operate to bring about this change, producing an effect that, judging from the shape of the curve, indicates the existence of a uniform process, reflecting the operation of some kind of ordering principle in response to "signals" both from the environment and from within the organisms themselves. At different points in time along the curve, latent qualities and reactions are evoked appropriate to survival, the program for which is coded in the germ plasm, which also contains an accumulation of control and regulatory factors essential thereto.

At the plateau stage of numbers, the individuals in the fly population would be expected to "behave" differently as compared with those alive earlier in the growth curve, *i.e.,* before the zone of inflection when different "problems" prevailed. The extent to which circumstances differ, at different points in time along the curve, is graphically suggested in Figure 5 by breaking the continuity at the point of inflection so as to create two curves, A and B.

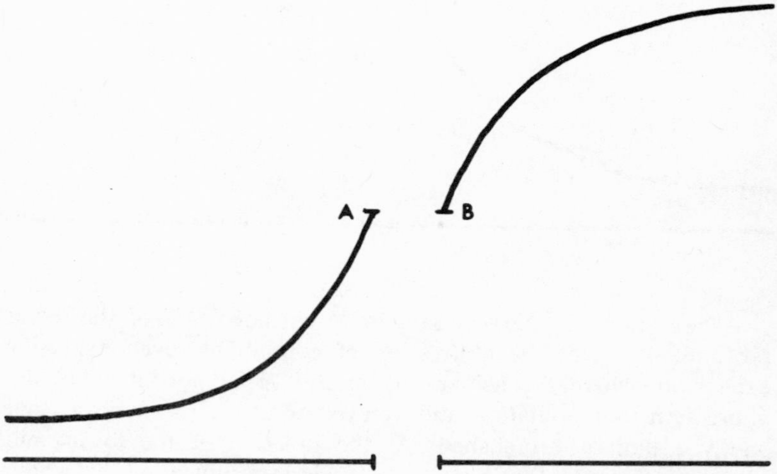

Figure 5.

These curves are intended to emphasize the difference in attitude and outlook in the two periods and help create a visual image of what can be sensed "intuitively." They also convey concretely what might be appreciated "cognitively" by means of an objective analysis of the increasingly complex problems generated by the growing numbers of individuals. In the discussion to follow, curves A and B will be used as symbols of the "shape" of the past and of the future, as we attempt to characterize each. When we speak of the fruit fly in anthropo-morphic terms, it is to suggest, using this caricature, the nature of the forces operating in the human realm. For example, if we speak of the flies as possessing, individually or collectively, a "sense of responsibility" and "insight and foresight," it is to suggest the existence of the equivalent of conflicting forces by which they would, were they human, be impelled to "judge" and "choose." Such judgment would be exercised according to the contesting "value systems" that would be in operation during periods as different as those suggested by curves A and B.

The fact that the fruit flies are a product of a long evolu-tionary history, whose survivors react according to their genetic programming, leads us to think that Man, who is of more recent origin and, moreover, at or near the point of inflection in his present curve of population growth on the planet, is about to find out whether he is programmed to behave in ways leading to a population growth curve similar to the fruit fly's, or to a curve of another shape. He has still to find out about the nature of the quality of life under circumstances that remain to be experienced. In being tested for survival, he still has a way to go not only quantitatively but qualitatively. The curves, how-ever, provide some insight, their shapes suggesting the character of the problems that prevailed in the past, those now existing, and those likely to be encountered as Man continues to move through evolutionary time.

Man differs from other living organisms in possessing another "control and regulatory" system, for response to environmental and other changes, in addition to that genetically coded and automatically operative as in the fruit fly, which has been tested and selected in the course of its evolutionary history. Man is able to exercise learned behavior. He also possesses individual will, which can be either in accord or in conflict with genetically coded patterns of response. In this sense Man is more complex and more unpredictable than the fruit fly. He can learn to behave in ways that are anti-life as well as pro-life, anti-evolution as well as pro-evolution. He remains to be tested for this pattern of response to all that is implied in the need for changing values to make the transition from Epoch A to Epoch B. In view of the greed and ideologies of Man as causes of his conflicts, attitudes as well as values will be put to test in the transition from Epoch A to Epoch B.

Genetic programming does not change as rapidly as the attitudes and values that also guide human behavior. Since genetically as well as culturally determined responses are "environmentally" linked, the circumstantial differences implied by the dissimilar "shapes" of the curves symbolizing Epoch A and Epoch B will be expected to evoke different sets of genetic as well as cultural potentialities. In Epoch B those attitudes and attributes which are of the greatest value will determine the "real" and not merely the "presumed" shape of the population growth curve and the quality of life. Value systems such as prevailed in Epoch A will, of necessity, have to be replaced by those appropriate for Epoch B, and new concepts will emerge about the nature of Man and his relationship to all parts of the cosmos. Since the conditions into which future generations will be born are not yet determined, it will be of interest to see how men in different cultures, with different genetic backgrounds and capacities, will respond to the human and planetary changes now well under way. It is not yet possible to see how Man will deal with attributes which dominated in Epoch A nor to foresee very clearly precisely what attributes will emerge in Epoch B.

Thus Man is being subjected to a new and possibly more severe challenge than ever before, for which he needs perspective and insight. He must become aware of the opportunities and the dangers that he will have to face when confronted by the conflicts resulting from a necessary inversion of such magnitude as implied by the diagram in Figure 6. The profundity of the change in values required for survival and for quality of life in the periods described by curves A and B makes it seem not only that what was of positive value in A may, in fact, become of negative value in B; but also, if "B values" had prevailed earlier they would have been of opposite value in the A epoch. From this point of view it is not difficult to understand the depth and meaning of the change that Man is now experiencing in the various forms that have already become manifest under the specific

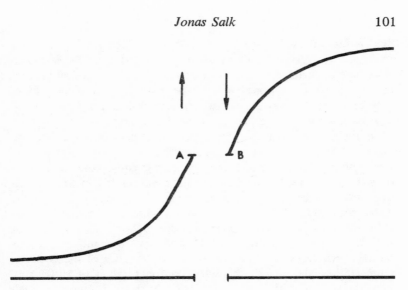

Figure 6.

historical circumstances in different cultures in all parts of the world.

This change is of such magnitude and significance that it may well be judged to be of major import in the course of human evolution. At this time Man seems to be seeking tolerable levels quantitatively and is being called upon to develop qualitatively satisfying ways and means for living with himself and with others that fit what might be thought of as the scheme of Nature. Man's choices will be "judged" by Nature, thus revealing the wisdom of his selections from among many alternatives.

We need to discern Nature's "game," as well as Man's. The choices that Man makes from the alternatives available to him will profoundly influence his own evolutionary destiny. The outcome will reveal the extent to which he will have succeeded in understanding the workings of Nature, at a time in his own evolution when he is being tested for his capacity to accommodate himself to change, and for his ability to create the possibilities for existence under circumstances as different from those of the past as suggested by the shapes of curves A and B. Until this point in evolutionary time Man has been selected for characteristics that were of value for survival during the A epoch. Now, quite abruptly, a new "selection pressure" has appeared, for which he is ill-prepared by experience but for which there may exist within him a reservoir of potential appropriate to the new circumstances such as are now developing.

In the course of evolution many more species have become extinct than have survived, each perhaps for particular causes very different from those which might cause the extinction of Man. For in Man's case, at this point in his evolution, his extinction might well arise for internal reasons. The way he deals with unresolved conflicts within himself individually and collectively might lead to his own destruction. The process of natural selection has developed survivors resistant to various infectious diseases and to some of the vicissitudes of the environment. It has also led to the selection for survival of those successful in escaping the ravages of war and those ingenious enough to escape human tyranny. Thus until now the qualities that have been selected for survival reflect the conditions and circumstances that have prevailed as much as the potentialities that exist in Man. As Nature continues its game of biological mutation and selection, and as Man plays his own games of selection of ideas and of cultural innovations, Nature will have the last word. Therefore it is up to Man to look closely and deeply into Nature's workings, not only at the molecular and cellular levels but also at the consequences of advancing knowledge and cultural practices as these bear on the question of survival and the quality of life. It is in this respect that wisdom will be required for which a balanced creative center for judgment is needed.

We must look to those among us who are in closest touch with the unfathomable source of creativity in the human species for an understanding of the workings of Nature and for insight into Nature's "game," as we enter upon an epoch in which new values are required for choices of immediate need as well as for those with longer-range implications. This is especially important when, as now, the number born in each new generation exceeds the number born in each of the earlier generations. For this reason, the character and quality of the individual that will survive and predominate in our period will have a very profound effect upon the character and quality of human life for a long time to come.

To what extent will we be able to affect the course of Nature, in the short or in the long run? That remains to be seen. Nevertheless, we are fully conscious of this problem. How will we deal with this opportunity and this responsibility knowing as much as we do? What more do we need to know, being as aware as we are now of our limitations and our capabilities?

To help our understanding of man's relationship to Man, and Man's relationship to Nature, in terms of their inherent complementary character, analogies have been drawn between the "games" of Nature and of Man. The point that has already been made is that the laws that govern Nature's game require, under certain circumstances, "double-win" rather than "win-lose" resolutions which Man must also develop.

Although each of us would like to be "winners," at least in terms of individual satisfaction and fulfillment, it is also clear that more luck, knowledge, and wisdom are required than are possessed by very many. Some are more fortunate than others, but none are born either fully knowledgeable or infinitely wise; hence Man's search for perspective and guidance in dealing with the unknowns and uncertainties of life in all its complexity.

Since many of the problems for which Man seeks solution are an inherent part of the process of human development itself, and since he is both a contributing cause as well as a sufferer, his position as both patient and physician is a difficult one. And yet he must be both. Fortunately, means do exist for self-correction, for self-cure, and for prevention even of those potentially harmful or lethal effects that are self-induced. The approach employed here in thinking about this dilemma has been to seek useful analogies in the self-correcting processes that are an essential and integral part of living systems. The assumption is that if individual man were aware of the existence of such processes and the way they operate, knowing that they are an integral part of his own self as well, he might develop the desire to learn how to use them consciously and deliberately not only for survival but for fulfillment in his lifetime. Such clues can be found in the way in which control and regulation operate in living Nature, where success is evidenced in the persistence of life in spite of vicissitudes, difficulties, and seeming impossibilities. On the assumption that metabiologic evolutionary problems (that is, those surpassing the ordinary limits of living matter) are similar to problems encountered and solved in biological evolution, analogies are sought to serve as models helping us to deal more realistically, and therefore more appropriately, with some of our unresolved problems, and even, possibly, to accept the existence of insoluble enigmas.

Referring to Man as a metabiological entity infers that he possesses self-correcting, self-controlling, and self-disciplining mechanisms, as well as biologically governed balance-mechanisms for each of his two distinct yet related evolutionary purposes, *i.e.*, for improving the quality of life as well as for survival. It implies, also, that change in human behavior that will serve both biological and metabiological aims requires many steps and stages involving both error-making and error-correcting. In spite of our prior limitations, due to ignorance of the character or details of the processes involved in evolution, can we, now, with our increased knowledge of the nature of living systems, and of Man, apply ourselves to conceive of ways and means of influencing the course of future events toward fulfilling Man's evolutionary potential? In Epoch A it appears that greater success has been achieved in reducing premature death than in improving the quality of life in terms of individual satisfaction. Hence, to the gains made in Epoch A, facilitating survival by better hygienic conditions and other measures for the prevention of disease, new challenges will have to be accepted in Epoch B, testing Man's ingenuity in developing the means to enhance the degree of fulfillment in the life of the individual and in the quality of life generally.

The difficulties and complexities involved in such a challenge are considerable; the mere existence of innate mechanisms for meeting them does not mean that the odds are in favor of success. Human history is replete with evidence that *de*volutionary processes also operate, with deterioration of the human condition, unless foresight, imagination, ingenuity, determination, and wisdom are brought to bear, to increase self-awareness and self-discipline in the choice of ends as well as means. To be able to prevent such deterioration, principles will be required by which to live, and by which to intervene judiciously in the process of biologic and metabiologic evolution with knowledge of the *de*volutionary as well as the evolutionary consequences of each action or nonaction when we face issues that affect our well-being individually and collectively.

The hypothesis has been proposed that if the mind of Man is exposed to the economy of Nature, as revealed in the workings of living systems, he will become sensitized to recognize the necessity of balancing values. Thus measure is established as the source of wisdom. By improving the quality of life, wisdom, thus, can influence the processes of metabiological evolution, just as the enhancement of physical fitness functioned in the struggle for survival in biological evolution. If Man can come to recognize that the use of wisdom in the game of life leads to the reward of a greater measure of fulfillment and satisfaction, then he will value the development of such special skills; nowadays more individuals have the opportunity to do so for more years than was generally true heretofore. In this, everyone has much to gain.

If, in the course of this quest, a struggle arises between the wise and the nonwise, the conquest or elimination of either one would result in loss to both, just as if Life and Death were to "conquer or eliminate" each other. The wise must avoid a "win-lose" conflict with the unwise, just as it was necessary in biological evolution for Life and Death to arrive at a "double-win" resolution in order for either one, and hence both, to persist. Even though Death eventually wins over Life so far as the individual is concerned, Life wins over Death in the perpetuation of the species. This is to say that Life "wins immortality" for the species and Death, mortality for the individual; the individual may be unwise, but not the species. For the quality of life to be improved, and for survival, Mankind will have to respect those who are wise and expect the individual to behave as if he were. If wisdom is, in fact, a new kind of fitness for survival, the operation of the equivalent of natural selection in the metabiological evolutionary processes will have been guided by the choice of human values.

In Epoch A Man acted effectively on the side of Life, both of the individual and of the species, by reducing the incidence of disease and the frequency of dying prematurely. Correspondingly, in Epoch B Man may be able to devise ways of improving the quality of life of the individual and of the species by reducing unwisdom or its adverse effects and by respecting and applying wisdom for increasing the possibility of personal fulfillment. Among individuals who now have less to struggle for personally in order to survive, as a result of the changes brought about in Epoch A, a new syndrome has developed, manifest in seeming purposelessness, for the treatment of which new experiences will be needed, possibly leading to new motivations.

Judgment is required in larger measure than ever before if Man is to succeed in balancing the adverse effects, both upon the species and upon individuals, resulting from the increased knowledge and improved technology that reduce the need for struggle and also the opportunity to learn how to experience a sense of satisfaction. This is seen among the increasing numbers of individuals whose lives have been prolonged and made more secure by the metabiological evolutionary developments that have occurred in recent times, without effort on their part.

There is a further undesirable side effect of the benefits brought about in Epoch A. Among the individuals who feel purposeless, some become wantonly and pathologically destructive, threatening and interfering with the development and achievement of fulfillment of others. For resolving such problems as these, far more insight is needed than has as yet been activated.

By suggesting the idea of survival of the wisest I mean not only that the more discerning will survive but also that the survival of Man, with a life of high quality, depends upon the prevalence of respect for wisdom and for those possessing a sense of the *being* *

---

* "Being" is the center in which exist the possibilities that, when unfolded, reveal the essence of the person, both as a member of the species and as an individual.

of Man and of the laws of Nature. These are necessary for choosing from among alternatives, for fulfillment as well as for survival. Man's metabiological questions and problems still need answers.

The idea of wisdom as a pro-health, pro-life, pro-evolutionary influence still leaves open and unresolved the question as to how this might be developed and applied. Man's capacity to bring this about is also not known. The role of religious and political organizations has been to enlighten and to guide. Now new means are needed for inner self-regulation based upon naturalistic rather than on arbitrary moralistic formulations. In spite of the difficulties involved in devising and developing such formulations, this could provide an important purpose *in* life and serve the purpose *of* life individually and collectively.

The extent reached by Man in his capacity to create, to destroy, and to move in space as well as over the surface of the earth has indeed been remarkable. To what extent does he have the ability to invent new ways to act wisely as a species even if his aptitude to so behave individually is relatively limited?

Exposing Man's mind to the laws of Nature may help him discover and apply whatever insight and foresight he possesses for dealing with the problems of relationships to himself and to others, and to the universe. This way of thinking about Man and Nature and relationship and wisdom is new to most, and to be of value will require modern patterns of perceiving one's self and others. New attitudes and behavioral patterns will follow.

It is simpler to conceive such notions than to apply them in everyday life. Nevertheless, it is far easier to reach objectives based upon sound concepts and hypotheses than upon those without basis. Hence the challenge with which Man is generally confronted at this point is to see himself as a biological and metabiological entity, possessing attributes capable of reversing some of the *de*volutionary trends. These attributes can also be directed and disciplined to facilitate and increase the probability of achieving a greater measure of fulfillment in life than has been possible until now.

Paradoxically, this challenge and hope exist in the face of enigmas more difficult to overcome than ever before, because greater opportunities for fulfillment are matched by correspondingly greater obstacles. For this reason, wisdom, understood as a new kind of strength, is a paramount necessity for Man. Now, even more than ever before, it is required as a basis for fitness, to maintain life itself on the face of this planet, and as an alternative to paths toward alienation or despair.

LIONEL TIGER
An Interview

LIONEL TIGER is a sociologist and anthropologist born in 1937 in Montreal, Canada. His book *Men in Groups* (1969) has proved a controversial entry in the debate over women's liberation. His other book is *The Imperial Animal* (1971).

MORAES: How would you define yourself?

TIGER: When I first grew up and had to have a job, I was defined as a sociologist because that is the degree I got—Political Sociology from the University of London. But since I had done research in Ghana (and hence studied black people), it was commonly felt that I must be something of an anthropologist. For a long time, when I was asked the question you asked, I would tell students that sociologists study white people and that that was the only useful distinction—the most parsimonious distinction—one could make between sociology and anthropology. I have since come to think that the distinction is more serious, chiefly because anthropologists still retain a lingering interest in human beings, while sociologists have become, in a certain sense, condemned to being concerned with systems. It was really through concern with the behavior of other animals and evolution and biology that I became an anthropologist. Professionally, I do not really identify myself as an anthropologist but as part of the larger enterprise of comparative zoology. I try to do my work as a zoologist, drawing heavily on the ethological tradition.

MORAES: How would you actually define the work you do?

TIGER: There has been a shift in the conception of what biology is, which I think can be linked to the development of ethology, as a science. Ethology is the study of the behavior of animals, including humans, in the context of the evolution of the animal and its behavior. And this is in a real way a kind of revolution. By that I don't mean a political revolution but a turnabout in the attitude to behavior, because for a long while the social sciences tried to distinguish themselves from any work based on the assessment of "instinct." In the United States and in the Soviet Union, there was, for a time, and for obvious political, antiracist, ideological reasons, a concerted effort to avoid making any kind of genetically linked statements about behavior. But, recently, this has become clearly an untenable attitude, particularly in view of the fact that human beings continue to be recalcitrant about their life cycles, they continue to exhibit behaviors that are plainly more related to their evolution as a species than to the social conditions in which they live, and also because of the vast amount of new biological information that we have.

A central notion of many social scientists, and I think this is not a totally impudent comment, is that, by and large, human behavior is principally constrained by other human behaviors—by circumstances we can generally call cultural. This has certainly been the tradition in sociology since Émile Durkheim, for example, who argued that we could only explain the social by the social. It was linked to an effort to break away from the natural sciences. However, there are such clearly biological events as the life cycle, for example, which must constrain, if not deeply influence, the social behavior of any individual human, another primate, a turtle, or whatever animal you care to name.

In the human, the life cycle, the aging process, is quite an astonishing biological event. You can take a tiny organism, which may be a foot long, and within reasonably close limits, predict its physical form over a seventy-years' span. That is under biological control. There is not much we can do about it. We can speed it up, reverse it a bit, repair it if it goes wrong, improve the system a little, but there remains the basic biological event, the life cycle, which constrains everything else. It would seem unlikely that something so important did not also have behavioral analogs.

Adolescence is one such behavior in which the organism suddenly shifts, becomes an entirely different thing, much more involved, much more charged, much more stimulating to members of the opposite sex and, presumably, to members of the same sex, perhaps with hostile stimuli. People are much more interested in different things in adolescence; they see things they did not see before—for example, secondary sexual characteristics. The biological event of the life cycle is a major constraint on the social phenomena of existence. And it seems that in sociology and political science, economics, and so on, the assumption is proudly made that humans are sapient, that we are governed primarily by a kind of reason and that we can explain everything we do without looking seriously at this biological substratum.

I realize it is a somewhat conventional argument to say that there is an "instinctive" behavioral base, but at the same time the ethologists come back to the question. They have given us some indication of how sophisticated this instinctive pattern is and how much there is a reciprocity between behavior in an animal and its genetic endowment. Not instinct in the old sense such as a knee-jerk reflex; it is far more complicated, far more sociological.

What results from an effort to study the biological substratum is, in fact, a greater attention to human similarities. Traditionally, social scientists have focused on differences between peoples; these were our stock in trade. The ethological approach permits one to begin to look, without being pious, anxious, or simpleminded, at human similarities—because we all share the same gene pool. The ethological conception demands that we see how behaviors, which are biologically governed, require sociological circumstances for their expression. That is to say, you can, for example, lower the age of puberty of female rats by subjecting them to sexual stimuli (and I would not be at all surprised if the reduction in the age of human menarche, or first menstruation, may not be subject to some similar influences). Thus, it is clear that biology now requires the understanding of sociogenic factors as well as purely physiological or other ones. In this sense, ethology becomes a subfield of comparative biology or comparative zoology and, from that point of view, the social sciences will have to become part of the over-all biological enterprise in the scientific sense.

There are two principal issues involved in adopting a biological perspective on the human condition. The first is substantial and has to do with the fact that we are primates and that we share many of the physiological characteristics of the primates, in terms of the composition of our blood and so on. Presumably, some behavioral similarities are also shared. That is a matter for discussion, examination, and testing. But the other aspect is theoretical or methodological and evolves from the origins of assumptions about what life is like. It seems to me increasingly, if painfully, clear that the tacit assumption we have been using before, that we are the total creators of our lives, may have to be tempered by an understanding that we are also subject to certain constraints that are deeply rooted in our evolutionary history. As someone said, those who do not learn from history are condemned to repeat its failures and its errors. In the human case we may be condemned to repeat our successes. For example, we have been a very successful breeding species; we maintain ourselves in the state of constant sexual readiness; we have a reproductive structure that permits repeated impregnations and births; and we do this extremely well. So well that in some parts of the world we approach disaster because of our very success as a breeding species.

Now, it is all very well to accuse people of being irresponsible for having children or not understanding the global problems they are creating. On the other hand, they are simply responding as very healthy organisms, tempered over several million years by high mortality, slow socialization of children, great risks for children, and so on, to breed enthusiastically and repeatedly.

MORAES: You say "very healthy organisms." But where we are approaching disaster is in the Third World countries. There the people are not very healthy.

TIGER: They may not be physically healthy, but their response to their existential condition is a healthy one. That is, they say, "Let us reproduce." Healthy in the sense that you can say that an animal in a zoo that is unable to reproduce for sociological reasons is really an unhealthy animal—and it is the success of particular zoos to have healthy conditions so that animals can reproduce. This becomes increasingly important as species approach extinction. In the human case it is healthy to be able to reproduce; it is the kind of health that represents our previous successes in having populated the globe.

Unless we understand the origins and contemporary manifestations of some of these forces, we will be condemned to repeat our successes, which will indeed be catastrophic. The line that produced us is some 70 million years old. Basic human adaptations occurred not earlier than 2 or 3 million years ago. To quote somebody fancy, "To the blind everything is sudden." My suspicion is that the sense of human life as totally contemporary is a form of blindness and that people concerned with understanding social arrangements must go beyond the obvious, the immediate, and try to see the historical depth of some of the phenomena that they observe. This may be imprudent, since it can easily generate an overwhelming and paralyzing sense of tragedy.

On the other hand, more tragic even might be an unfettered sense of optimism about the human condition, which, as we know, leads political leaders to adventures that may or may not work —to the peril of the people for whom they should be responsible. The biological perspective also has the capacity, I think, to replace a sense of tragedy about reality by providing a rounded and multifaceted vision of what the nature of existence is. As we are forced to live in a world increasingly compacted, in which there are more people and relatively fewer resources, we are going to have to become delicately aware of what we are, who we are, why we are; and in the crudest sense we are going to have to take an almost veterinarian view of the species and ask ourselves under what conditions does this animal not beat itself to death, not overpopulate itself to death, not run riot, not commit acts hazardous to the over-all survival of the human group. And this is not solely a sociological enterprise; it has to involve comparative biologies since we are dealing here with the very nature of life itself.

There is emerging in the field of genetics at the moment, a remarkably powerful new conception called the "genetics of altruism," which begins to make even clearer why human beings have so many children. The genetics of altruism in its simplest form asserts that humans as well as other animals become aware of the genetic implications of having children. I don't mean that in any simple sense, but people are aware that their own children are more meaningful to them as organisms than children of somebody else, though children of relatives have a greater claim on their attention than nonrelatives. Why do people have children at all? They are such utterly inconvenient and costly creatures and persist in troubling parents for extensive periods of time. Yet, routinely people continue to have them. The "genetics of altruism" argument makes it a little clearer why people suffer such inconvenience and difficulty in order to reproduce themselves. This is, after all, what a species is about: reproduction. The kind of argument being developed suggests that reproduction is not a blind, selfish activity but is very broadly based in a social system and is one of the principal underlying factors in the persistence of kinship systems and family structures of various kinds. In addition, of course, children are biologically able to be stimuli that provide joy and interest to parents and therefore pay their way, as it were, by making adult organisms feel a kind of connection to the world that is very difficult to have purely with other adults. Being with children is to social life as sonatas are to traffic noise.

MORAES: Is it not also true that in rural societies they were *useful?*

TIGER: Certainly in agricultural communities, and in others as well, children could provide useful labor. But I suspect that was not all. Since they existed they were made useful. We find them existing even when they are not useful, so that it could not be simply utility that is responsible for fecundity, though it is undoubtedly a factor. In India, to cite one case, there are very important social-security implications in having large families.

It is unwise to ignore this, which happens even in highly sophisticated countries. The Rumanians had a very elaborate abortion system, the birth rate had fallen very low, and it was discovered if they continued with their abortion practice there would be too few births to support the adults presently in the population. (Children, in time, would not generate enough pension funds.) So, abortion practices were curtailed; the birth rate is now going up. That is very much like the case of the Indian family. It may gleam with the veneer of sophistication, but its effect is similar in the end to what the Indian peasant does because of his alleged craven ignorance "of the real forces of life." The more sophisticated kind of bureaucratized biological process will become increasingly important as we begin to live in a world in which the fixed relationship between resources and people becomes ever more perilous.

Bureaucracy is often seen by sociologists as the most elaborate expression of rational social arrangement, yet I suspect that over the next thirty or forty years we are going to become aware of how unnatural it is. Not that I can foresee any alternative ways of organizing governments or any large corporation, for example. But nonetheless, bureaucracy places enormous strains on individual human beings. Bureaucratic structures precisely maximize the lack of control that individuals can have over their circumstances by demanding that individuals not intrude their own personal passions and fears and enthusiasm into a situation but rather act as any other human in that office might act. Max Weber set up a distinction between the office-holder and the office or the person and the office. He described this distinction, which is an immensely powerful tool to use in organizing communities, because it reduces, if you will, all the primate passions and enthusiasms I described. However, at the same time as it reduces their importance it may also reduce the commitments of people to the job they are supposed to be doing.

I think we can see this most clearly in the corporate business system on this continent, in which it is routine for business personnel to be frequently moved from place to place on the grounds that having proved that they can be good assistant general managers of X that they should then become general managers of X and that requires moving them from one part of the continent to another—a decision made on the impersonal bureaucratic grounds that the person does not matter. But what about that person? What about the wives and children, who are shifted endlessly from place to place in the name of some supposed efficiency, which is really profoundly antiprimatological? We know that children are extremely conservative creatures and require long periods of exploration and consolidation. They respond very well to known stimuli and are not at all pleased or reassured by totally novel stimuli, particularly when everything is varying all the time and at once. So business people, who are extremely important in deciding the form of the community, live in a kind of critical isolation from it, a profound isolation from their own community simply because they have been moved around so much. Many people move every year or two in order to conduct themselves in a professional manner in the business world. The human implications of this are simply staggering, and the thought that people making important decisions about other people are so unrooted in communities is, in a primatological sense, quite frightening.

For migrants to run power structures is rare, but I think what we see in American business is a government by migrant people. Some of the consequences, in terms of social irresponsibility, in terms of lack of concern for local communities, in terms of a simple lack of understanding and concern about what people feel in communities, may be due not only to the venality of capitalist procedures at their worst—and to simple greed—but also to a kind of profound misunderstanding of the nature of existence, which rootless migratory executives practicing a kind of scorched-earth policy may engage in. Looking at the Marxist conception of alienation in a biological sense—biological in that Marx claimed that people were alienated when they were no longer in touch with the fruits of their labor—how much more alienating it is not to be in touch with one's life as a result of one's labor. When one has to move constantly in order to work, it is profoundly alienating.

I am sure that were Marx able to observe this pattern as it

has come to full fruition in the modern world, he would see the problem of surplus value as possibly less critical than the problem of reduced opportunity to live in a primatologically compassionate way. In this sense, Weber's "rationality" is uncomfortably close to Marx's "alienation," an interesting connection between Marx and Engels and biology, which has neither been explored nor understood. It is not widely known that Marx offered to dedicate *Das Kapital* to Darwin on the grounds, it seems, that he felt they were both preparing cognate major systems of thought. Both Marx and Darwin were concerned with reciprocity and with interdependence of organisms; both were thinking on a grand scale—Marx studying the economic reciprocity, Darwin concentrating upon other reciprocities. But I think Marx understood something that his successors or followers have not understood: Biology is not the enemy of reciprocity but in fact the agent or the basis of it.

It is commonly assumed that biological thinking is reactionary in political terms chiefly because it has been all too often associated with racism, elitism, and various other reactionary social patterns. But that is a perversion of biology, because the problem of organic social interdependence is profound. Both Marx and Darwin approached it, but their successors have not successfully assimilated their various systems.

In the Soviet Union, for example, one finds a devoutly anti-Darwinian conception that culminates in Trofim Lysenko, who as late as 1964 said that genetics does not matter and that by changing the environment of an animal you can even change its genetics. The same pattern emerges (with a somewhat different nuance and, certainly, with less political implication) in the United States, where a symbolically equivalent figure, B. F. Skinner, also assumes that by changing the reinforcement schedule (basically, this is also the environment), you can also change the nature of an animal. Skinner, however, does not go so far as to assume that you can actually change the genetics of the animal. Typically, Skinner doesn't deal with the problem of what you do with the offspring of this changed animal, because he would be obligated to recognize that he would have to undertake the reinforcing and scheduling all over again. That would, of course, be very tedious, to say nothing of being unlikely to work. The lack of appreciation of biology in Marxism originally has led in this perspective to an ignorance of what the human organism brings to the human community; what is in the black box, if you will. Skinner is not terribly interested in the black box. Lysenko figured he had a way of changing the black box. But in neither case does it seem to me there is any quick compassion about what that black box itself might be, and in that sense I think a structural anti-humanism exists in these sciences.

My sense of what is likely to happen in biology is that it will emerge as a much more progressive or ameliorative science in the years to come. I keep thinking of the analogy between economics and the Fabians in England: when the Fabians understood that in order to change social conditions in England, they first had to understand what was happening and engage in an extensive demanding process of examination of English society. I like to think that it might be possible to generate a biological Fabianism that will do the same thing on a species-wide kind of perspective to try to find out what are the real biological conditions in terms of which humane social policy can be created. What are the limits of our opportunity? What sorts of things can we do well? What sorts of things can we do badly? What strengths have we as a species that we can utilize? What weaknesses have we to be understanding about as we try to change the consequences of these weaknesses?

I suspect that we are going to see a rather different place for biology in the policy sciences in the years to come and I suspect that ethology as a science will find an important application in social medicine, in seeking ways to maximize the opportunities for humans to live in unstressful and pleasing ways and minimize contrary experiences. Yet it may be a characteristic of the human brain that we try to make distinctions between nature and culture, and it may be difficult to break that down in any real way. If we can't, then this kind of provident biology that I am somewhat piously anticipating may never become effective, because powerful people in the world such as politicians will continue to maintain rigorously a distinction between themselves and the rest of the natural world.

There is also a general, very perplexing problem about ideology, which is that ideologies really *do* matter to people; there are whole hosts of communities who organize themselves on the basis of some belief in some promise, or some particular tryst with destiny or another, or some particular ethical syndrome. Then they act on those bases rather than on the basis of what they see around them. They make up complicated schemes in their minds that come to define their reality for them.

I sometimes become depressed at the receptivity of the human imagination to ideological statements. I presume this represents a personal antipathy that arose out of an early experience of mine in a Labor Zionist group in Montreal, the Habonim. Part of the assumption of membership of that group was that you would go to Israel and live there. I was never wholly convinced that the people running the organization would have me emigrate to Israel for my benefit, and I finally concluded that it was primarily for their benefit. So I became very suspicious, in that rather indecently naïve period of life, of any effort to tell people how to run their lives and of ideologies in general.

In that sense, the brain is probably the most dangerous organ in the body, because it can create the most spectacular pathologies of real behavior; it is the brain that decides that it is desirable to kill people of group A, simply because one is of group B, or that people of group B can make the decision whether it is extremely useful and desirable to kill people of group A because they are not of group B. And this is a symbolic distinction. The brain, in that sense, is a very treacherous catalyst for potentially dangerous behavior. An Irish Ambassador to the United Nations said "the most underdeveloped area in the world is under men's hats." In a real sense, yes, because the brain magnifies all the other forces that go on in the human being and not all of these forces are in the direction of sobriety, thoughtfulness, restraint, and so on. Often the brain magnifies enthusiasms and frivolities and treacheries we could well be without. I am looking at the brain here as a kind of megaphone: The new part of the brain, the cortex, amplifies the other messages in the brain and enables us (endlessly and with very sophisticated means) to extend what is happening within us.

MORAES: How did you come first to be interested in biology and sociology?

TIGER: When I was doing my dissertation research in Ghana, two things happened. First of all, I became impressed with how similar Ghanaians were to Canadians. I had formerly studied Canadian bureaucrats; now I was with Ghanaian bureaucrats. There seemed to be very little difference. Clearly, a good deal of similarity had to do with the common British socialization the administrative systems shared, but even so, that was not a sufficient explanation. When I began to move around the countryside and saw the people who were not bureaucrats but just mere Ghanaians I compared them with my own family and my extended family in Montreal and the kind of ethnic squabbles that one grew to understand mainly in Quebec and in Canada. I could see no spectacular difference to justify the great apparatus of explanation that sociologists and anthropologists had generated.

Secondly, I was introduced to a South African political refugee, Walter Pope, a marine biologist, who had been working with some of the people involved in excavations in Southern Africa in general. He told me about the implications of those finds and of Louis Leakey's work, Raymond Dart's, Robert Broom's, and then of the work of the animal behaviorists. It was very exciting to begin to think in the generous terms that biology permits. The biological perspective seemed to me more generous because it permitted an expansion of sociological imagination to include all members of the species with equal validity; one ceased instantly talking about advanced and backward people. You ceased instantly talking about progress, you ceased instantly to be concerned about primitives and so on.

One of the things that marked me from my time in Ghana was that I developed an unshakable hostility to any notion that would say that people such as Ghanaians are backward by virtue of the fact that they don't have complicated electronic factories. When I talk to students who are usually irresistibly drawn to the notion that technology confers superiority, I ask them, when they describe how important technology is, if they can make a typewriter. Of course, none of them can, and I then point out that in terms of their technology they are as primitive with respect to it as they could possibly be. Yet persons supposed to be less sophisticated could make their own canoes and their own clothing.

Working in Ghana made it very plain to me that there was enormous prejudice in talk about things like modernization and industrialization, which traditional societies are supposed to lack. Now, we are beginning to see that you can modernize all you want and you can still end up having Pakistan and India fight, just the way you get Americans and Vietnamese fighting. This has nothing to do with technology. It's a simple function of the passions of the participants. You can have as skillful a dictator in a rich country as in a poor country—there is no difference.

I should add that I am very grateful that I was trained sociologically, because sociologists learn very clearly how to deal with systems; it is this ability to think systematically that I perhaps most value from my sociological training. Thinking systematically is, of course, biological in the provision of social interdependence.

MORAES: Can you trace any influence in your life that led you to this search you are now pursuing?

TIGER: I spoke before about why I got originally interested in biology. Being a Jew growing up in Montreal in the '40s and '50s made it somewhat clear to me that social arrangements were fragile and that you had to at least try to understand them for self-protection. I grew up in Montreal—a city in which everyone thinks himself to be a member of a minority group, including the majority. It was probably a very special crucible, because it provided a kind of formal cynicism that you simply had to have. It was a good way of becoming quickly skeptical about systems.

It has taken me a long time to realize that I was very fortunate that I belonged to a community such as the Montreal Jews, because it was an extremely tenacious, powerful, skilled, and assertive community—a group of about 140,000 people living, on the one hand, with white Anglo-Saxon Protestants and, on the other, with French Canadians and Greeks, Italians, Poles, and so

Voices for Life

on—and it has managed to retain its own sense of integrity as a group. I still am routinely rebellious against all of its dictates and that has given me a kind of certainty about who I am and who I am not. Still I have to admire the real commitment to the social group involved in that particular community, and I am very sorry that both the requirements of my job and the skepticism of my way of approaching my job and my life even, have made it quite impossible for me to cultivate wholeheartedly that particular garden.

All this underlines for me the importance of a stable childhood. I know how important it is when I return to Montreal to see faces from my childhood that are now in my stage of the life cycle, and it provides a kind of reassurance that cannot be achieved any other way. The vast mobility of much of the world seems to me as dangerous as nuclear weapons in terms of creating consternation and fear and uncertainty and a kind of heady sense that nothing matters among people whose experience of life is that it is always in the state of becoming something else, because one is always moving on somewhere else. So that experience in Montreal I always knew was very important, if only because one had to struggle against it.

But now I think it is even more important than I knew to have been part of what was an actively ongoing, self-confident and self-aware group of human beings of all ages. For example, I have been involved with an Israeli sociologist in the study of the kibbutz movement in Israel in which we have been looking at the situation of females. We are still analyzing the data but it looks quite clear that all the major ideological efforts of the kibbutz have been achieved. Communism, agriculturalism, Zionism, communal child-rearing, etc. Except for the question of sex differences where it has become clear that females do not participate in higher management or in politics or security matters and so on in any way, shape, or form such as one would have expected—even though they don't depend on males for their income, and they don't have to raise their own children, and so on. Here is a case where ideology has failed to tell people how to behave in a way that will be effective from their own point of view and where some kind of biological perspective might help in a real way to achieve the ideological ends. Because with ideological conceptions alone, I think, that system has failed to achieve its goals as far as sex roles are concerned, and since sex is, of course, a biological category my expectation is that a biological perspective on the problem will be at least as rewarding, if not more so, than the ideological ones that have so far not succeeded.

MARGARET MEAD

MARGARET MEAD, born in 1901 in Philadelphia, has been one of the shaping forces in modern anthropology. She is now Curator Emeritus of the American Museum of Natural History and a Professor of Anthropology at Columbia University. Among her extensive list of publications are: *Coming of Age in Samoa* (1928), *Growing Up in New Guinea* (1930), *Sex and Temperament in Three Primitive Societies* (1935), *From the South Seas* (1939), *Male and Female* (1949), *Growth and Culture* (1951), *Technique and Personality* (1963), *Culture and Commitment* (1970), *Blackberry Winter* (1972).

I turned twenty in December 1921. I was halfway through college and still uncertain about which of the human sciences I would specialize in, but I was fairly sure that I would reject my other alternatives: painting and politics. My father was an economist who had worked on the quantity theory of money; my mother was a sociologist who did some of the first work on the assimilation of immigrants into the United States. I knew about the comparative study of cultures; I knew that all human groups had the same kinds of varying capacities; I knew how economic institutions changed; and I knew about the consequences of the United States Senate's failure to honor the promises that President Woodrow Wilson had made on our behalf.

Although the hopes engendered by World War I were still with us, I also knew that the seeds of World War II were already being sown because of the failure of the United States and Russia to join the League of Nations. Those of us who were aware of what this meant knew that however much our lives were in our own hands, another world war might indeed destroy civilization.

We had not yet come to fear the destruction of all life on this planet nor the possible destruction of the planet itself, but we were acutely aware that civilization had been built laboriously over centuries by human beings and that it was within the power of human beings to destroy it. The English comment about World War I, "The lamps are going out all over Europe; we shall not see them lit again in our lifetime," echoed in our minds.

To us, "civilization" meant Europe and Europe's offspring. Although we knew that the great Asian countries had ancient and impressive traditions and that Japan had entered the war as one of the modern nations, civilization as a concept was actually confined to the Graeco-Roman tradition in government and the Hellenic, Judeo-Christian tradition in religion, philosophy, and science. "Democracy" covered a wide range of hopes: freedom from tyranny, freedom from slavery, freedom of thought and enquiry, freedom of religion, and freedom of opportunity for all. But we actually did not yet think of the world as a whole. There was the European tradition, of which Americans were a part; there was the tradition of freedom from tyrannical monarchical and colonial regimes, which the countries of South America shared with those of North America; and there was the belief that the overthrow of the Czar in the Russian Revolution was a harbinger of freedom for the Russian people. Germany was to become democratic; battleships were to be sunk; and the warring world was to disarm.

There were many things that we did not understand. Malthusianism was not popular, nor had the Depression ushered in the practices of burning crops and slaughtering little pigs. There had been famines, but during and after World War I, the American people had responded to calls for help. Without war it seemed that supplies of food could be plentiful. I had no sense yet that the resources of the earth were so limited and so distributed that the question of how they were to be used would be a crucial one. Nor did I have any idea of the changes that would be wrought by the introduction of automation.

The possibilities of new resource uses with automation were not realized until about 1930, when Howard Scott, who founded the very premature and prophetic movement called Technocracy, began to talk about joining together in economically viable units regions—in North and South America, China and India, Europe and Northern Asia—having resources and technical knowledge. The various kinds of socialist utopias, including guild socialism, were components in our thinking about the future of the world. We had no hint yet that the labor theory of value would have to be replaced by kilocalories, which combined energy (human and resource-based) and our assessments of our capacity to produce food or control the rate of growth.

For myself, I had a sense of an open future, that I would be free to pick a career, marry or not marry, have children or not have children, be a politician, a painter, writer, or social scientist. Many of the old debates that had agitated my grandparents' and my parents' generations seemed to be over: the battle between science and religion; the acceptance of Freud's documentation of the importance of the unconscious, especially in creative activities; the right of women to vote, to organize, to participate in political life, to work as the intellectual equals of men in a new atmosphere of freedom, to combine a career and marriage, or to choose either one. I combined a sense of the possibility of developing an increasingly more just world with plenty for all with the sense that a second world war was nevertheless hanging over us. The young people five to ten years my senior were already being spoken of as "the lost generation." For my college generation, the expectation of another world war meant a shortened time perspective within which to do what needed to be done, rather than a profound pessimism.

As a girl I had read various books on utopias and counterutopias and science fiction dealing with prophecies of the twenty-first century: *Caesar's Column,* in which the author Ignatius Donnelly invented airplanes but not automobiles; *The British Barbarians* by Grant Allen, where the disillusioned time traveler returned to the twenty-first century disgusted with the provincialism of nineteenth-century British natives; H. G. Wells's *War of the Worlds* and Sir Arthur Conan Doyle's *The Lost World*; Jules Verne's *Twenty Thousand Leagues Under the Sea* and *Around the World in Eighty Days,* with their precursors of modern technology; Jack London's *Before Adam,* with its first speculations of the way in

which man's membership within biological orders and families
would later have great significance; and *Erewhon* by Samuel
Butler, in which criminals were treated as sick and deserving of
sympathy, and the sick treated as criminals. Among the poets, there
were the usual prescient whisperings of later disaster. The American poet Edna St. Vincent Millay had published in 1921 "The
Blue-Flag in the Bog" with its picture of a world destroyed:

> God had called us and we came;
> Our loved Earth to ashes left;
> Heaven was a neighbor's house,
> Open flung to us, bereft.
>
> Weary wings that rise and fall
> All day long above the fire!—
> Red with heat was every wall,
> Rough with heat was every wire—
>
> But the earth forevermore
> Is a place where nothing grows,—
> Dawn will come, and no bud break;
> Evening, and no blossom close.

The science fiction writers and the poets were slowly building
up the consciousness with which, twenty-four years later, I could
understand that the discovery of the atom bomb meant the end of
the world in which I had been reared, that not one line of a book
that I was writing on the post–World War II world could now
stand. I tore the manuscript up and threw it all away. But in
1921 the specter of a future that would be less bearable than
the present and the fear of new forms of tyranny that would
replace the old monarchical forms that had been our shorthand
for tyranny then, were not yet with us.

The word "international" was the word we knew. Ideas like One
World of the early 1940s and Planet Earth of the 1960s were not
yet born. The map in my mind at that time was shaped like a
globe, old style, not like Buckminster Fuller's map, which really
shows how the land masses are related. There were vast spaces
on my map about which I knew almost nothing. Africa was an
unknown continent, fitfully illuminated by books like *Batouala*

or plays like *The Emperor Jones,* by the influences of African wood sculpture on European art. India was a place where Gandhi was trying to restore to themselves a people who had been grievously exploited by a colonial regime; China was a vast and different civilization so far away that one knew hardly anything about it. I knew that there had been pre-Columbian high civilizations in Mexico and in South America and that these civilizations had developed independently along quite different lines from the rest of the world. But these, too, had been destroyed by invading Europeans on horseback. In 1921 Mexico was a scene of revolutions against dictators who somehow belied the democratic processes that were supposed to accompany representative government.

Of the various groups of primitive peoples who lived in remote jungles and forests and on the islands of the South Seas, whose study was to become my principal task for the next forty years, I knew very little beyond current claims: by missionaries, that these people needed to be rescued from their heathen ways; by artists, that the clothes the missionaries brought spoiled the islanders as subjects for aesthetic appreciation and gave them new diseases; and by anti-imperialists and socialists, that these primitive people were being exploited. Imperialism was represented in my mind by Kipling's tales and poetry and by Thorstein Veblen's *Imperial Germany and the Industrial Revolution,* the coming economic world by Maynard Keynes's *Economic Consequences of the Peace.*

If I try to reconstruct what I believed then to be the quality of life for which all human beings should strive and what I believed were the necessary steps toward attaining it, I find that peace came first (obviously, since war destroyed lives, towns, the countryside, hope), and after that came economic justice, a resolute willingness to revise our social system so that everyone could have the necessities of life. I would not have been able to list these necessities as food, housing, education, medical care, etc. I do not think that I had any concept of the possibility of eradicating the great scourges of the world—tuberculosis, for example. My friends were still being sent to sanatoriums for many years' "curing." I knew that there were terrible plagues that attacked everyone, native and foreigner, and that these diseases (cholera in India, for example) had something to do with hygiene and poverty. But the vision of a world freed from these great scourges was as far from my mind as was the idea that there could be too many people in the world—too many hungry people, too many unschooled people, too many people who lived under tyrannical political regimes, too many people who toiled under terrible conditions in mines and factories, too many women veiled and housebound, too many children forced to engage in child labor.

Yes, I knew these were conditions that required enormous efforts—possibly revolution, possibly reform—to correct. But I myself hoped to have six children in an era when childbearing was not very popular with the intellectual middle class, many of whom had no children or only one. I wanted to have six children because I enjoyed children, and having children and a life of responsible usefulness seemed to fit together. In those days I expected to live in a country parsonage and work in local communities. I ended up with only one child (who has one child), and I now work, not in a country parsonage, but in the World Council of Churches programs in church and society, and theology and science. And my present community is the world.

Today we associate improvement in the quality of life with radical changes in our cities, new designs that will correct the terrible urban sprawl that the automobile has made possible and bring people back together again into multigeneration, multiracial, multiclass, multi-occupational communities—not households but communities—where people can know and trust their neighbors, and into a living style where much of the natural world of farm and wilderness is within walking distance of the very young and the very old. When I was twenty-one, the present urban style, which so many people now feel has always been with us, was still in the future. There was still good public transportation; even in the big cities people lived in neighborhoods. Only a few grandparents, affluent and footloose, went to Florida or California. The word "baby-sitting" had not been invented, but there were families who had no kin or neighbors to help. In college I organized my friends into baby-sitting groups, because

I thought it was bad for us to spend so many months without contact with children. But the dreadful loneliness of the isolated nuclear family of today, isolated in transient slums, isolated in developments, isolated in suburbs, had not yet become a way of life for a large proportion—and the style-setting section—of the population.

My mother was interested in cooperative laundries, more cooperative relations between households, and in ways of giving domestic servants dignity. But the world of today—the world in which it is taken for granted that each couple will live wherever they can find housing they can afford, within driving distance of the husband's job, or both their jobs, and will expect no help from anyone; the world in which gadgets replace helping hands, where telephone conversations with distant mothers take the place of visits over the back fence, where driving substitutes for bicycling, walking, and riding streetcars—was only foreshadowed. Today we know that in order to restore a human quality to living, town and country roads and transportation systems must all be redesigned, not to conform to the old image but nonetheless in a way that will recreate some of the values that were destroyed with the development of our automobile-based society.

In 1921 I knew a good deal about racial and social injustice, and I knew how precious basic dignity and opportunity were to the minorities—Negroes, European and Asian immigrants, Jews, and Catholics—who were often accorded neither dignity nor opportunity. Since then I have lived through the period in the United States when we fought for the integration of individual members of minorities as students, physicians, lawyers, travelers, property owners. And we have seen the rise and fall of totalitarian terrors—massacre and genocide—of newly liberated countries emulating their former colonial conquerers in savagery and racial prejudice. But here, I do not think that my perceptions have changed very much. For the quality of life that we want for all cannot be attained until no human beings are demeaned or denied dignity or an equal chance for a livelihood because of race or color, nationality, or ideology of their parents. People of every physique must have a world to live in where they can find beautiful both their own parents and very different peoples' parents. I believe I was fully conscious of the way in which the culture in which one was born and reared, one's class position, whether one was rich or poor, determined whether genius was to flower or not. I was fully conscious that there is a wide range of intelligence in every human group, and that, to date, civilizations have wasted large numbers of their gifted. I would have phrased this thought then in the words of Thomas Gray's "Elegy Written in a Country Churchyard":

> Perhaps in this neglected spot is laid
> Some heart once pregnant with celestial fire;
> Hands, that the rod of empire might have sway'd,
> Or waked to extasy the living lyre.
>
> But knowledge to their eyes her ample page
> Rich with the spoils of time did ne'er unroll;
> Chill penury repress'd their noble rage,
> And froze the genial current of the soul.
>
> Full many a gem of purest ray serene,
> The dark unfathom'd caves of ocean bear:
> Full many a flower is born to blush unseen,
> And waste its sweetness of the desert air.

But in my youth I was not as conscious of how much the quality of a culture depended not only on the way it provided for expression of the gifted but also the way it treated its crippled and unfortunate. I think if someone had made the point then and had suggested a program on birth defects like that of the American March of Dimes today, with half the funds going to research to prevent the birth defects in the future and half to care for those who are born defective today, I would have understood it. But no one did. And no one had yet formulated the idea of the interrelationship between the climate of opinion in a society and what changes the members of that society can make. That was in the future, too.

These are the issues that concern us today: the prevention of war; the protection of the environment; the balancing of population and resources; the management of energy so that we will neither exhaust our resources with unbridled growth nor contaminate the environment; the distribution of resources among nations and groups who have been differently dowered in the past by nature and history; the humanization of technology so that technology can be used for human ends and not primarily for profit or for power; the replanning of towns and cities so that neighborhoods can again be a microcosm of three-generational wholeness of life; the creation of transcendental values that will no longer set members of one religion against another, or of one ideology against another, so that all human beings can move in new ways without being traitors to the old. Of these, only the need to prevent war was as clear to me then as it is now.

Perhaps most important of all, I did not have any doubt then that the world was changing, that change was in the very air we breathed, absolutely unpreventable and absolutely necessary. I think this too is part of the quality of life, that human beings must have a chance to learn to cherish the past, act in the present, and leave the future open.

E. F. SCHUMACHER

E. F. SCHUMACHER is an economist and writer, born in Germany and now living in England. He is founder and chairman of the Intermediate Technology Development Group, as well as director of the Scott Bader Co., which is a pioneer effort at common ownership and workers' control. His books are: *Export Policy and Full Employment* (1943), *What Will Planning Mean in Terms of Money?* (1944), *Roots of Economic Growth* (1962), *Small Is Beautiful* (1973).

> Schon in der Kindheit hört' ich es mit Beben:
> Nur wer im Wohlstand lebt, lebt angenehm.
> (Even as a child I felt terror-struck when I
> heard it said that to live an agreeable life you
> have got to be rich.)
> —Bertolt Brecht

Only the rich can have a good life—this is the daunting message that has been drummed into the ears of all mankind during the last half-century or so. It is the implicit doctrine of "development," and the growth of income serves as the very criterion of progress. Everyone, it is held, has not only the right but the duty to become rich, and this applies to societies even more stringently than to individuals. The most succinct and most relevant indicator of a country's status in the world is thought to be *average income per head*, while the prime object of admiration is not the level already attained but the current *rate of growth*.

It follows logically—or so it seems—that the greatest obstacle to progress is a growth of population: It frustrates, diminishes, offsets what the growth of gross national product would otherwise

133

achieve. What is the point of, let us say, doubling the GNP over a period, if population is also allowed to double during the same time? It would mean running faster merely to stand still; *average income per head* would remain stationary, and there would be no advance at all toward the cherished goal of universal affluence.

In the light of this received doctrine the well-nigh unanimous prediction of the demographers—that world population, barring unforeseen catastrophes, will double during the next thirty years —is taken as an intolerable threat. What other prospect is this than one of limitless frustration?

Some mathematical enthusiasts are still content to project the economic "growth curves" of the last thirty years for another thirty or even fifty years to "prove" that all mankind can become immensely rich within a generation or two. Our only danger, they suggest, is to succumb at this glorious hour in the history of progress to a "failure of nerve." They presuppose the existence of limitless resources in a finite world, an equally limitless capacity of living nature to cope with pollution, and the omnipotence of science and social engineering.

The sooner we stop living in the Cloud-Cuckoo-Land of such fanciful projections and presuppositions the better it will be, and this applies to the people of the rich countries just as much as to those of the poor. *It would apply even if all population growth stopped entirely forthwith.*

The modern assumption that "only the rich can have a good life" springs from a crudely materialistic philosophy that contradicts the universal tradition of mankind. The material *needs* of man are limited and in fact quite modest, even though his material *wants* may know no bounds. Man does not live by bread alone, and no increase in his *wants* above his needs can give him the "good life." Christianity teaches that man must seek *first* "the kingdom of God, and his righteousness" and that all the other things—the material things to cover his needs—will then be "added unto" him. The experience of the modern world suggests that this teaching carries not only a promise but also a threat, namely, that "unless he seeks first the kingdom of God, those material things, which he unquestionably also needs, will cease to be available to him."

Our task, however, is to bring such insights, supported, as I said, by the universal tradition of mankind, down to the level of everyday economic reality. To do so, we must study, both theoretically and in practice, the possibilities of "a culture of poverty."

To make our meaning clear, let us state right away that there are degrees of poverty that may be totally inimical to any kind of culture in the ordinarily accepted sense. They are essentially different from poverty and deserve a separate name; the term that offers itself is "misery." We may say that poverty prevails when people have enough to keep body and soul together but little to spare, whereas in misery they cannot keep body and soul together, and even the soul suffers deprivation. Some thirteen years ago when I began seriously to grope for answers to these perplexing questions, I wrote this in *Roots of Economic Growth*:

> All peoples—with exceptions that merely prove the rule—have always known how to help themselves, they have always *discovered a pattern of living which fitted their peculiar natural surroundings.* Societies and cultures have collapsed when they deserted their own pattern and fell into decadence, but even then, unless devastated by war, the people normally continued to provide for themselves, with something to spare for higher things. Why not now, in so many parts of the world? I am not speaking of ordinary poverty, but of actual and acute misery; not of the poor, who according to the universal tradition of mankind are in a special way blessed, but of the miserable and degraded ones who, by the same tradition, should not exist at all and should be helped by all. Poverty may have been the rule in the past, but misery was not. Poor peasants and artisans have existed from time immemorial; but miserable and destitute villages in their thousands and urban pavement dwellers in their hundreds of thousands—not in wartime or as an aftermath of war, but in the midst of peace and as a seemingly permanent feature—that is a monstrous and scandalous thing which is altogether abnormal in the history of mankind. We cannot be satisfied with the snap answer that this is due to population pressure. Since every mouth that comes into the world is also endowed with a pair of hands, population pressure could serve as an explanation only if it meant an absolute shortage of land—and although that situation may arise in the future, it decidedly has not arrived today (a few islands excepted). It cannot be argued that population increase as such must produce increas-

ing poverty, because the additional pairs of hands could not be endowed with the capital they needed to help themselves. Millions of people have started without capital and have shown that a pair of hands can provide not only the income but also the durable goods, i.e. capital, for civilized existence. So the question stands and demands an answer. What has gone wrong? Why cannot these people help themselves?

The answer, I suggest, lies in the abandonment of their indigenous culture of poverty, which means not only that they lost true culture but also that their poverty, in all too many cases, has turned into misery.

A culture of poverty such as mankind has known in innumerable variants before the industrial age is based on one fundamental distinction—which may have been made consciously or instinctively, it does not matter—the distinction between the "ephemeral" and the "eternal." All religions, of course, deal with this distinction, suggesting that the ephemeral is relatively unreal and only the eternal is real. On the material plane we deal with goods and services, and the same distinction applies: All goods and services can be arranged, as it were, on a scale that extends from the ephemeral to the eternal. Needless to say, neither of these terms may be taken in an absolute sense (because there is nothing absolute on the material plane), although there may well be something absolute in the maker's *intention*: He may see his product as something to be *used up*, that is to say, to be destroyed in the act of consumption, or as something to be used or enjoyed as a permanent asset, ideally forever.

The extremes are easily recognized. An article of consumption, like a loaf of bread, is *intended* to be *used up*, while a work of art, like the Mona Lisa, is *intended* to be there forever. Transport services to take a tourist on holiday are intended to be used up and therefore ephemeral, while a bridge across the river is intended to be a permanent facility. Entertainment is intended to be ephemeral; education (in the fullest sense) is intended to be eternal.

Between the extremes of the ephemeral and the eternal, there extends a vast range of goods and services with regard to which the producer may exercise a certain degree of choice: He may be producing with the intention of supplying something relatively ephemeral or something relatively eternal. A publisher, for instance, may produce a book with the intention that it should be purchased, read, and treasured by countless generations or his intention may be that it should be purchased, read, and thrown away as quickly as possible.

Ephemeral goods are—to use the language of business—"depreciating assets" and have to be "written off." Eternal goods, on the other hand, are never "depreciated" but "maintained." (You don't "depreciate" the Taj Mahal; you try to maintain its splendor for all time.)

Ephemeral goods are subject to the economic calculus. Their only value lies in being used up, and it is necessary to ensure that their *cost* of production does not exceed the *benefit* derived from destroying them. But eternal goods are not intended for destruction; there is no occasion for an economic calculus, because the benefit—the product of annual value and time—is infinite and therefore incalculable.

Once we recognize the validity of the distinction between the ephemeral and the eternal, we are able to distinguish, in principle, between two different types of "standards of living." Two societies may have the same volume of production and the same *income per head of population,* but the *quality of life* or life-style may show fundamental and incomparable differences: the one placing its main emphasis on ephemeral satisfactions and the other devoting itself primarily to the creation of eternal values. In the former there may be opulent living in terms of ephemeral goods and starvation in terms of eternal goods—eating, drinking, and wallowing in entertainment, in sordid, ugly, mean, and unhealthy surroundings—while in the latter there may be frugal living in terms of ephemeral goods and opulence in terms of eternal goods —modest, simple, and healthy consumption in a noble setting. In terms of conventional economic accounting they are both equally rich, equally developed—which merely goes to show that the purely quantitative approach misses the point.

The study of these two models can surely teach us a great deal.

It is clear, however, that the question "Which of the two is better?" reaches far beyond the economic calculus, since quality cannot be calculated.

No one, I suppose, would wish to deny that the life-style of modern industrial society is one that places primary emphasis on ephemeral satisfactions and is characterized by a gross neglect of eternal goods. Under certain immanent compulsions, moreover, modern industrial society is engaged in a process of what might be called ever-increasing ephemeralization; that is to say, goods and services that by their very nature belong to the eternal side are being produced as if their purpose were ephemeral. The economic calculus is applied everywhere, even at the cost of skimping and paring on goods that should last forever. At the same time purely ephemeral goods are produced to standards of refinement, elaboration, and luxury, as if they were meant to serve eternal purposes and to last for all time.

Nor, I suppose, would anyone wish to deny that many pre-industrial societies have been able to create superlative cultures by placing their emphasis in the exactly opposite way. The greatest part of the modern world's cultural heritage stems from these societies.

The affluent societies of today make such exorbitant demands on the world's resources, create ecological dangers of such intensity, and produce such a high level of neurosis among their populations that they cannot possibly serve as a model to be imitated by those two-thirds or three-quarters of mankind who are conventionally considered underdeveloped or developing. The *failure of modern affluence*—which seems obvious enough, although it is by no means freely admitted by people of a purely materialistic outlook—cannot be attributed to affluence as such but is directly due to mistaken priorities (the cause of which cannot be discussed here): a gross overemphasis on the ephemeral and a brutal undervaluation of the eternal. Not surprisingly, no amount of indulgence on the ephemeral side can compensate for starvation on the eternal side.

In the light of these considerations, it is not difficult to understand the meaning and feasibility of a culture of poverty. It would be based on the insight that the real needs of man are limited and must be met, but that his wants tend to be unlimited, cannot be met, and must be resisted with the utmost determination. Only by a reduction of wants to needs can resources for genuine progress be freed. The required resources cannot be found from foreign aid; they cannot be mobilized via the technology of the affluent society that is immensely capital-intensive and labor-saving and is dependent on an elaborate infrastructure that is itself enormously expensive. Uncritical technology transfer from the rich societies to the poor cannot but transfer into poor societies a life-style that, placing primary emphasis on ephemeral satisfactions, may suit the taste of small, rich minorities but condemns the great, poor majority to increasing misery.

The resources for genuine progress can be found only by a life-style that emphasizes frugal living in terms of ephemeral goods. Only such a life-style can create (or maintain and develop) an ever-increasing supply of eternal goods.

Frugal living in terms of ephemeral goods means a dogged adherence to simplicity, a conscious avoidance of any unnecessary elaborations, and a magnanimous rejection of luxury—puritanism, if you like—on the ephemeral side. This makes it possible to enjoy a high standard of living on the eternal side, as a compensation and reward. Luxury and refinement have their proper place and function but only with eternal, not with ephemeral, goods. This is the essence of a culture of poverty.

One further point has to be added: The ultimate resource of any society is its labor power, which is infinitely creative. When the primary emphasis is on ephemeral goods, there is an automatic preference for mass production, and there can be no doubt that mass production is more congenial to machines than it is to men. The result is the progressive elimination of the human factor from the productive process. For a poor society, this means that its ultimate resource cannot be properly used; its creativity remains largely untapped. This is why Gandhi, with unerring instinct, insisted that "it is not mass production but only production by the masses that can do the trick." A society that places its primary emphasis on eternal goods will automatically prefer production by the masses to mass production, because such goods, intended to last, must fit the precise conditions of their place;

they cannot be standardized. This brings the whole human being back into the productive process, and it then emerges that even ephemeral goods (without which human existence is obviously impossible) are far more efficient and economical when a proper fit has been ensured by the human factor.

All the above does not claim to be more than an assembly of a few preliminary indications. I entertain the hope that, in view of increasing threats to the very survival of culture—and even life itself—there will be an upsurge of serious study of the possibilities of a culture of poverty. We might find that we have nothing to lose and a world to gain.

MOCHTAR LUBIS

MOCHTAR LUBIS, one of Asia's best-known journalists, was born in 1922 in Sumatra. Imprisoned during the Sukarno regime, since 1966 he has been editor of the *Indonesian Raya*. Some of his books are: *Perkenalan di Asia Tenggara* (1951), *Perlawatan Ke Amerika Serikat* (1952), *Twilight in Djakarta* (1965), *Djalan Tak Ada Udjung* (*A Road with No End*, 1968).

When I became aware of life around me in my early childhood, I lived in the district of Kerinci, Central Sumatra, where my father was a district commissioner with the Dutch colonial administration. It was highland country, spotted with lakes and rivers, terraced rice fields, forests, and tea and coffee estates. Automobiles were few in number. Dutch military airplanes flew over once a year. People lived close to nature.

We played in the lakes and rivers; we snared birds in the hills and fields. The forests were fearful places where tigers, bears, elephants, and mysterious beings lived. But we villagers were happy.

From generation to generation the old wisdom, the old crafts, and the old ways of living had seeped through. We built our houses from wood and bamboo and were proud that we never used a nail in our buildings. Roofs were made from pieces of split bamboo neatly placed upon each other or from the strong black fibers of the *tuak* tree. We made our own tools of bamboo to snare animals and birds or to catch fish in the lakes and rivers; and the village smith made whatever iron implements were needed to work the rice fields and carve wood.

141

Being a son of the district commissioner I lived in a house with a tin roof and rode in one of the few cars in the district. But at that age my greatest pleasure still was to ride on the back of a black buffalo or to race downhill on a Dutch-made bicycle, or to swim in the lakes and the rivers, to sit still on a big boulder in the midst of a lovely stream, and to listen to the birds singing.

I felt happy and contented.

Then a Chinese entrepreneur built the first cinema in the district capital. We saw alien life-styles that exerted a strong attraction. We began to long for the big cities we saw on the screen, to board the big ships, to fly around in an airplane, to be able to push a button and get electric light, and to want the machines that moved and made things.

Eventually I moved to bigger places to pursue my education. I saw my own people no longer able to make things with simple tools and with their own hands. They had to buy everything they needed to live, including the most simple things, things that could be made by little boys or girls in the Kerinci district. But at my age then, between eighteen and twenty-three, the new things were very attractive. They were modern, and therefore I felt they were good. Without realizing it I was growing away from the natural life that I had lived happily as a child. In the big city there were other attractions. Completely unaware of ourselves, we cultivated new needs and new values.

When after World War II new synthetics appeared to replace wood and bamboo, they were welcomed because they were new, the product of modern science and technology. Plastic tabletops replaced wood; synthetic cloth replaced beautiful and natural cotton and silk; plastic bottles, glasses, cups, and plates replaced natural glass. In the big city people began to depend on certain services to survive. They became cut off from the old wisdom of personal family and group survival techniques. They became cut off from nature. Slowly the younger generation who lived in the great cities forgot the names of trees and plants, could no longer identify birds by name. They lost their affinity with the soil, the lakes and rivers, the mountains and forests. They lived in an artificial environment. Their pace of life quickened; their life-ways changed.

International trade and industry are imposing and have imposed on the big cities of the world similar consumption patterns and life-styles. Modern communication and transport systems too have imposed similar life-styles, similar desires for consumption goods, and even similar values. The big cities themselves grow to look like one another. Tokyo and New York, London, Manila, Jakarta, Singapore, Hong Kong experience similar traffic problems and similar pollution problems. Only the intensity of these is different.

As I continued to live and work in Jakarta, I, too, perhaps through a process of osmosis, developed certain values and attitudes about the quality of life ideal to me at that time. I was quite confident that to become a great and strong nation Indonesia must acquire all the modern industries that the powerful nations possessed. My friends and I dreamed of seeing chemical, steel, fertilizer, plastics, automotive manufacturing, and textile factories all over Indonesia. We dreamed of superhighways crisscrossing the main islands of the Indonesian archipelago, connected to each other through undersea tunnels, choked with trucks and automobiles day and night. We dreamed of great cities being built on the islands. We dreamed of boats plying throughout the archipelago, and airplanes flying in the skies. We talked about skyscrapers. We talked about highly mechanized farming and sea fisheries. We put great faith in what science and modern technology could do to improve the quality of life of our people.

We also thought that to be a great nation, we had to possess a great arms industry. We had to be able to manufacture weapons of all kinds, build our own warships and guns. The most modern weaponry, jet fighter planes and bombers, rockets, radars, tanks, artillery, bombs, and other fearful means to kill and destroy were regarded as prerequisites to a modern nation—part of a special quality of life.

With each new discovery of science we rejoiced, for we believed that everything science and technology offered was good and improved the quality of life for man. Science and technology in the hands of man would enable him, we believed, to remain master of his destiny. We could overcome any problem that might arise: grow food in abundance; build good houses for our people cheaply; eradicate all the traditional diseases—malaria, tuberculosis, cholera, typhus, and dysentery—that had been a scourge to the population in the past. The use of DDT was welcomed, for example, because it would mean the eradication of malaria, which for centuries had been a plague to many parts of Indonesia. The new synthetic fertilizers were regarded as a miraculous solution to our food problems. We even welcomed the new electronic communications system, putting up with its endless ear-shattering blaring for commercial ends.

Nothing—not even life itself—seemed to be beyond the ability of science and technology to create. Man seemed at the threshold of being able to interfere in the biological process and through the manipulation of genes and chromosomes to create special personalities, copies of persons. The research into the processes of the human brain promised that human behavior could be controlled and moved in certain directions.

We thought that whatever was good for the industrialized nations must also be good for us. And many of us thought that a good life should include at least one automobile per family, a telephone in the house, a refrigerator, an air-conditioning unit, a TV set, a hi-fi set, and other gadgets in the kitchen, bathroom, bedroom, and living room. The good life was to be found in the big cities only, however. The thought of the simple life in the villages where big-city facilities were completely absent was horrifying.

I was as enthusiastic over the rapid development of science and technology as anybody in any developed country who "reaped" the benefits of science and technology in his society. My first disillusionment with technology came only when I went to Korea after war broke out there. The cruel destruction to life and property caused by the machinery of war shocked me and made me question the wisdom of those who handled the vast resources of science and technology and used them to kill and destroy.

Later, when I visited the United States of America and read Rachel Carson's *The Silent Spring,* I started to look at science and technology with a new awareness of how unthinkingly nations have used the fruits of science and technology. In many cases we have poisoned our lakes and rivers, and our seas and soil, destroyed our forest and fields for generations to come. We have polluted the air we breathe, and our economic statisticians, politicians, and government leaders have asked the people to rejoice with each new smokestack that belches black smoke into the sky, because this means economic development and modernization and will raise the quality of life for our people.

My next shock, during a visit to America, was the sight of the automobile graveyards that pockmarked the landscape throughout the United States. And the next was on a flight to Mexico City, when I had to stop for half a smoggy day in Los Angeles. My eyes smarted and became red and painful, and it was with considerable relief in my heart that I boarded the airplane that flew us to the Mexican capital.

Another disappointment came on a visit to Calcutta some time after that. It frightened me to see how the quality of life for human beings could become so degraded in a big city. It made me fear the same experience would one day befall our own great cities in Indonesia.

My many flights across the wastelands of Persia and the Arabian Peninsula, the deserts of North Africa, and parts of Northern India forced further painful adjustments upon me. Looking at the dead earth through the window of the airplane, the green islands of Indonesia flashed before my eyes, and I asked myself then whether our islands would one day end like these wastelands: despoiled, violated, destroyed, and murdered.

I remember also a ten days' stay in Tokyo without seeing the sun through the smoke and smog that hung low above the city. Each day when I came back to my hotel, my shirt collars were blackened by soot, and I could actually feel the dirt that had settled in my hair, my nostrils, my ears and eyes, and on my skin. Those were scary days, when shops offered whiffs of oxygen from special bottles, and everybody was walking around with mouth and nose masks. I felt I was on an alien planet, menaced by evil beings lurking in the dark clouds that hung heavily over the city.

Since then I have attended a number of seminars on ecology and environment, and I have become convinced that we should strike out in other directions and try to formulate for ourselves our own development goals and the kind of life-style we in Asia want. It should be different from those we have seen so far in countries like Japan or the United States.

In some cases we have already gone too far in copying or repeating the mistakes of the developed countries. For example, Jakarta today gives the same impression of traffic snarls and overdependence on personal transportation without air-pollution controls rather than on public transportation. The island of Java is today only 11 per cent covered by forests, while some experts claim that the safety margin against unchecked erosion should be 33⅓ per cent of the total land area. Our indiscriminate use of pesticides in the national effort to increase food production has caused some negative side effects, like the killing of fish in ponds and rivers. And the overuse of synthetic fertilizer has caused the quality of the soil to deteriorate.

It would be idle to wish to return to the old days of the Kerinci district. Most of the developing countries have woven their life patterns into the international framework of industry and commerce, and international advertising, using subtle methods of persuasion, is imposing similar consumption patterns and life-styles on our societies. We must, however, deliberately free ourselves from this hypnotic influence. It serves no good purpose to denounce science and technology today. I believe we should continue to expand them, but we should endeavor to keep man in control.

It is not the automobile that should dictate policies on transportation systems, on the building of highways, and broader economic, social, and political priorities (the shortage of gasoline recently even dictated a change in foreign policies by many developed and developing nations). I think we should limit the size of our cities and the size of our cities' population; building codes and the strict enforcement of zoning laws could enable us to do this. Some urban development experts feel that cities of a million or under are manageable. The monstrous cities, such as Tokyo, New York, Chicago, Los Angeles, or Calcutta, phenomena of our times, have proved themselves to be out of control and have also created undesirable side effects in both individual and group behavior. They have become breeding grounds for crime and in-humanity.

We still have to learn how to create comfortable areas for living and working in the great cities, how to relate individuals and groups to each other. I believe we should learn to build new cities in a different way. For example, to build in the tropics sky-scrapers and concrete fortresses sealed against the elements as in North America or Europe seems not only stupid but a waste of our resources. I think we should build light and airy homes. We should learn to cool our buildings with shadows, trees, and shrubs. Why copy expensive building techniques from the developed countries? We should use science and technology simply to make our natural materials like wood, bamboo, and plant fibers more durable and resistant to fire.

We should learn to use more of our biodegradable materials for wrapping and packaging. Before plastics appeared, rice, sugar, coffee, tea, and many other articles were transported in jute sacks, wooden chests, or woven bamboo packages. Smaller amounts were wrapped in banana leaves and other woven plant fibers. But today we see plastic bottles, containers, and sheets thrown away everywhere to dirty the landscape. The old jute sacks and leaf packages would have rotted under the sun, and we would have given back to the earth what we took from it. All this may sound simple. But truth is simple; only lies are complicated.

We should learn to keep the ecological balance in our environment; we should learn how to use fertilizers and pesticides wisely and in moderation and stimulate plant production organically and control pests biologically. We should keep our rivers, lakes, streams, and ponds clean and healthy, guarding against the spillage of dangerous elements such as mercury and poisonous chemicals from our industries, which should be equipped to defuse dangerous waste.

To be happy and comfortable one does not need to be rich. We should revise our concepts of economies of scale away from the mass-production values developed in the highly industrialized societies. The goal and the main purpose of every endeavor should not be maximization of profit but how to keep people constructively engaged for themselves and society. Traditionally in many societies in Asia the mere pursuit of wealth and pleasure is not the real purpose of life, nor is it the key to happiness and peace of mind. Man's life can be much enriched by the mysterious spiritual realm, by the mysteries of nature and the cosmos, and by the source of all life, call it God, Buddha, or whatever.

Our societies in Asia teach us moderation in everything we do, for we believe it is not for us to conquer nature but rather to live in harmony with it. Thus, we should preserve our sense of time and space, refusing to be enrolled in the rat race that causes high blood pressure, ulcers, and heart attacks in industrialized societies.

The crucial question is this: Can we liberate ourselves from the values of those highly commercialized societies and develop our own—gaining control of science and technology, so that our culture can handle them wisely and constructively?

As an Indonesian the quality of a good life seems to me to consist of living simply, closer to nature, taking what you need from the soil, and giving back to the soil what you have used; developing warm and compassionate human relationships, being rational but at the same time accepting the mysteries of life and existence, and living in peace with these mysteries. And since the quality of life obviously does not rest only upon abundant material facilities and resources but also upon those cultural resources from which we can draw inspiration and spiritual sustenance, I also believe that we should live in a free and open society that guarantees basic human rights and freedoms such as the freedom of expression and, no less important, the freedom of choice.

If he lives in human dignity, man can sustain a happy and peaceful life on very little material wealth. We do not need most of the wasteful trappings of the highly industrialized civilizations. We should learn—from their sorrows of today and their deep anxieties about the future—to be content to fulfill our basic needs and to further enrich our life from the cultural resources we have inherited.

GEORGES WALTER *

GEORGES WALTER, writer and critic, born in 1924 in Hungary, now lives in France. After having his own radio show for some time, he has become TV critic for *Le Figaro*. His novels are *Les Prêtres mariés* (1969), *Les Enfants d'Attila* (1967), *La Ballade de Sacramento Slim* (1971), *Des Vols de Vanessa* (1972).

As with food and love, language to me has always seemed to be a function full of mystery that deepens with the process of writing. Are not words, which are so necessary and yet equivocal, like that strange woman that the poet Verlaine saw in a dream?

> who's never quite the same
> and never quite another . . .

From our very first years the flutter of words surrounds us, and little by little we get into the bird cage of society, having in turn acquired the few sounds that bring about laughter or tears and on which the sun will never set till the end of time. Ever since man opened his mouth, ever since he started writing, confusion has accompanied expression as our shadow follows each one of our steps. The story of the Tower of Babel has not yet ended: The Tower is still rising toward the divine and the workers still do not speak the same language.

Though it is difficult for me to give a figure of strictly scientific value, I feel that I have spent more than a quarter of my life in the act of writing. Since I am fifty years old, this means I have

* Translated by Leela Moraes.

spent something like fifteen years of my life working with a typewriter or a pen. Seen in this way, this long succession of years makes one think of being purged of a criminal offense, of having to go through with a silent and inexorable prison sentence. In fact, the act of writing, which has always appeared to me to be my one and only vocation, has always been fraught with pain and suffering.

Since my adolescence I have wanted to be a writer. Truthfully speaking, I have never considered that I was or could be anything else; my only problem was to prove this. As far as I was concerned, I did not need to prove it to myself with even a single line, but was it not a question of showing the product to others? I would have been very surprised then if anyone had talked to me about "communication." Of course, as I approached manhood, I did feel that the writer needed others. But those others, that is to say the public, appeared to me to be a remote pretext for an entirely different kind of communication: with myself, with what was most secret in me and what was even beyond my own self. I ended up asking myself what any of this had to do with the public and what the public had to do with it.

My work as a writer was awaiting me like waves ranked on the horizon, like a Himalayan range that was inaccessible yet familiar. Then circumstances forced me to become a journalist. I say "forced me," because from the start using words from the same language for so different a purpose from what I had intended seemed to me something profane, like prostituting myself.

It is, however, through journalism that I have been able to understand the terribly dangerous influence of words, the power of those who write them and of those who spread them. In the air we breathe they act like the mephitic fumes of those factories that handle the most dangerous products, for which we slowly lose all sense of smell.

I began as a journalist during the war, in the U.S. Army press. I was not a war correspondent but sort of a peace correspondent, since I worked in Nice for the Public Relations Office of the U.S. Riviera Recreational Area. (The French Riviera was a rest and recreation area for the GIs.) I wore a U.S. uniform, no doubt to blend into the background, and my work had mainly to do with writing about the well-being of the troops and the way such and such a GI spent his day—a short piece meant for the GI's home town, nothing more obnoxious on the surface.

For example, one would write:

> John P. Norton of Little Creek (Arkansas) of the 102nd Airlift has spent two days furlough on the French Riviera. After a dream of a night at the Hotel Negresco, in the room once occupied by Winston Churchill, he visited Monte Carlo and ate crêpes suzettes at the Sporting. My friends, what a day! John is in splendid shape and the USRRA has organized things well, etc. . . .

In fact, on the Riviera, in 1944, it was euphoria for the liberated people who had been starved for years and the same for the GIs who, for a few days, forgot about the war. But in hospitals one began to see weird specters still dressed in striped pajamas, survivors of concentration camps, who, in agony or madness, would sit up to salute the visitor, taking him for an SS officer. As for the GIs, while some visited Monte Carlo, others continued to die in Germany or even nearer—and a few kilometers from the Hotel Negresco, I saw trucks full of sacks being unloaded into a hangar.. These sacks contained the corpses of GIs, each one ready to be sent off to some little town to which the Public Relations Office was sending news of another soldier on rest and recreation. This also was part of reality, but it played only a very discreet part. Newspapers, as is normal in wartime, took part in constantly bolstering the morale of the armies and the people.

I was twenty-three years old, and I could already understand that what one calls information is in many cases just the contrary: a system that, in giving the illusion of reporting facts, acts as a cover-up for them. As the years went by I saw more and more clearly the strange machinery of a press that still had the tendency, although the war was over, to distort things for the sake of a supposed public, of imaginary people. The aim was no longer victory but how to remain in business, which amounts to about the same thing.

The work of a journalist brings about many different feelings: the surprise of discovery, joy in certain encounters, the feeling of impotence when one cannot change anything, and the feeling of being ill at ease with the very instrument of communication—the newspaper—where the worst and the best are side by side. This is the kind of admixture whose taste, over the years, became to me as familiar as tobacco.

With the addition of radio loudspeakers and small TV screens, and now gradually such constant background noise in our lives as the nonstop traffic in our cities, aren't the information media like a great weight on the very quality of our lives? Information is certainly a sign of essential freedom in world communities. When it is enslaved, it becomes a precious symbol. But when it is free, what does it do with its freedom? Communication is only valid in terms of the message it conveys. So, what is the message? Why is it conveyed? How is the message experienced? Two types of lies blur channels simultaneously: the lie of omission, a subtle censure from the outside or the inside; and also the lie of excess, an attachment of too much importance to the insignificant. It is more and more difficult to find information between these lines of dissimulation and exhibitionism.

In this whole process one must not forget the role of speed. Napoleon died at St. Helena on May 5, 1821. Do you know when the French got the news? In *July* 1821 (without taking into account that much of the world then never knew that Napoleon had died or even that he had ever existed). Today the international press agencies feel triumphant when one of them has beaten its competitors by a minute or two in transmitting an item of news on its world news relays. Satellite television enables us to see "live" an attempt on someone's life. But there again, when speed, which is the powerful slave of our times, becomes our master, it is a source of danger.

After some years in the jungle of information I returned to the silence of writing as if I had stepped into another world. Here, to start with, no one awaits the manuscript except oneself, and the act of completing it is constantly postponed by doubt. Knowing how to complete a book is very much an art and a trial, but one is oneself responsible for a suffering that no one else has inflicted. All the same, there are moments of grace: when characters that never existed anywhere come to life in areas of the imagination, carry one away, and refuse to be anything but themselves; when the pen leads the narrative to chase after it; when language is like the voice of a child one didn't know. What is inspiration? Never an aimless concept, often a memory or reminiscence, the eruption of incongruous elements from that flea market that clutters every corner of our brain, elements that unite in a way that can sometimes astonish or please. The deepest inspiration is no doubt more mysterious. It is a sudden communication with others and the universe, and it is part of what one calls true culture. It happens with popular songs that have come from two most distant parts of the world and yet are similar, like different dances and musics. One invents a story, and suddenly it seems that one has not invented anything at all. The stories that the world has told itself since its creation, isn't their source so far beyond our vision that we do not know where they come from? Few writers reach such purity, but isn't a writer someone who has more or less a share in this? How does one recognize him? His readers will say so. Then from the writer's solitude will emerge authentic communication, not just fleeting excitement. It goes without saying that the writer who is in that state of grace is not bothered about any ideas of success, but in addition he is the only one who will reach another, because the secret center that has awakened in him will awaken the secret center in each of us. "The one who wants to save his life will lose it; the one who is prepared to lose his life will save it," says the Bible.

But the one who returns from the silence of writing to the tumult of information will see that here, like there, one judges the tree by its fruit and it is the tree that determines the fruit. The writer, for many reasons, should not disdain the journalist. Enthusiasm or caution are not more forbidden to one than to the other. One can lie about what is imagined as one can lie about reality. A lie in the field of information is seldom conscious. Because of that, and because things have evolved with shattering rapidity, we must be all the more vigilant and scrupulous.

The power and prestige inherent in what is written is slowly being replaced by the overblown power of a voice or face. For several years on the radio, every day at a certain time, I used to provide an editorial, my personal comment on an event. Listeners would write to me to agree or disagree with what I had said the day before. But there were others, people who would ask me for strange advice, granting me abilities I had never laid claim to. One mother asked my advice about her daughter's marriage, and a woman who thought her husband had been poisoned begged me to make the truth "burst out." In spite of my insisting that I was not a detective, that I had no special powers, that I was simply a journalist, she refused to believe me. This is highly revealing. It proves that the audio-visual medium meant to enlighten the mass more often than not sinks it into confusion, if not into a state of mental infancy.

One of the misfortunes of the press is that its need to be everywhere and to pretend to know everything leads it to know too much, to create a confused mentality. Children living in hovels do not hold press conferences. The press gets to them and transforms their misery into beautiful photographs. Quite naturally the great misfortunes of humanity make for big headlines in the information media. But just when it would be best to ponder and understand them, the furious noise of the press and of the audio-visual machinery turns the individual into a stunned, tired, and desensitized spectator. There came a time when the Vietnam War no longer affected anyone, though it was more atrocious than ever. On French television producers screened footage on it not in terms of the latest political news but in terms of the public's supposed saturation point. In such a case, it is no longer the real importance of the event that matters but its entertainment value. Then everything is turned around: Instead of information being subservient to reality, reality has to comply to the media. The newspaper page, the microphone, and the camera have become the dictators, and the crowd listens.

Because this whole machinery is aimed at crowds, it shapes those crowds, which is why the individual is as ill at ease before it as in one of the crowded constructions of our cities, where one has to hear what one is not listening to and to see what one is not looking at. Publicity being precisely what one does not listen to but hears, what one sees but does not look at, its being coupled with information is the most striking phenomena in the world of communication, in this electronic clamor that surrounds and encircles us. Only by living on a desert island is it possible to escape this din. Today children can see, as if they were there themselves, an enormous number of events that they could only distantly relate to through adults' descriptions. As for adults, don't they in turn carry within themselves a mass of information, through word, sound, and the screen images that reach them?

Thus, the marvelous world of communication, which enables us to have at hand the most refined techniques, from the Chinese ideogram and Egyptian hieroglyphics to the televised message, contains one of the most threatening dangers that weighs on the human quality of man. Moreover, we do not yet know what will come about in the next few years in terms of even more subtle techniques, like records that produce pictures, one's own cinema, or satellites. Should one, from now on, impose a ban on radio, television, and newspapers on certain days, or plan for oneself periods of fast that could give one back a taste for such things? Should one destroy the apparatus, build bonfires, chuck the sets through the window? That would be like saying one should stop all scientific research because of all the ill effects of the technical world, close all the factories because of the pollution they cause.

If we find ourselves with too much power too soon, maybe it is time for us to learn how to use the toys we manipulate, to know that what contains the worst can also contain the best. The information media is sometimes like that huge machine a humorist conceived of, as big as a locomotive but, though full of cogs, pistons, and bolts, only able to crack a hazelnut. If all too often communication conveys insignificant matters, it does happen that the publicity that goes with information brings out what was kept hidden and acts brutally as the voice of justice. When a paper has no other power than a fact whose truth it proclaims with obstinacy, with substantiating evidence, then it shows real strength. Television can inflict the face and words of a nitwit upon us; but it can also reveal the sincerity that goes with the face and words of a valuable man, and it can show up the impostors.

Here and there are signs of lucidity. The demand for immediacy that prevents thoughtfulness and the speed of transmission that leaves no time to distinguish between the essential and the accessory finally creates the need for their opposites: analysis and calmness. The very instruments of communication are starting to criticize themselves, either by showing the wounds that their own inventions have inflicted on man today or in seeking out pictures of what is neither famous, nor out of the way, nor spectacular.

If everything depends on the attitude of those who transmit and the attitude and attention of those who receive, it would be advisable, from now on, for the men at both ends to become aware of the good and the bad use of communication, remembering the remark made by the ethnologist Claude Lévi-Strauss: "90 per cent of what we call progress consists of attempts to make up for the inconveniences that stem from the advantages provided by the remaining 10 per cent."

In Pedro Calderón de la Barca's great play, *Life Is a Dream*, one sees the hero, Sigismund, shut away since his birth in a cave in the mountains, because it had been predicted to his father, the King, that the child would be bad and dangerous. When the prince is twenty, the King, feeling guilty, wants to try an experiment. He sends messengers to the cave in which Sigismund is chained, makes him drink a potion that puts him to sleep, and has him dressed up in finery. Sigismund wakes up to find himself sitting on a throne, surrounded by courtiers. He thinks he is dreaming and at once pursues a woman and throws out of a window a man whom he finds irritating. The potion puts him to sleep once more, and he is taken back to the cave where they chain him up again. Alas, thinks the King, those predictions were right. In the course of time, however, life once more gives Sigismund access to power. This time he is careful. Whether it is a dream or reality, he says, one must be careful to behave; if not, it would be too dangerous.

Millions of words have been in circulation for thousands of years, between dream and reality, like small interplanetary machines, and one doesn't know what to do with them. We are heading more and more toward signs on an international scale, returning perhaps, in a way, to a world before Babel. René Etiemble, the philologist, reminds us that Gottfried Leibnitz saw in Chinese characters the possibility of a universal script, where in each character one could find a word from his own language. Etiemble himself suggests one alphabet for the world. Possibly communication's cacophony will prompt us to simplify. All the same there will always be words, words, words, in which to lose or to find ourselves. There is, however, a secret area within each one of us where the river of words flows into a deep and silent ocean. Communication with others has meaning only when we have established communication with ourselves.

JULIAN MITCHELL

JULIAN MITCHELL, novelist and playwright, was born in 1935 in England, where he lives. Though he has written and adapted several television plays, he is best known for: *Imaginary Toys* (1961), *A Disturbing Influence* (1962), *As Far as You Can Go* (1963), *The White Father* (1964), *A Circle of Friends* (1966), *The Undiscovered Country* (1968).

I lived my childhood at the ends of lanes. The first house I remember was in the middle of an Iron Age camp. There were three other houses inside the great earthworks and ditch that surrounded and guarded the camp, but two of them were invisible and the other was our gardener's cottage. No traces of Iron Age life remained, except the earthworks themselves, now overgrown with trees, and the round stones we sometimes found in the ditch and firmly believed to be attacker's slingshots. There was also a cork tree, under which Queen Boudicca, who led the resistance to the Roman invasion in the first century A.D., was supposed to be buried. The tree has gone now, and with it, I suppose, the legend. But our old house is still there, with the copper beech my mother planted and the old fir in whose branches my elder brother and I built our treehouse. The drive still crosses the ditch where the prehistoric people entered their camp. Revisiting Wallbury recently, I experienced all the familiar sensations: Everything was smaller; the vast distances I used to bicycle would now scarcely stretch my legs; the steep hill down to the canal is a gentle slope. But one thing has not changed. Wallbury is still extraordinarily isolated. A little road comes up to the entrance of the camp but then shies away and runs around the outside of the defenses.

And at every possible entrance there is a notice marked PRIVATE.

When I was a young child, I very rarely went to the neighboring but invisible village, and never without an adult. There was nothing to go for, except sweets, and there were quite enough of those at home. For another, my family took no part whatever in village life. We did not go to church, for instance; my father did not go to the pub, nor my mother to any of the women's organizations. Those things were not for us. We were not villagers. We lived behind our ancient defenses, and when we came out to shop, we went to the nearest town. When the war came, our isolation was intensified, for without gasoline it was almost impossible for our friends to visit us or us them. It was only then, under the pressures of war, that my brothers and I were allowed to play with the two boys of our own age who lived in one of the other Wallbury houses. Peter and David were not really quite our sort of people. Their mother talked a great deal about Pinner, the salubrious London suburb from which she had moved, and clearly longed to go back there. With her husband, like my father, away at the war, she found country life lonely and boring. My mother, who had moved from a commuter town of very little higher social standing, smiled and said nothing. She was delighted to have escaped from middle-middle-class life to her upper-middle-class isolation. For the middle-middle she had one utterly damning adjective: common. If my mother said a thing was common, it was beneath contempt. Peter and David were very common and not to be imitated in any way just because they were the only available playmates for several miles. They couldn't help it that their mother knew so little that she hadn't even had their adenoids out, of course. But she hadn't, and that was always a sign. Their commonness put a certain reserve on our relationship. They were eager to please, and I had to remember not to like them too much.

My two brothers were four years older and younger than I, respectively. The distance in age was then vast, like the distance to the end of the drive; besides, my elder brother went to boarding school when I was five, so I only saw him at holidays. Thus, in spite of Peter and David, my childhood was quite a lonely one, and I think I must often have been bored. I'm told I read enormously, though I don't remember it. What I do remember is bicycling: up and down the drive and out of the camp and up the road to a "suitable" neighbor's for lessons with his governess —I hated him; he was sly and accused me of peeping through my fingers at prayers—and down along another lane to fetch the dog meat, sloshed with a vile green paint to discourage people from eating it and so getting more than their meat ration. I also remember wandering by myself for hours round the wooded ditch and down to the canal below the bluff on which the camp had been strategically sited. I felt I knew every leaf on every tree of the woods, every hollow stump and bird's nest. When I went to boarding school myself, I planted a great bullrush in the middle of a little marsh and proclaimed it King, and ordered the trees to obey him loyally in my absence.

The outside world did occasionally intrude. A German bomber, trying to escape from British fighters, unloaded its bombers across the camp and destroyed our great old barn. But we weren't there when that happened and for excitement had to make do with V-1 and V-2 rockets and the wreck of another crashed German plane in a swamp the other side of the canal, from which we filched thrilling notices in enemy language. Occasionally, troops came and maneuvered. A soldier offered me a taste of his lunch from his canteen; when I burned my tongue, he laughed. When my father came home on his rare leaves, he brought me maps, on which I marked the allied advances in Africa, then Sicily, Italy, and France. But reality was mostly a long way away, and far more important to me than bombs and guns were two small incidents that puzzled and frightened me.

The first happened when I went one day on my bicycle into the village on an errand for my mother. I wore, as a good little upper-middle-class boy should, a tweed cap. I had no objection to the cap—I think I may even have liked it and thought myself rather grown-up. On my way home, I was stopped by a gang of village boys, who teased and tormented me and threw my cap in some stinging nettles. It was an utterly trivial occurrence, and I'm sure not one of the gang remembered it for more than a week; but I have never forgotten it. I had gone outside the defenses; I had entered hostile territory. I had had my first inkling that there might be people who didn't like people like us and the way we lived. I fled home as fast as my legs would pedal me, burst into tears, and refused to wear the cap again.

The other incident was quite different. Wandering through the woods one day, I found some men in shabby uniforms digging out a ditch. They were Italian prisoners of war, it turned out, and so harmless that the authorities did not even bother to guard them but sent them out under the command of one of their own officers. Scared at first, I gradually grew bolder, approached, and began to talk to them. The officer was very friendly. He came from Milan, he said, which was in the North of Italy. The North was much better than the South: People in the South were lazy and never did a decent day's work, but Northerners worked very hard and were honest. He gave me sweets and a puff of his cigarette. He had a marmalade factory in Italy, he said. I had no idea what a factory was like, though I knew all about marmalade, of course. His factory sounded like Heaven on earth. The officer had a wife and family; he showed me their pictures. He put his arm round me and asked for a kiss.

Now our family, like many in our class, was not good at kissing and cuddling; indeed, we scarcely went in for that at all, apart from a formal kiss at bedtime. Isolated from the world beyond the defenses of our camp, we were physically isolated from each other within it. So I was quite nonplussed to be asked for a kiss, and though I submitted for a moment or two, I quickly wriggled away. The Italian seemed amused, but I was not. I had felt it wasn't quite right, in any case, to fraternize with the enemy, and this seemed to prove it. I went home feeling an interesting afternoon had turned tediously adult in a way I didn't understand. I had not been frightened, only embarrassed, but when I told my mother and our cook about the marmalade factory and how Southern Italians were disgracefully lazy, and how funny it was that the man had wanted to kiss me, there was immediate consternation. I was closely questioned: Was that *all* he had done? Was I quite sure? Was I *positive?* They had instantly assumed the Italian officer was a sex maniac. Not knowing what sex was, let alone a maniac, I could not understand what the fuss was about, but I could tell they were genuinely frightened, and that, naturally, frightened me. When they wouldn't explain, I became more frightened still. What appalling danger had I undergone? What was the *matter?* Why was my mother going to write to the commander of the prisoner-of-war camp? Why was I not to go near the prisoners again?

Prisoners—it seems to me now that we were the prisoners, prisoners of an idea about what life, and our kind of life in particular, should be like. I have often wanted to find that poor, lonely man, who hadn't seen his children for so many years, or cuddled anyone else's, and apologize to him. He was obeying a much healthier instinct in wanting to kiss and cuddle a child than my family was in assuming his motive must be base. Not only did we have notices at the gate saying PRIVATE, we had them hanging round our necks: TRESPASSERS WILL BE PROSECUTED.

After the war, when I was ten, my family moved to another part of England, to a house at the end of another lane, with no other house near it at all. It was on the side of a Cotswold valley, surrounded by beechwoods, and though nearer to a village than our last house, it was even more isolated, for beyond us were only woods and fields for several miles. By now I was at a boarding school for eight months of the year, herded about with a hundred other small boys of my class, learning irregular Latin verbs, reading the novels of Captain W. E. Johns, and kicking and hitting balls of various colors and sizes. One Christmas shortly after the war I came home with a common skin disease, and my parents decided I was "run down" and had better have a term off from school. It was the shortest term of the year, so I wouldn't be missing too many lessons, and I would be able to enjoy the benefits of the country life and air for which my father slaved all week on our behalf in an office in London (as he did not fail to remind us). My mother had been able to find only one boy for me to play with in the village, partly because there were very few children in the village at all and partly because though he was extremely common, the others were even worse. (To be worse than common was, perversely, to be better—less pretentious, more honest, more down-to-earth, somehow more "natural," but also, of course, less suitable for me to play with.) Unfortunately, John Sparrow, my common playmate, got me into terrible trouble one day by saying as a joke that Mr. Chamberlain, the thrice-married patriarchal village farmer, had died that morning. It never occurred to me that anyone could joke about death, and, completely deceived, I told my mother. She at once wrote a letter of condolence to Mrs. Chamberlain, who was stone deaf and found all jokes difficult to appreciate even at the best of times. She was very much surprised by my mother's letter and not at all amused, and John Sparrow was not often invited to play with me again. In any case, he still had to go to school, even if I didn't. So for ten weeks I was virtually without any friend of my own age at all.

Everyone in that part of the country rode. (Everyone, that is, of our class and anyone in the lower classes who could possibly afford to. This did not, naturally, include the farm laborers who occupied most of the cottages in the village.) My parents, therefore, decided to buy me a pony; riding him and learning to look after him, I would get plenty of fresh air and exercise. He was a good rough pony, distinctly "common" in looks and character, with a buck that would have tested a rodeo rider. Sometimes he ran away with me or bucked me off, whereupon I would thrash him and curse him in the foulest language (quickly picked up at the pony club). Sometimes, after a titanic clash of wills, he would submit and do what I wanted. After a while, except when one or the other of us became overexcited, which was too often, we got on splendidly, making instant joint decisions about who was to be in command at any crucial moment and trusting each other not to do anything too stupid. I frequently fell off, but he usually waited for me to get on again. And though he once kicked me in the stomach, it was entirely my own fault for trying to currycomb him in his field, which he rightly regarded as bad horsemanship and an unwarrantable interference with the business of his eating. He was called Flicka, after an American film.

I grew out of Flicka in time and had another pony, much better bred, a mare called Goldie. She went like the wind and had the sweetest, gentlest nature, and I loved her. I never *loved* Flicka; our relationship was too masculine for that, a constant struggle for mastery. But I much preferred him, too, to any human being

I knew, and, though I had my friends at school and at the pony club, there was never anyone to whom I felt as close as I did to those two animals.

It's years since I rode a horse, but I've never had any difficulty in understanding how someone could happily spend his or her life with horses or how the legend of centaurs arose. I have been a centaur myself, half a man, half a horse. That is what it is like when you and your animal are in perfect understanding. Nowadays Western writers, revealing the ghastly mechanical, denatured state of their civilization, seem quite unable to imagine any state of union and empathy that is not simply sexual. I don't deny that there was a sexual element in my feelings of oneness with my ponies. Why should there not have been, when we all have partly sexual natures? But the sexual was only a minor element, even a trivial one. The joy in my heart as I rode at a fence was in the heart of my pony, too, as I could feel along the reins and between my knees. And as we jumped, and I leaned forward along the pony's neck, it was my legs springing us over and my toes on which we landed.

I don't believe the feelings I had then would have lasted into adulthood, for a man does not ride like a boy, and a horse is not a pony. The relationship becomes more formal. But then I thought of my ponies as more understanding than any human being, and when I was happy or sad or lonely, it was into their exquisite velvet ears that I poured out my heart. They really did seem to understand, to feel the sympathy with me that I felt with them. One of the most beautiful sounds in the world was my pony's whinny of greeting when I came home from school. Of course, ponies cannot talk, which made my interpretation of our conversations easier to believe, but they can show when they're bored or indifferent. I don't think I have ever felt so rejected as when, one summer evening, full of the vague discontented yearnings of early adolescence and finding my family quite unsympathetic, I went to talk to my little mare and found her unapproachable. She was in heat; though my brothers' ponies were both geldings, they were as excited and nervous as she was. It was a situation from which all humans were excluded. I felt utterly crushed.

Besides my romantic feelings for animals, my sense of symbiosis, I also had moments of what I suppose were transcendental experience, in which I felt I knew the meaning of the universe and the principle on which it worked: that everything went on forever, and each individual or animal or plant or stone was part of the process, and each death led only to more life, so nothing mattered, nothing was said, it would all go on going on forever. I remember feeling enormous joy at such moments and wanting them to go on forever *then*. Afterwards, I would feel sad that the vision had faded so quickly, and that I couldn't remember it exactly right or recapture its absolute certainty. It was a little like postcoital sadness, though the experience itself was not in the least like orgasm. I could not say how much those transcendental moments have influenced my later life. Many adolescents have them, of course, and perhaps no one ever quite forgets them. But what they mean, or whether they mean anything at all, I have never been able to decide.

Some years later my parents moved again, to a house down yet another lane, that fulfilled most of the conditions of a particularly English upper-middle-class ideal. It was built of stone and had an eighteenth-century front that was not quite symmetrical and perfect but had an unmistakably Georgian feeling. A stream ran through the garden, with trout in it, and there were two magnificent evergreen oaks, ilexes, that exuded a sense of time passing very slowly and serenely and with perfectly disciplined order. But what gave the garden its ideal character was not the trees or the stream, but the 10- to 12-foot-high stone wall that surrounded it, cutting us off from the outside world. We could hear the clock striking the hours and quarter-hours from the village church, but we could not see it. What we saw above our wall was an avenue of elms that marched down the drive. Our other houses all had various aspects of the ideal: They were isolated; they stood apart from life; they kept themselves to themselves. This one was beautiful, too. But by then I had almost left home.

Growing up like that, at the ends of lanes, and spending most of the year at school in the exclusive company of other boys of my own class (with high walls round us there, too), my knowledge of ordinary life at eighteen was quite amazingly small, and I fear it still is—though not quite as small as that of my school-friends who went on, as I was supposed to go on, to banking and accountancy and the law, then married, and bought houses of their own, down other lanes, in different shires. For very little has changed, and if I had been what my father wanted, I should have found life at forty very much what at eighteen I imagined it would be: a continuation of my parents' pattern, with minor differences, such as more washing machines and no housemaids, but essentially the same gentlemanly life, with my greatest ambition a Georgian house with tall windows, and a garden with a stream, an oak tree, and a high stone wall. In a way, I still want those things, though I know I shall never have them and now feel it is wrong to want them, as well as useless. The whole ideal with which I grew up now seems utterly wrongheaded, even antilife.

I had been slowly feeling my way toward this conclusion, living in London, but making frequent long visits to the country, when I was invited in 1973 to go to Nigeria. I had traveled in Europe, America, and North Africa but never before to the tropics, and my notions about them were highly literary, derived from the novels of Joseph Conrad and Graham Greene. To prepare myself, I read as many Nigerian books as I could find and was greatly impressed both by the writing and by what the books revealed of African, and particularly Ibo, life. There seemed to be a quality in both that I felt was missing from English life and books, but I couldn't quite see what it was. It had something to do, I thought, with the highly democratic system of Ibo life and a feeling for place that wasn't the same as any English writer's. When I got to Nigeria I found out what it was. All the Nigerian writers I admired came from small villages, and though they had left them, often for years, to travel round the world and to work in the great cities, their roots remained in the collection of huts under the great trees of the forests from which they came. The soil—they knew the soil where the yams and cassava grew. They knew the village stream, the village elders, the village idiot, the village meeting place. They knew the village.

Seeing such villages myself, I suddenly knew what was missing in my own life and writing: a village of my own. I had always thought of myself as a country man, but living at the ends of lanes, on the farthest outskirts of villages, I knew nothing of the life of the country. I had never watched a field being ploughed for more than a minute or two, never cared about growing crops except as a nuisance round which I had to ride when I wanted to gallop straight across them, never thought about harvest except as a time for fun, for standing in the new stubble and watching the combine-harvester devour a shrinking patch of wheat so I could shoot the terrified rabbits as they came bolting out for the safety of the hedges. I knew the land only in the sense that I knew what it looked like. I knew the people only in the sense that I could put names to most of the villagers' faces. I treated the country like an eighteenth-century gentleman, as my private pleasure ground.

It doesn't say much for my intelligence or imagination that I had to go to Africa to learn what any of those villagers could have told me, though England's class system being what it is, none of them ever *would* have told me. The more I think about my childhood, the more extraordinary it seems, almost an aberration; it upsets me very much to think that people go on bringing up their children to unfit them for what I now see as the important things of life. I feel desperate for the deliberately, expensively stunted lives of my own class. At my school, one of the most famous public schools in England, they kept telling us how privileged we were and that with privilege went responsibility. They taught us that it was necessary to suppress our feelings and often our thoughts. But the great teachers have always been the ones who encouraged their pupils to ask questions. At home my father kept telling himself and us what a wonderful life we lived. And in some ways, of course, it was everything he said. But I now think the price of privilege is too high. My father could not bear to be questioned about his own beliefs and values, and I wonder now if he wasn't afraid of his own doubts.

It's too late for me to learn about real country life; in any case, I never wanted to be a farmer. But I hope one day I shall leave London, in which I have always felt a stranger, and settle in some isolated place and enjoy the country in the only way I know how. It is a solitary way, but I work best in isolation. Unfortunately, as soon as I have finished working, I like to see people, and that may be more difficult. But I know I shall never have roots anywhere now, not like my Nigerian friends. I see myself as a curious horticultural specimen, carefully planted in an artificial landscape, part of someone else's view. I can always be dug up and transplanted. It's not at all what I ever imagined I should think of myself, but I get some comfort from remembering I once felt with all my soul that all life was one. Perhaps that feeling was right, and even exotics have their place in the scheme of things.

DIPAK NANDY

DIPAK NANDY, a writer born in India, is now living in England. A frequent contributor to newspapers and periodicals, he is a specialist on the problems of race relations in England and has written *How To Calculate Immigration Statistics* (1970).

> Each torpid turn of the world has such disinherited children,
> to whom no longer what's been nor yet what's coming, belongs.
>
> RILKE

There are times when partial truths, soberly set down, are preferable to global claims—the sort that inspire and move men into action—which no one could claim the authority to advance. I write out of a conviction that we are living through a period when one ought for a time to make a point of saying, not "The world is . . ." but "This is what the world looks like to me . . . now. . . ." What follows is fragmentary, in part because the world it is about looks badly fragmented. This can easily, I recognize, become a cop-out: An essay on boredom need not itself be boring; sorting and ordering, making and seeing patterns are very specifically human urges, and the more essential when old orders break down and accustomed patterns disappear. In part the fragmentariness of this essay follows from a desire not to indulge in the vanity of dogmatizing, from an unwillingness to invest a personal and private set of perceptions with a (very likely) spurious generality, from a desire to speak with the correct degree of tentativeness.

One of the most vivid memories of my childhood, in Calcutta, shortly after World War II, is of sitting in a theater watching a visiting Shakespearean company playing *Macbeth*. In Act V, as Macbeth reached his celebrated lines, "Tomorrow, and tomorrow, and tomorrow . . . ," a hushed murmur rose in the hall, as half the audience, word-perfect, repeated the lines along with the actor on stage. It was, as Edward Shils observed, a provincial culture. Here we were, scarcely two years since the formal granting of independence and all the turbulence that had accompanied it. On the walls outside the "Quit India" signs were still fresh. Yet inside the theater sat the intellectual elite of a formerly subject people, still in the thrall of the culture of the departed conquerors. There seemed nothing odd in wanting to study English literature, nor in wanting to teach it—it seemed odder to the English than it seemed in the India in which I grew up.

What observers of that culture do not seem to me sufficiently to emphasize is the fact that—provincial and derivative as it was —it had its own distinctive and valuable qualities, qualities that even then were disappearing from the European culture of which it was a part-descendant. The atmosphere in which I grew up was suffused with vague but generous idealisms: We believed in freedom, equality, and justice without qualification; if we did not actually subscribe to a belief in "the effecting of all things possible," we did not wish to circumscribe the bounds of the possible either. We never seriously questioned the value of education; it was so indubitably a good thing that everyone, we felt, ought to have it. Even in our rebellion against some of the values of that traditional society, one could not but be aware of the tradition one rebelled against. For myself, it never occurred to me that a social order could ever be changed, except in the name of another social order, or that a tradition could ever be replaced by anything other than another tradition. What held these unexamined beliefs and enthusiasms together, anchored them down and prevented them from flying off into the empyrean, was the constant, inescapable perception, out of the corner of one's eye, of the ubiquity of hunger and misery. Few Indians of my generation (rather like the "penitent aristocrats" of late nineteenth-century Russia in this, I sometimes think) could help but be guiltily aware of the wretched and starving masses who constituted "the people," help but feel that our privileges were in some measure given in trust.

The England to which I came as a student was, in the mid-'50s, a smaller, more shrunken place than I had expected. In the aftermath of Empire it was beginning to withdraw into a sullen insularity from which it has not yet recovered. I witnessed the gradual shrinking of horizons and, with it, the narrowing of human sympathies that I now take to be the central problem in the relationship (or lack of it) between the rich nations and the poor. I witnessed the emergence of racial fears and hostilities in a society alleged to be superior to this affliction of vulgar people—such as the Americans and the South Africans. Because these fears have more to do with the collective insecurity of the English people than with the million and a half colored men and women who have settled here, their growth has been accompanied by a sometimes pathetic nostalgia for an English identity that can no longer be recovered and perhaps never existed. It is an interesting possibility that, because the culture in which I had grown up was indeed provincial and fifty years out of date, the England that I knew intimately in books, on film, in the theater, and that had all but disappeared in the deluge by the 1950s, was a closed book, another country, to my English contemporaries. "What can they know of England who only England know?" asked Kipling. One might add: "What can they know of the world who do not even know their own country?" I *should* have felt a provincial colonial. I do believe I felt that I not only knew a great deal more about the great non-English world beyond these shores; I also felt that, by a historical paradox, a provincial colonial had a stronger sense of English culture than did those of my contemporaries who, in virtue of being English, should have enjoyed a securer possession of their own culture.

If there is a hint of arrogance there, it is entirely unintended. The possession of a dying culture does not qualify one much above the state of a curator in a museum. Each generation likes to flatter itself, I think, that it is in some respect the last generation before the flood. But equally, every so often in history, the iceberg does turn over, and habits and values and mores that had seemed merely natural disappear without trace. My generation, Third World in origin, European (or American) by residence, rootless by choice, mostly left-of-center in politics, does at times seem the last of a line rather than the start of anything; its most distinguished members, men like V. S. Naipaul, unite the practical impotence and the acuteness of perception of men in a free state. The disinherited have no reason to feel superior.

The disappearance of consensus

> If a lion could talk, we could not understand him.
> WITTGENSTEIN

Nearly a century and a half ago, Alexis de Tocqueville said to Europeans: If you wish to see the future of democracy, look at America. (In the vividness and range of his insight, Tocqueville remains a unique authority in any account of the evolution of Western societies.) Today we can say to the rest of the world: If you wish to see the future, look at the societies of the West. It is not an altogether unequivocal invitation.

I do not mean merely the issues that have achieved notoriety in the last decade: the Galbraithian paradox of private affluence and public squalor, the environmental and ecological costs of economic growth, and so on. In a Baconian world these would be regarded simply as problems to be solved. But the reasons why these have come more and more to seem insoluble has to do less with the spoliation of the natural and much more with the transformation of the social and spiritual landscape of Europe.

Tocqueville first pointed out how industrial and urban democracy steadily breaks down the links between men and classes, and between the future and the past, until society becomes a lonely crowd of restless, autonomous, and anomic individuals, each man forever thrown back upon himself alone. Since his time the loss of community has become a major theme of sociologists, journalists, and moralists.

But the loss of community is—what? Societies can be characterized by acute and deep-seated conflicts and yet possess a moral consensus, a shared sense of what matters about human life. People in such societies will disagree, often violently, about the value they put on particular things. Underneath their disagreements will be a tacit agreement about their scale of values. The reason why European societies present such a signal warning to the rest of mankind lies in the specter they raise of a state of mankind that has gone beyond conflict and disagreement, a state in which there are only hostile uncomprehending, and noncommunicating groups. To each of us the other is a lion: He talks, and we do not understand him.

In the last hundred years or so, community in that sense has disappeared from most advanced European societies. This is why those, like Lord Devlin (in *The Enforcement of Morals*), who think that the purpose of law is to enforce the common morality of a society are mistaken, not so much about law as about its relevance to their society: There *is* no common morality that the law could seem to enforce.

I can make the point quite simply by juxtaposing a few names and comments. Professor J. H. Plumb, in *The Death of the Past*, has observed recently how industrial society,

> unlike the commercial, craft and agrarian societies which it replaces, does not need the past. Its intellectual and emotional orientation is towards change rather than conservation, towards exploitation and consumption. The new methods, new processes, new forms of living of scientific and industrial society have no sanction in the past and no roots in it. The past becomes, therefore, a matter of curiosity, of nostalgia, a sentimentality.*

This new-found dispensability of the past is more than contingently connected with what sociologists call "privatization" and

---

* Professor Plumb is concerned to distinguish "the past," which is unscientific and often reactionary, from "history." His eloquent hope that history will rise, phoenix-like, from the ashes of "the past" and fulfill its function in human life is indeed a consummation devoutly to be wished, but not one that convinces the present writer as being very likely.

with the paradoxical fact that the most interdependent forms of social life so far developed by mankind are devoted today in the West to the most private forms of living. It is not that such a fragmented society does not need a past so much as that it does not know what to do with it.

In an earlier essay, *Secularization and Moral Change,* Alasdair MacIntyre had sought to show that the disappearance of a moral consensus in England was to be traced to the evolution of industrial capitalism:

> The religion of English society prior to the Industrial Revolution provided a framework within which the metaphysical questions could be asked and answered, even if different and rival answers were given: Who am I? Whence did I come? Whither shall I go? Is there a meaning to my life other than any meaning I choose to give it? What powers govern my fate?
>
> The dissolution of the moral unity of English society and the rise of new class divisions lead to a situation where within different classes there appear different aspirations, and different attempts to express and to legitimate these in religious forms. But the compromises and abdications consequent upon the class co-operation of English life produced a situation where it was impossible for any one group plausibly to absolutize its own claims and invoke some kind of cosmic sanction for them. . . . Yet it was equally impossible to establish or re-establish coherent social unity. . . . The consequence of this is that there remains no framework within which the religious questions can be systematically asked.

The result of this loss of consensus, MacIntyre suggests, is a situation in which the traditional language in which the hopes, aspirations, the sense of the point of human and social life, had been expressed—the language of Christianity—is felt to be increasingly unsatisfactory; and yet it survives, because no more satisfactory language can be found in which to articulate these concerns.

This is linked with that steady denudation from social life of any coherent and shared sense of purpose that Max Weber attributed to rationalization, intellectualism, secularization. It is not, of course, secularization that causes this loss of collective purpose. Societies that have lost a shared sense of what matters about human life are unlikely to agree about social or political purposes;

secularization, the jettisoning of a religious sense of the world (what Weber in a strange and beautiful phrase called "the disenchantment of the world"), merely throws this lack of agreed purpose into relief.

Consequent upon this disappearance of consensus, and demonstrating it, is the disappearance from Western societies of those institutions in traditional societies that guided and gave shape to human life. At the height of their material power, Western societies have only to look at the traumas of their young to realize that Margaret Mead's backward societies are more truly civilized in their ability to assist the young to make the transition from childhood to adulthood, similarly, with that other great transition in human life—death. Again, in the same essay, MacIntyre puts it extremely well:

> The inability to cope with death is of course not simply a matter of ignorance or agnosticism about an after-life. What we say of a man when he dies always reflects an attitude to human achievement. It is our uncertainty about what genuine human achievement consists in, about what it is to live well or badly, that disables us.

As these institutions—churches, the family, friendly societies, and trade unions, those first human responses to industrialization—recede, the vacuum they leave behind is filled, if at all, by the state and its agencies. As a socialist this ought to gladden my heart, for increasingly there are functions in modern societies that only governments can perform. And yet the consequence is depressing, for socialist and liberal alike. For as governments intervene in wider and wider areas of social life, they merely serve to underline the impotence of government in the face of the primitive and recalcitrant vitality of human societies. And this practical impotence, when set against the rhetoric that governments are increasingly obliged to adopt, breeds too easily a kind of collective manic-depression in which whole peoples oscillate between states of euphoric hope and sour cynical apathy.

Our pessimism or optimism, our hopes and fears, ultimately grow out of our sense of the shape of the world. This is mine:

There are immense peaks of industrial and social development, mostly clustered around the North Atlantic—highly developed industrial societies with high and increasing standards of living but unable any longer to say what all this is *for*. These peaks rise sheer out of a surrounding swamp of poverty. One is only intermittently conscious of that swamp: occasional rumors of famine or disaster, together with the presence of a helot class of migrant laborers, economically indispensable and socially undesirable, who are drawn up from it to perform the menial and undesirable chores of the rich. There are occasional bursts of xenophobia. When they succeed in their object—the repatriation of the offending aliens—the place of the expelled helots is filled discreetly and rapidly by others, perhaps of a different color of skin or shape of cranium. As to that swamp of poverty that is the setting for these exits and entrances, varying quantities of foreign aid are released, much of it to prevent or forestall social reform, accompanied by much juggling of statistics to demonstrate that the swampland is gradually but inexorably being reclaimed from the sea. From time to time, all the same, there will be sporadic outbursts of the disease called social revolution. These will be brought under control, and law and order restored, by sorties of well-trained and superbly equipped policing forces from the white man's laager.

No doubt there is in this, as in the writing of all scenarios, an element of exaggeration, of selective falsification, of caricature.

But here is the testimony of a humane, much-traveled man of the world, Conor Cruise O'Brien, in *The Suspecting Glance:*

> The world by the turn of the century is likely to present some terrible aspects. The comfortable countries, assuming that they can keep their hands off one another's throats, will be more comfortable, or at least more affluent than ever. But the poor world is likely to be drowning in the excess of its own population, a human swirl of self-destructive currents, of which the Nigeria-Biafra war may be a type and forerunner. The advanced world may well be like, and feel like, the closed and guarded palace, in a city gripped by the plague. There is another metaphor, developed by André Gide . . . : this is the metaphor of the lifeboat, in a sea full of the survivors of a shipwreck. The hands of survivors cling to the sides of the boat. But the boat has already as many passengers as it can carry. No more survivors can be accommodated. The captain

orders out the hatchets. The hands of the survivors are severed. The lifeboat and its passengers are saved.

How, one asks, can the author of this nightmare vision survive the experience? But his real problem is not personal but social: It is the difficulty, in contemporary Western societies, amongst the men in the lifeboat, of finding a language to convey the urgency of the need (assuming one knew what to do about it.) I think at this point of lecturing to university students on just this subject— the widening fissures between the rich world and the poor—and wondering whether they can understand the words as well as hear them. It is like sensing for a moment what it must feel like to be a lion who has learned to talk, only to discover that no one can understand him.

The failures of radicals

> The best lack all conviction, while the worst
> Are full of passionate intensity.
>
> YEATS

The loss of belief afflicts not only the established societies of the West but also its grave-diggers.

My politics were for many years communist. If I do not write of the God that failed, it is because I never did think of it as a God, simply as the most promising road for poor countries to take. But the failure of a promise can take some getting used to also.

I would not wish for a moment to underestimate the immensity of the material achievements of the Marxist countries, nor play down how essential a sufficiency of bread is as a precondition of human dignity. But bread was not all that Marxian socialism was about.

In our time, by which I mean for the seventy years of this century, socialism carried forward the legacy of the Baconian and rationalist dreams of a world of hope and human possibility. It promised the transcendence of man's alienation from man—at least the end of man's exploitation by man. (And woman's too.) If in one aspect it was a stern, unsmiling rationalism that had no truck with mysteries and mystification, in another it promised to reinfuse human life with a larger and more generous sense of purpose than the mere pursuit of individual or sectional self-interest.

In place of the Baconian dream, there seems only a stale and tarnished repetition of the consumerism of the West. The cost, in terms of human freedom and dignity, has been forbiddingly high, and not all of it by any means dictated by the necessities of the Cold War. (Surely socialists of all people should have known that institutions, even in socialist societies, will fight for their survival long after they have ceased to be necessary.) The foreign policies of the socialist countries owe more to Bismarck than to Marx. And nowhere in the socialist East, not even in China, is there a glimmering of that alternative way of regarding human life, that alternative sense of what matters in the transitory life of human beings and the now increasingly fragile life of human societies, which in the end is the only conceivable justification for all that terror and pain.

Generations of socialists, however, have survived the discovery that their kings were, after all, merely human. I think myself that something more profound occurred in the 1950s. What had saved socialist regimes up to that point had been their very backwardness in economic terms. So long as they remained poor and backward, they not only attracted the sympathy which that generates, they also appeared morally less corrupt than the capitalist West. Indeed, whatever one might choose to regard as moral corruption could be plausibly attributed to capitalism itself. But when the Soviet Union ceased to be a poor and beleaguered country, when it began to match and sometimes surpass the West in terms of technological progress, growth rates of gross national product, nuclear warheads and delivery systems, and consumer goods, then it began to dawn on socialists that socialism itself might be subject to many of the frailties that flesh is heir to, and that to many of the pressing and legitimate worries of modern men the faith of our fathers did not always provide a satisfactory or sufficient answer. I believe this is what happened in the 1950s, and that one of its consequences was a fragmentation of the Left that matched pretty nearly the fragmentation of belief and purpose in Western society as a whole.

But there is one further stage. The first generation that discovers that God is dead goes about preaching its discovery with all the earnestness of true believers. Or so its younger critics are apt to point out. To us, of that first generation, it seems that it is the next generation that has the problem. To us they seem mere nihilists at best, incapable of knowing what it would be like to have beliefs, standards, values.

It is possible to be too finicky in saying what one means. I am troubled increasingly by the thoughtlessness and ahistoricism of young radicals in the West. Their contempt for my generation appears to be matched only by a radical unwillingness to ask for the sake of what they wish to engage in political or revolutionary action. They are for all the right causes; but it remains unclear whether their commitment is to people they can touch and hear, or whether it is an existentialist gesture to soothe some private anguish or deprivation. The privileged intelligentsia of tomorrow has nothing but contempt, it would seem, for the intellect and reason of men. Too easily the politics of gesture and rhetoric give place to the politics of the act (I am thinking of the Olympic village, Munich, 1972). If there are radicals who disapprove of the gratuitous violence, the barbarism of the politics of the act, I do not hear them very clearly.

America, which has produced a unique brand of reaction in my lifetime, now obliges us with a new kind of revolutionism. I read of the activities of a small but widely publicized organization in California whose manifesto declares that its aim is to overturn, by violent revolution, "all forms of racism, sexism, ageism, capitalism, fascism, individualism, possessiveness, and competitiveness." The mind boggles.

The phenomenon is not entirely without precedent. Turgenev was worrying about Bazarov in the 1860s. Yeats evidently knew something similar in Ireland at the beginning of this century. So it may be that we shall survive this outbreak of contemporary nihilism. But the suspicion grows in one's mind that this kind of radicalism is to be taken seriously, not on its own terms but as part of the pathology of the Western world. I mean as part of the pathology that, fifty years ago, Joseph Conrad sensed with remarkable prescience when in *Under Western Eyes* he described how

> The ferocity and imbecility of an autocratic rule rejecting all legality and in fact basing itself upon complete moral anarchism provokes the no less imbecile and atrocious answer of a purely Utopian revolutionism encompassing destruction by the first means to hand. . . .

If the wisdom of our fathers has failed us, there is no hope, it would seem, in the innocence of the young.

To the ancient and traditional stridencies of class and nation, there are now added the conflicts of race and color and perhaps soon now of age. If we have not managed conflict too successfully so far, our collective capacity to cope in the future seems even more dubious. A shrinking, depleted world, which should be united in the common perception that there is only one world, discovers in this instead new reasons for division and conflict. A world whose people are more interdependent than ever before rediscovers tribalism with a vengeance. Tribalism in a world of tribes calls for no comment; tribalism in a world that contains the United Nations is insufferable. It is, however, easier to protest against this insufferable reality than to change it.

Transformed by the jet engine and the electronic media of communications into a global village, the reluctant villagers become more acutely aware of what differentiates them than of what they have in common. Messages travel virtually instantaneously in the new communications media and serve merely to emphasize the depths of our mutual misunderstanding.

It would be impertinent to prescribe values in this state. Perhaps I can set down instead three qualities essential for survival. The first is a readiness to acknowledge the provisionality of all truths. The faith of our fathers speaks to us in a strange and moving language—but it is not moving us *to* anything. The passionate intensity of the young too often masks a vacuum of belief—a vacuum for which we perhaps are more responsible than they, but a vacuum nonetheless. It seems essential to survival for us to develop the capacity to be tentative rather than dogmatic.

But the problems of a poor, miserable, divided world will not wait while we establish the right tones of voice. Maybe the hardest discovery of all is that in a world bereft of certainties, the need to act and act urgently, *as though the certainties existed,* is greater, not less. So my second quality is the willingness to act decisively while acknowledging the possibility of being mistaken. We have not seen such a quality in our leaders so far, and perhaps it cannot be achieved.

The third is a readiness to see that leaders are only human—a readiness to see this on the part both of the rulers and the ruled. "Cursed is the land which breeds no heroes," says a character in Brecht's *Galileo,* to which Galileo replies, "Cursed is the land that *needs* a hero." Our need for heroes is, in other words, a measure of our ordinary incompetence. If I sense that ordinary people need to have restored to them more of a sense of their competence, I also sense that political leaders need more and more to deny themselves the irresponsible privilege of promising more than they can deliver. There is no exploitation of the poor and the powerless so cruel as raising hopes that are bound to be frustrated, as when we promise to do in ten years what could not possibly be done in less than fifty.

From where I write, these seem important virtues in a fractured world. They seem essential, at any rate, for its survival. When we have survived, perhaps we can begin to think then of more daring ones.

BARBARA WARD

BARBARA WARD, economist and writer, born in 1914 in England, since 1968 has been Schweitzer Professor of International Economic Development at Columbia University. Her best-known works are: *The International Share-Out* (1938), *Turkey* (1942), *The West at Bay* (1948), *Policy for the West* (1951), *Faith and Freedom* (1954), *The Rich Nations and the Poor Nations* (1961), *Spaceship Earth* (1966), *The Lopsided World* (1968), *An Urban Planet?* (1971), *Only One Earth* (1972, with René Dubos).

We have perhaps witnessed a tragic irony in the unfolding of World Population Year.

If one change more than any other has recently marked expert thinking about the problem of stabilizing the size of populations, it is a growing realization of the link between higher and more human living standards and smaller families. This perception is, no doubt, part of a wider shift—away from development strategies aiming almost solely at economic growth and toward an acceptance of greater social justice and wider popular participation as basic requirements of successful modernization. But its relevance to population policy is very direct.

Where, as in Taiwan or Korea or, above all, in China, rural investment has bettered conditions in the villages and where, as in Hong Kong and Singapore, urban living has been purposefully improved, very high traditional birth rates have started markedly to decline. Whatever the reasons for the change—greater confidence in the survival of children, greater belief in the possibilities of educating sons and daughters for a better life, greater expectation of community support in old age—these are sufficiently widely established to ensure that social equity and personal dignity and opportunity are accepted as a critical element, possibly *the* critical element, in any successful attempt to diminish the rate of population growth. As Pope Paul VI said to the leaders responsible for the U.N. Fund for Population Activities and the World Population Conference:

> Any population program must therefore be at the service of the human person. It must reduce inequalities, fight discriminations, free man from various types of servitude and enable him to be the instrument of his own material betterment, of his moral progress and of his spiritual growth (*Populorum Progressio,* 34). Hence it must remove everything that is opposed to life itself or which harms man's free and responsible personality.

But then comes the paradox. Just as the link between social justice and stable population is more clearly recognized, the means of realizing it become much less secure. If we take the forty poorest countries with per capita incomes below $160, they include some of the most populous lands—India, Pakistan, Bangladesh among them—and make up at least 40 per cent of the human race. And here, in the last two or three years, the chances for social betterment, economic opportunity, and personal self-determination have dangerously deteriorated. The farm sectors of all these states depend upon critical imports of fertilizer. All must buy food abroad to supplement uncertain harvests at home. Most of them produce little or no domestic petroleum. Their major exports—tea, jute, cotton goods—have tended to be depressed. At the best of times development has been precarious. And since 1972 what has set in has been the worst of times.

Most of the major elements in the cumulative crisis are well known. In 1972 bad harvests in Russia and India led to the buying up of the whole American grain reserve. This emergency tripled grain prices in the following year and led to a cut of two thirds in America's Food for Peace programs. In 1974 it was expected that wheat shipments under Public Law 480 would be less than a third of 1972 levels, rice, food grains, and vegetables less than half, and there would be no milk at all. Domestic inflation and a lag in the building of new fertilizer plants pushed up the price of fertilizer. Months before the fuel crisis the food and fertilizer bill of the "Fourth World" of poorest states had more than doubled. Indeed, it began to look as though fertilizer would not be available at any price and that the 1974 harvests would be cut by millions of tons as a result. It has to be said that this phase of the crisis crept up on the world without headlines or audible cries of alarm, because the pressures were being felt by the poorest peoples while the United States was adding several billions to its export earnings and visibly strengthening the value of the dollar. The storm broke when petroleum prices tripled. Now the rich states were suffering, and their balance of payments showed the strain.

Yet it was once again the poorest of the developing peoples who felt the full shock of the tripling of petroleum prices in a couple of months. The earlier drain of rising food and fertilizer prices had added at least $5 billion to the import bill. Now came the energy squeeze. The energy bill of the non-oil-producing developing states looked as if it would increase from $5.2 billion to $15 billion in a single year. Even if they threw in all their reserves, all their normal gains from exports, and all their expectations from official foreign aid, it seemed as though an absolute gap of at least $3 billion had opened up in their balance of payments. If it could not be met, the risk was imminent of their falling into a deteriorating spiral: less fertilizer producing less food, less food requiring more food imports and thus cutting still further fertilizer imports from abroad, in turn again decreasing food supplies. This was the prospect in the months before the World Population Conference: a sharp deterioration in the economic and social prospects of the poorest, most populous states, just when the realization had begun to take hold that a more human and promising social context is a precondition of stabilizing the size of families.

Nor should we simply concentrate on the tragic paradox of 1974. It is even more urgent for us to understand that it is not self-liquidating. On the contrary, there are longer-term forces at work that suggest a steady worsening of the dilemmas posed by rising population pressure and economic and social deterioration. Let us take one category only—the most vital, it is true, and the one that most determines whether parents will believe in the survival of children and a future of hope. This is the category of the world's food supplies. As we advance into the 1970s, evidence accumulates of a number of profound environmental changes at work in the world that could drastically reduce the reliability of future food supplies.

Some reflect ecological damage inflicted by faulty human activity. Quite apart from the problems of immediate drought, the Sahel region on the fringe of the Sahara is being overgrazed and the land denuded. Some surveys suggest an advance of the desert of thirty miles a year. In Northern India deforestation and overuse of the Himalayan foothills are increasing the short-term risk of devastating floods—Pakistan's floods last year were the worst in history—and the longer-term danger of failing water supplies. Another example of human overuse can be seen in the world's fisheries, where a number of edible species look as if they are being fished into extinction. After phenomenal increases in sea harvests and new technological methods that literally suck the fish, mature or immature, out of the oceans, the world's fish catch has fallen for the last three years. Continued rapacity could accelerate the trend.

Another set of constraints is posed by the physical limits of quickly available land. In the early 1960s the United States had 50 million acres of crop land in reserve—the equivalent of a harvest of 70 to 80 million tons of grain. Today, those reserves are under cultivation, and no other areas have comparably productive soil withdrawn from use. Although much of the world's tropical belt is not yet farmed to the full, tropical soils are fragile and unsuitable for crash programs. How, then, can critical protein supplies like soybeans be increased, when growth depends upon increased acreage—and there are few more acres to spare?

Further obstacles are technical. What will be the cost of fertilizers, giving a doubling of the price of oil, which is both a fuel and a feed stock? How, in general, can the crop increases of the "Green Revolution," which depend upon fertilizer, water, and improved seed, be secured and extended, if fertilizer is too costly and water supplies are coming under pressure?

Nor should we forget our present lack of reserves for dealing with short-term meteorological disasters. There is some evidence of the monsoon pattern becoming less reliable. At the same time the North American "breadbasket" is known to undergo phases of drought of the dust-bowl type from time to time. To offset the dangers of short-term disasters, the U.N. Food and Agriculture Organization suggests a reserve of grain equal to at least 15 per cent of present annual consumption. This would supply 180 million tons of grain. The present figure is less than half that amount and could keep the world going for less than a month. One can only conclude that if all these interlocking circuits of difficulty and obstruction continue to reinforce each other, the chances of a reasonably human context for life in the poorest and most populous states look remote indeed.

But the obstructions, many of them caused by man, can also be reversed by man. And this is precisely the point of the World Population Conference, the World Food Conference, the Law of the Sea Conference, the U.N. General Assembly's special session to consider raw materials this year and development strategy next and, beyond these consultations, the U.N. Conference on Human Settlements planned for 1976. For all their size and unwieldiness, such conferences do represent *all* the nations' efforts to conduct a sane dialogue on issues that surpass the capacity of any one of them, acting singly, to resolve. They are an attempt to get away from drift and to concert strategies that offer some openings for constructive action. True, it is not yet clear whether the changes in food and energy costs in the last two years have wonderfully concentrated or woefully distracted the minds of men. The weight of disaster and difficulty has fallen with different emphasis, dividing the "old rich" from the "new rich" and creating quite new categories of "haves" and "have-nots." As a result, the process of disentangling fear, self-interest, enlightenment, and potential paranoia is still going on. But the fundamental issue that needs to be brought out with every possible emphasis, particularly at this year's U.N. conferences on population and on food, is that a number of concrete policies are available to the nations, that they do serve the aim of both more stable population and better human existence, that they are not beyond the planet's physical means, and that the alternative to adopting them is the almost certain defeat of any prospect of an orderly and hopeful planetary life.

The main features of such an "agenda for survival" are already being discussed. They include: an immediate fund of about $3 billion contributed by the industrial and oil-rich states to take the poorest lands over this year's balance-of-payments crisis and to prepare the way for a new world monetary system more responsive to the needs of developing lands; the restoration of a world food reserve adequate for a year's consumption; a new commitment to long-term transfer of funds through increased aid and through a possible linking of special drawing rights with development assistance; a new emphasis upon investment in agriculture, particularly in fertilizer production and small-scale agriculture, to permit the doubling and trebling of acreage yields that can still be achieved on most developing farms, given better techniques more research, and more capital; a new investment effort to match agricultural expansion with jobs in manufacturing and services set up in intermediate urban settlements where markets, education, health centers, and family clinics provide more of the opportunities of modern life; a new look at international trade, not only to stabilize primary prices and secure the opening of industrialized markets to the exports of developing lands but also to ensure reasonable access by all states to what are likely to become increasingly scarce supplies; a new awareness of the balance between development and environment to prepare the way for a more stable planetary system.

It should also be added that in spite of the strains of inflation and the jolting increase in energy prices, the rich nations have the resources for such a program. The United States, leader of the old rich, has at least $2 billion already authorized under its Food for Peace programs. If the old rich gave an example of generosity in helping the neediest nations with their problems of food, the new rich, the Gulf oil states, could be encouraged to dip into the extra $25 billion they earned from petroleum sales in 1973–74 to help on the side of fertilizer and energy.

Clearly, there are the makings here of a general strategy capable of relaunching the world's process of economic and social advance. The various elements reinforce each other. Short-term funds and reserves take away the risk of imminent disaster and pave the way for a sustained effort in which investment at research dedicated to food-expanding agriculture and job-expanding industry bring present scarcities under better control and provide the context of hope required for more stable populations. The vicious circles become less vicious. The interlocking cycles begin to move upward, and the various elements make, as it were, the interdependent context or ecosystem of successful development.

For those who dismiss these possibilities as the wildest of Pollyanna optimism, one can only recall that such an effort has been made before in the face of a comparably worsening situation. As President Houari Boumédienne of Algeria reminded the recent special session of the U.N. General Assembly:

> Marshall Plan aid, which was dispensed by one developed country for the benefit of other developed countries and nine-tenths of which consisted of grants, amounted to 3% of the GNP of the United States of America. This aid, which was put into effect fully and rapidly, shows that in the developed countries financial means can be readily mobilized when the political will to do so exists.

Nearly thirty years later, with nearly five times the wealth and who knows how much more experience, skill, and educated talent, are the old rich industrialized powers incapable of a new Marshall-type gesture? Can they not by their example encourage the new rich to cooperate? Can they not together hold out to the poorest and most populous peoples the kind of realistic hope of progress upon which future stability, whether of population or social order or planetary existence, in fact depends?

ARNOLD WESKER

ARNOLD WESKER is a playwright, born in 1932 in London. The realistic, working-class settings of his plays reflect his early jobs as furniture maker's apprentice, carpenter's mate, bookseller's assistant, plumber's mate, road laborer, farm laborer, seed sorter, kitchen porter, and pastry cook. These plays include: *The Kitchen* (1957); the trilogy *Chicken Soup with Barley* (1958), *Roots* (1959), *I'm Talking About Jerusalem* (1960); *Chips with Everything* (1962); *Menace* (1963); *Their Very Own and Golden City* (1964); *The Four Seasons* (1965); *The Friends* (1970); *The Old Ones* (1972); *The Journalist* (1972); *The Wedding Feast* (1973).

A coincidence! The invitation to write an essay about "the way the world is—should go" comes while I'm in the middle of directing a play I'd written eight years ago called *Their Very Own and Golden City*. It opened then, in London, in a form different from the one I'd written, and now I'm rediscovering it, changing it back here and there, learning to love and respect the child I'd been persuaded to dismiss as crippled, almost stillborn.

It's a play about four youngsters who, in 1926, while out on a day's sketching in Durham cathedral, are so stirred by the daring and madness of the Gothic architecture that they're moved to consider "the way the world is—should go," and to plan what they'll do to help it go that way. As they talk about the future, the play, through a series of "flash-forwards," then enacts the future they plan. The protagonist, fired by the dreams of a socialist upbringing, plans to become a young architect and conceives the idea of persuading people to pool their money in order to build their own cities. He plans six cities, to be given their commerce by the co-ops and their industry by the unions.* Though their lives begin as they hope, yet at a certain point the future and their hopes for it begin to diverge. The reality separates from the dream. What goes wrong, and why, is the play's story.

Writing a play that attempted to cover the years 1926 to 1985 confronted me with many problems. If the problems were merely technical—how do you get through thirty-two scenes in sixteen settings on one stage in two and a half hours?—then I'd not think mention of the play would be relevant to this essay. But the problems were more, and even now, as I direct the work for myself, with almost ideal conditions, still changing the text around—the version performed in London was about the thirteenth draft; plays, cities, societies need constant rethinking—even now I'm not sure that the problems are solved. Actually I *am* sure they're not solved.

But what are they that they have relevance to this essay? First, just as the play could not be an architectural blueprint for a real city, so an essay such as this cannot possibly be a philosophical or political blueprint for "the way the world should go." Yet, just as it was necessary to create interest, excitement in the city itself—otherwise who would believe anyone would give money to build it, or be distressed if it didn't turn out as hoped for—so it's necessary to evoke an image of a real world for this essay, however short it must be.

To do this, some abstraction is necessary, as it was in the play. Here from the play is an evocation of the city that reflected the values I thought necessary for society's survival.

Halfway through, at the end of the first act, the youngsters, in a state of high excitement composed of part horseplay, part mock revivalist meeting, part the defiant prophecies of innocent youth, chant:

> JESSIE: What kind of cities shall we build, Andy?
> ANDY: Cities of light and shade, Jessie, with secret corners.
> JESSIE: Paul, what kind of cities?

* John Kenneth Galbraith, speaking at the Sunday *Times* conference on The Exploding Cities, was quoted in the Sunday *Times,* April 7, 1974: "The most urgent need is to accept that the modern city is by its nature a socialist enterprise."

PAUL: Cities for lovers, Jessie, and old men and crawling children.

JESSIE: Stoney?

STONEY: Cities for crowds and lone wolves, Jessie.

ANDY: With wide streets and twisting lanes.

PAUL: Cosy cities, Jessie, family cities.

STONEY: With warm houses, low arches, long alleys.

PAUL: Cities full of sound for the blind and colour for the deaf.

ANDY: Cities that cradle the people who live there.

PAUL: That frighten no one.

STONEY: That sing the praises of all men, Jessie.

JESSIE: Who will help you, my ragged-arsed brothers?

ALL: Labour!

And later, when, as older men they're actually talking to people trying to persuade them to join the scheme:

PAUL: The city's spirit? What will be the city's spirit? Look, look more closely at these plans. What do you see?

STONEY: Variety! That's what you see. Roads that are wide and alleys that ramble.

PAUL: Bold squares and intimate corners.

STONEY: There's colour in that city and sound.

PAUL: And movement of line and patterns of mass.

STONEY: Not a frightening city, not intimidating.

PAUL: And its heart? What do you see as its heart? Industry may be a city's backbone but what should be a city's heart?

STONEY: You can't seriously place a town hall at the city's heart, not a place where functionaries meet to organize our tax affairs and drainage problems?

PAUL: No! Our city's heart is its gardens, concert halls, theatres, swimming pools.

STONEY: Dancehalls, galleries and meeting rooms.

PAUL: Restaurants and libraries . . . Politicians are men we hire to mend roads and tend to the sewers.

STONEY: The Prime Minister is an accountant. Give the city to its teachers and artists . . .

The play was conceived in 1964 and probably represented the priorities that had come together in me as a mixed heritage from my family and my reading. Priorities based on values that have a long-fought-for and treasured history: socialist, humanist values founded in a society where the means of production are owned in common; where all men earn their living; where privacy and independence are respected in the form of each man's owning his own home; where every man is permitted his imperfection, since that is the nature of humanity; and where material possessions have their value measured by usefulness, personal association, and the individual's estimation of their beauty. Values based on a love and respect for and belief in art and knowledge. These were fundamentals for me. It was all very clear.

What was not so clear, and I'm not sure that it is even now, was what is *basic* to human nature and what is *artificially superimposed* upon that nature. If it's true that man is imperfect and weak, then it must be conceded he can be abused and imposed upon. For example, though I disapprove of it, yet I must ask: How instinctive *is* the profit motive in man? Is the desire for material profit—which can be termed "acknowledgment of his achievement"—the more basic? And if acknowledgment of his achievement is what really matters to him, then why is not his "neighbor's respect" sufficient acknowledgment of that achievement? Is the fact that material profit has developed over the centuries as the one universally accepted measurement of achievement sufficient evidence of its "naturalness"? *I* might think there should be sufficient profit in my neighbor's respect, but is that natural? I don't know. The answers are locked in sciences with which I'm not familiar. But such questions must be pursued each time a city is built or rebuilt.

Some things I do know though: that I need to have my own house, inviolate, the one place on earth from which no man or state can evict me, where I can rejoice in family, extend hospitality to friends and travelers, pursue in privacy my private passions, retreat and lick in unpublic shame my foolishly acquired wounds, or in isolation from, and despair with, men and their world, protected from scorn and public approbation. I owe and must account for much to my neighbor, but not everything. I know, therefore, that I need a house. But how much of what I've described is basic and evergreen in human nature, and how much is due to the way society has developed it, *that* I don't know. And since development itself is a natural human process, then what is a *distorted* and what a *true* development? Such questions must be asked because the city should be molded to man's true nature rather than his nature be crippled to fit the city's shape. My play argued for a society perfect enough to accommodate man's imperfection as well as organize for his material well-being.

"In the way you build a city you shape men's lives," cries Andy, therefore cities were important. But since men were various and complex, the cities you built had to be for all kinds: "lovers, old men, children, lone wolves, crowds," answering differing temperaments with "light and shade and secret corners and wide streets and twisting lanes." Human cities that "cradled people and frightened no one." Compassionate cities where functionaries had their place but not the most important place. Politicians were servants and not rulers, and in my list of priorities the teacher and artist had pride of place.

The play echoed my own efforts to form in England a huge arts center that was to have been a prototype for the rest of the country, and, like the hero in the play, I hoped the trade unions, as representatives of the vast majority from whom the experience of art had been alienated, would finance the project. It was called Centre Fortytwo. Something of its history is written elsewhere; now it's enough simply to report that I failed to raise the funds necessary to continue its work, and to ask: What do I feel now? Do those same priorities persist?

For those of us living in the West these are difficult times in which not to be confused and intimidated. Guilts are there to be felt daily, and men are there to ensure we feel guilty. (Does ensuring the guilt of others in some way assuage one's own, I wonder?) With so much of the world underprivileged, dare anyone still maintain pride of place for the teacher and the artist? Not that it's such an easy thing to do in this philistine country where teachers are underpaid and the artist is more a decoration than a need. It is a curious fact that large sections of the bourgeoisie and certain elements in the militant Left share with the Nazis this twitch of loathing, moving them to reach for guns at the mention of culture. I use the word "culture" in this context, because it's commonly recognized. But in fact we ought to begin acknowledging the distinction between art and culture, the one being used to describe the entire life-style of a society of which art is only one part.

Two anecdotes illustrate this. The first is very disturbing. The British playwrights David Mercer and John Arden, both known for their—albeit ideosyncratic—Marxist positions, were once invited to lecture in Sussex University, a university known for its student militancy. They were barely given a hearing. Stink bombs together with abuse were hurled at them.

Later, a student approached Mercer and said, "We must burn all the books, start again, from the beginning, burn them all."

"What?" asked Mercer gently, "Marx and Engels as well?"

"All of them!" cried the student. "Burn them all!"

"Excuse me," said Mercer, "but that worries me a little, for the last time people said that was in the days of the Reichstag."

"The *what*?" asked the student.

Second: an Arab friend visited me not long ago. She was once involved in the theater but now, between professional commitments, was deeply engaged in Arab politics, a reassessment of which had been brought about by the ill-conceived and senseless Arab-Israeli war, "I now believe all art to be irrelevant," she said. It was a familiar refrain. I had some sympathy with the feeling but felt angrily opposed to where it led her.

Every time art is thrown out of the window it is because men have found the emotional, ethical, or intellectual demands of art too bothersome to contend with. The gun becomes a simpler solution. And because it is a simpler solution it is enthusiastically taken up by simple-minded men, and the times become frightening. It is easier and—to begin with—more glamourous to be a heroic man of action than a thoughtful man of letters. The act of pulling a trigger takes less time than thinking a thought through. Its effect is immediate; it commands the attention of greater numbers—or their fearful obedience, at least—and it appears to reflect greater courage. Where four-fifths of the world are undernourished, they are also undereducated, and there the report of a gun is a language more comprehensible and accessible than a poet's report. Who would not understand this or not feel intimidated when huge numbers respond to such a simple tongue? I sympathize, and yet I despise it. I do not believe in the simple wisdom of the people. That has always seemed to me insulting and patronizing, stirring the heart of the man who utters it but commanding little more than ephemeral loyalties from those it briefly flatters. I do, however, believe in the ability of the deprived and wretched to confront and assimilate knowledge and art and through them to become wise. (I say "through them" by way of suggesting that though experience is often the first and most powerful teacher, yet it is not sacrosanct. Experience frequently needs help to be illuminated.)

The courage and intelligence of George Jackson, one of the Soledad brothers, form a saga I shall remember for a long time, reminding me of the cancerous evil the United States has still to cut out from itself, but even intelligent men have loose tongues that produce a rhetoric lesser men become intoxicated with and misuse. His cry "Let the voice of our guns express the words of our freedom" must be such a comfortable slogan for lazy minds to live with. Similarly Ché Guevara was an honorable man, a real hero, a man to be loved and yet, paradoxically, he unleashed much mindlessness into the world with his cry to "hate! hate! hate!" I can't bring myself to be grateful for that.

To my Arab friend I sent a copy of a poem by the late Francis Hope (killed in the terrible Paris air crash, March 3, 1974). In it are some lines I'd like to have written:

> At times like these, he cried aloud
> That not to be a poet is
> The worst of all our miseries . . .

"*Not* to be a poet is the worst of all our miseries . . ." I think I'll always feel that. I know, of course, that in times of great evil not to be a poet *and* not to have a gun is a double misery. But evil must be carefully measured and accurately named. I believe poets, or statesmen who are poets—and there are some—are possibly the best people to do that. Perhaps they should be the keepers of the armory. Hitler was evil; Nixon is not—he is corrupt. Stalin was evil; Brezhnev is not—he is authoritarian, possibly cynical. Or another thought, equally unpalatable: Imperialism led to evil but, though we may believe in the socialist ethic of cooperation, yet we may have to recognize that British capitalism has, so far, given greater happiness to greater numbers than Soviet socialism appears to have done. That's not easy to explain away. Qualifying observations are possible and necessary but not easy to form; men are unpredictable with mixed appetites and diverse motives. Corruption and authoritarianism may lead to evil, but they are not the same beasts; evil may finally demand arms to destroy it, but corruption and intransigent authority must be met by the tried processes of argument and legislation. The bullet may be a short cut for short tempers, but blood is too precious to sacrifice at the altar of impatience. Evil must be carefully measured and accurately named, because the gun is a dangerous weapon and the world a complex place; neither charge of the one nor understanding of the other should be given to unsubtle minds.

Ah! Unsubtle minds. To whom then is to be given the task of developing the subtle mind? Do I still believe in the function of teacher as well as the value of the poet? I must affirm, categorically, yes, I do! And more! The man who does not share that affirmation is not, in my book, a true socialist, no matter what extreme position on the Left he assumes for himself.

"Give the cities to its teachers and its artists!" They will keep it free and vibrant and alert to the dangers of tyrants and demagogues and thus fit for the people to live and organize their lives in.

Now I'd like to start this essay again.

Part Two: Definitions of Experience

Surfacing to the top of one's hesitancy to describe "the way the world should go" is an awareness of the very, very slow potency of words. Decisions, we suspect, are inspired by other than books and made by other men tempered by God knows what, if anything, who have none of those lovely blessings of reason and culture with which we touchingly imagine a sad reading of history and literature tempers *us*. And so the reasons for reaching their decisions engage criteria quite alien to *our* civilized ones of liberty and happiness. "Liberty to do what?" some kinds of "other men" ask. "Happiness? Hah! Two-thirds of the world are starving. Don't talk to us about human happiness just now," say other kinds of "other men."

But people have been starving, suffering, and fighting tyrants and one another since the beginning of time! Does that mean we will never pause to consider the question of human happiness, only mere existence? We seem always forced to concentrate our energies upon coping with the miseries caused by the tyrant and never get to asking the question how he got there in the first place. The result usually is that we're led to destroy one tyrant with an embryo tyrant at our head. Demagogues lead us to fight demagogues, not to free us but simply to take over. Bellies have always needed to be filled (I do not say "always will"), and so the question "why have men persistently allowed tyrants into their midst or demagogues to turn them against one another?" goes unanswered, except among a few tiresome artists, unreadable philosophers, and weary, embattled academics.

Which artist, then, would presume to spell out panaceas knowing the enormity of man's problems and how little notice those in power—and those "revolutionary" leaders aspiring to power—take of artists anyway. And they have good reason to feel safe in not taking notice of them: It has always been a simple task persuading society to denigrate its artists. So well has it been done in the West that the artist himself has been coerced into denigrating his own powers and dignity. "Why!" he cries in spiritual self-flagellation, diminishing his role like an old-fashioned sinner, "what *is* an artist anyway? All men are artists!" thus making it easy for himself if, by chance, it is discovered he has no real talent. Or: "Why should my blueprint be worth more than another's?" the presumption of his calling having been made more than he can bear.

Guilt for the presumptions of art! How cleverly that argument has been used to reduce the artist to an impotent, apologetic thing, inhabiting only gargantuan cities in whose streets it's easy to lose him or fatten and confuse him with flattery. Yet it's an argument to be faced and demolished, for it is true, we do presume, constantly, for each other. But whereas I, personally, don't mind presumptions in others—especially those to do with art, which presume I might be moved by this man's novel, that man's poem, another's interpretation of world events—yet other men are *encouraged* to mind such presumptions. It seems as though politicians—or commercial entrepreneurs with huge profits to earn—mindful of the questioning spirit engendered by art and artists, seek to divert that questioning spirit by perpetrating the myth that all art is an imposition, a presumption. Some artists, terrified of such accusations, have been known to race apologetically to the other extreme and declare that all art is Fascist, since it dictates a view of the world on its (in the theater) captive audience. This is, of course, an absurdly perverse definition of the process of art and one that I believe has been cleverly insinuated into the consciousness of societies all around the world by those who fear the revelatory qualities of art.

But even with the presumptions tolerated, the problems remain enormous. More than that—and this I feel should be the cornerstone of any essay into helping men live the lives they think (or could come to think) happiest—more than recognizing that the problems are enormous, is the recognition that problems are a constant, and that built into a philosophy of society must be both the awareness of this and the provision of machinery to cope with it. Having located a problem, it is society's responsibility not merely to look for a solution and then impose it, but to be prepared to recognize that by the time the solution is ready the nature of the problem may have altered, or that the chemical reaction of the solution applied to the problem may produce a related problem. Further, we need to remember that, if either occurs, then the men and women trained to think and apply their solutions may be people deformed by vanities or stultified by unsubtle minds, which will prevent their conceding mistakes and changing course, and there! there's the rub!

When all our blueprints are mapped out, then men—poor, vulnerable, soured, and tired men, with perhaps unhappy lives— must apply them, and who knows into what unimaginative, crude hands the beautiful dreams will fall. What a Marx may dream a Stalin may be left to enact. Or, not to take easy examples, what an enlightened minister of social services conceives, a bitter spinster behind the counter of the local office for social services is left to apply.

Machinery for coping with the ever-recurring problems, there I would begin. But the questions come begging: What machinery for what order of problem? Problems of communication? Improved machinery of the media? No, not that. Problems of political machinery? Should there be a proportional or representational system of counting votes? No, not those either. Nor problems and machinery to do with transport, mighty though such problems and their machinery are. No, I'm now talking about the more fundamental problem of informing the people who will have to name and then solve those problems, the people who will have to decide whether to accept the machinery for solving them, the people who may have to operate the machinery, and then, the people—all of us—who will have breadth of education to handle the problem of developing those subtle minds! And here let me tell a personal story that brought these questions into sharp focus.

When the question arose of where my children were to be educated it seemed to me that there was no problem. As a socialist I wanted them in a comprehensive school; * as someone who'd seemed not to have lost out as a working-class boy in a working-class school, so I felt my children would benefit from one also; as a doting Jewish father I wanted them near me—not boarded out; as a writer I wanted them to have the kind of school life that would offset the highly specialized atmosphere of a house constantly humming with the discussions of artists and intellectuals. So, the school down the road with a 60 per cent immigrant and working-class population was just the answer.

One day, my eldest son, aged thirteen then, was standing outside his school talking to some friends. He's a big boy, with very long hair and those irritatingly happy, intelligent eyes. Two older boys from the school approached him. One kicked him in the backside. He ignored the kick. "Get stuffed," said the other boy to him. "Alright, I will," replied my obliging son, and he continued to ignore the two fourth-formers. "Get stuffed," said the other boy again. My son assured him, confidently, that as he'd promised, he *would* "get stuffed." The boy drew back his arm and with a heavy ringed fist smashed into my son's right eye. "Good God!" said my son, reeling back, unable to believe any-

* An alternative system of education to the public and grammar schools, so called because it brought together children of mixed abilities and thus, more than previously, of mixed social classes.

one could do that or that it could happen to him. And then he came home.

Many months later I received a communication from a group of teachers calling itself The Right To Learn. Their opening paragraphs announce them sufficiently:

> London education is in a state of crisis. The degree of staff turn-over and number of unfilled positions is alarming. The truancy rate is very high. On paper, London children appear to be less intelligent than those in other parts of the country. We think that this results more from what goes on in the schools than from any alleged social or cultural deprivation.
>
> Many schools are turning from education to 'socialization.' Opinions about the children and their families now intervene in educational provision.
>
> Educational discussion seems to have polarised at present. On the one hand, the 'community' educationists like Eric Midwinter push for 'relevance' and immediacy, calling for massive change in the curriculum:
>
> > "When you get on the shop floor, in the supermarket, or when you're going to ask a girl to marry you, the symptoms of the Black Death or the ability to recite 'A View From Westminster Bridge' doesn't always appear to be terribly significant."
>
> This is a cheap attack on learning. Dr. Midwinter should study the reality of good subject teaching *now*. He should also beware of suggesting that the working-class do not need, or are not interested in poetry, art or music; or that they, unlike the middle and upper classes, do not need a good general education as the basis for forming critical judgments.

Though I knew standards in education were low and that the concern shown in this document confirmed what other teaching friends had told me, yet one sentence was disturbing: "Opinions about the children and their families now intervene in educational provision." It was a shock to learn that in these days a family was still investigated, judged, pronounced able to produce only fodder for factories, and its offspring handled accordingly.

Yet if it *is* true that a student's cultural limitations are imposed by his family life, then you have to give education a more basic foundation than either Midwinter or The Right To Learn group concede. If you are merely telling the child what the symptoms of the Black Death were, or asking him just to learn the poem by Wordsworth, then Dr. Midwinter is right: That's just dabbling, confusing. But he's criminally wrong to imagine that his own "relevant" and "immediate" approach are the only alternative approaches to education. On the other hand The Right To Learn group must accept the full implication of their belief in the edifying value of poetry, art, or music. These are "languages" that have complex structures. If you pretend that they are easy to assimilate then they will be pursued in the wrong way and perhaps, subsequently, for the wrong reasons. I believe we need to begin further back.

I'm slowly coming to my point, bringing the ends together. You are not simply asking a child to learn more facts to enable him to pass exams that will tear him out of his family's intellectual strait-jacket; you are expecting of him the qualities of courage to face the scorn often thrown out by friends, neighbors, and others in that family; you are hoping for the qualities of tact and modesty that will enable him to resist flaunting such new and challenging aspirations; you are trying for the quality of compassion that will prevent his judging and despising those who've been unable to accompany him. And that's only the domestic half of the problem. At a national level the problems can lead to terror. I put the point to the teachers of The Right To Learn group: "Look," I said, "the last war produced a monstrous state crime. The decision to exterminate 'inferior' men was elevated to a carefully defined philosophy that men seriously considered, then accepted, and then executed in the form of gas chambers. Now what do you propose there should be in education to help ensure that such an event never happens again?"

It was out. Simple. Education meant absolutely nothing unless the gas chambers of Nazi Germany hung constantly before the consciousness of the pupil. Alongside it should be measured history, science, literature, politics. Now, how do you do this? What basic kit has education formulated in order to enable such measurements to be made? There was no time to pursue in depth the question I'd posed, and my only reason for relating this long episode here is that it brought me to articulate something that had been nagging for a long time. Was the punch in the eye a mere casual act of thuggery? Were resentments at work there that neither the bullies nor my son understood? And how much more of what children experience or do to each other—which is the basis for what adults experience and do to each other—how much more is not understood by the child? And what is there in a school curriculum anywhere in the world that handles the subject of—what shall it be called? "Definitions of Experience"— that might illuminate history's massacres and thumps in the eye for the child and help him recognize its causes and its signs in order that they're forestalled, prevented? Who knows how to maintain definitions watertight enough for outrage not to drain away?

Definitions of experience—that's the nearest I can get to naming the "new school subject." But I'll illustrate it further. Take a word like "intimidate." Intimidation describes a sensation some people feel and a behavior others enact; and the fear, unease, confusion *felt* by the one, and the menace, distress, insecurity *caused* by the other, must surely be among the most basic of experiences felt between men in their relationships one to another. Now, is there a moment in any school where an imaginative, fully trained teacher takes that word in front of a class and shakes it inside out for its meaning, for its appearance in the contemporary world, in history, for its application to the pupil's own life, for its illustrative presence in art, literature, film? Is it possible that through a discussion of the word in my son's school he might have come to understand that it was not the thug intimidating him but he—with his long hair, colorful clothing, disregard for the school uniform, extensive vocabulary, his entire personality and output of confidence—it was *he* who was intimidating the thug?

I don't know what the other boy would have gained from such a class, perhaps the realization that to have been intimidated by such qualities was an admission of personal defeat of which the thump was visible evidence, and so he'd have been ashamed to produce such evidence. That, I think, may be overestimating the power of discussion. How reasonable, reasonable men expect men to be! But though the thump was on its way to my son from the day his star began shining on him, as indeed are many thumps of one sort or another, yet I can't help feeling that he might, just might, have got out of its way, had he understood the nature of intimidation. Such understanding can't keep a swelling down, but it might have prompted him to move on at the first sign of danger, or to have faced it squarely to show he was going to hit back.

And what of the child of whom it's expected that he break from the cultural inhibitions of his family? What value might a discussion of words be to him? He must leave his family, but with love. He must reject the values of his parents, but retain honor for them. Perhaps he can feed back to them what he has acquired, but he must not impose on them, shame, or diminish them. How important, therefore, are words for him! Culture, inhibition, values, honor, imposition, shame, diminish—all are words containing concepts of behavior, concepts essential to that child's life, if he is to break the pattern of his inheritance without a bitterness that might one day sour the achievement. Words!

Vindictive. Lilliputian. Mockery. Superficial. Spurious. Greed. Relativity. Doubt. Reason. Faith. Freedom. Demagogue.

It is not simply a question of building up a vocabulary but of fitting together the jigsaw of experience, of building a battery of concepts. I don't know what words they should be. Men with other qualifications could list the basic kit needed for understanding the human condition—not guaranteeing it, nothing can guarantee an understanding of the human condition—but a basis, upon which there exists a *possibility* for understanding, *that* basis, that "beginner's kit" does exist. Men have built it up over centuries, giving names to their actions and sensations, pinning them down for all time. And when once a word was found inadequate, they found another to describe the nuance.

Nor is the nuance a mere quibble. There *is* a difference between jealousy and envy. One is passive, the other active. The first wishes he had something the other had, the second wishes the other didn't have it at all. The one is a wistful feeling, the other malicious. The first is permissible, to be forgiven, the second is reprehensible; a man should know that he might be feeling the one and not the other in order that he doesn't judge himself too harshly or that he may defend himself when wrongfully described and accused.

It has been said before by men of authority: Language is our most precious instrument, the currency of our existence, however inadequate, imperfect. Despite abuse and all that has been done to language and committed in its name, it is the most extraordinary piece of equipment forged by men for their better understanding of themselves, one another, and the world in which they live. Words describe and give names to what men feel, think, see, and do, and so command of them is of paramount importance, and, yet, nowhere that I know of is their importance sufficiently appreciated for them to be—in some form or other, with a title like Definitions of Experience—number-one subject on the curriculum. Words! To define experience! We learn now to write them nicely, to spell them (some of us!); we learn how to construct them into sentences that accord to rules of grammar; we apply them to the *facts* (rather than the interpretation of) history, sociology, science. But we're never taught to understand them for what they were originally intended: as descriptions of what we do, what we are, or what we experience. Is it any wonder that time and time again men can be persuaded to commit acts of brutality against one another? Or that they can be led to pursue policies that history has repeatedly proven fruitless? Or build cities that are self-destructive?

Yes, I know, perhaps it is history that should have a greater prominence on the school curriculum. I've considered that one also. But the *facts* of history *especially* require a conceptual understanding of words before their lessons can be interpreted and then learned.

So, this essay seems to have become a defense of language. Is it so far from the notion that art and learning must be the priorities in men's cities? Of course, some experiences, some feelings, some of what we see and think cannot be put into the language of words. And so man, incredible man, made other languages for himself: music and painting. But still, visual, musical, or verbal, each language is crucial as a basis for developing sensitivities, perceptions, and critical judgments.

Panaceas, we're long agreed, there are none. Guarantees for

civilized behavior neither. Two acts can be expected of men: that they survive first, and then, if they can survive, that they be brotherly. Helping the young to identify, locate, define what's happening to them and what they're doing to other people must surely contribute to a basic arsenal for survival and fraternity.

YEHUDI MENUHIN

An Interview

YEHUDI MENUHIN, internationally renowned violinist, is more than a musician. Born in 1916 in New York City, after making his debut as a child prodigy, he went on to play with most of the world's orchestras and conductors and is largely responsible for introducing Indian music and musicians to the West. He is founder of the Yehudi Menuhin School of Music and author of *Violin: Six Lessons* (1971) and *Theme and Variations* (1972).

MORAES: You have been set apart in my mind from most other artists by your concern for human beings and by the way you involve yourself with activities directed toward the welfare of people. How did this come about?

MENUHIN: That is, of course, going back to my own background. My concern for those around me began in my childhood. From my earliest years I was concerned through my parents with the human condition. Both my parents were, each in their own way, extremely concerned in their thoughts, and their hearts, with those around them: my father, in a more general way, with social problems, perhaps not quite in the abstract, but in the general public area; my mother with individuals, with specific human beings who enlarged her own family. I could hardly separate the life of our family, each daily routine from the world. We were in some mysterious way, although isolated, in our own concern with music and languages, connected very intimately with issues and movements that were not within arm's reach. Thus, what happened in Europe, what happened in Russia, what happened in New

York and in England were as close to us as if these events were happening in San Francisco. So it was no great extension of this concern in later years for me to embrace the whole world, in particular India and the other countries that I came to know. It was no extension to play Indian music or to get to know the gypsies in Rumania; it was no great extension, in fact, to enlarge my human horizon or musical horizon to include all ages, races, periods, and geographical areas. So it came about that my first vision was that music would be able to bring peace to the world, that, perhaps, if I played well enough, I could stand on some street corner and play and begin a wave of good will and love and compassion and concern that would soon bring peace to the whole world—a child's vision but nonetheless representing what, in fact, I have tried consciously and unconsciously to follow all my life.

I have often found that different waves of thought and fashion and conviction are shared by groups of people where one person, who may be at the apex of the movement, may see a little farther, though he may not have a completely original idea. He may be one of the body of people who are aware of a change in the world, aware of the point that we're now reaching, where the child has to turn into an adult after so many thousands of millions of years, in the sense that he must now be more and more responsible for not only his own condition but the condition of everything on earth. Until now he could blissfully ignore this because of the limitations on his abilities to inflict damage and his relative innocence.

MORAES: It is often thought in the world that the people who are going to bring about any change will be scientists rather than artists. What do you feel is the role of the artist in contributing to any change that takes place in the world?

MENUHIN: I believe that the scientist is viewed in the role of a specialist, like a doctor with a degree in the field of medicine in which he has specialized, and people go to him in a group to get cured. I do not see that the ills of humanity will be cured by specialists who are accorded the privilege and the right of deciding on the fate of the patient as they attempt their cures. Sometimes these people are experimenting, and then, when they become more proficient, in newer sciences that are not as securely founded as, say, mechanics or perhaps chemistry, they build a few towns here and a few schools there.

I see scientists, rather, in a limited role, because they are aware of means geared to very specific ends that reflect an often one-track-minded conception of human existence and life in general. It is usually concerned specifically with having either enough food for people or the right quantity of people for the food available. It is concerned with keeping society in a state of order, whether through voluntary or involuntary methods; there is a science of torture today. All these are universal technical achievements that are regarded in an abstract light, as if the conquering of space and the conquering of human nature were one and the same thing. I do not see the scientist as offering the ultimate solution for mankind. I respect the scientist, and I respect, particularly, the scientist-artist who has gone far enough to realize that eternity and infinity, and the mystery of these, are probably with us forever and are part and parcel of life, and whose scientific discovery of this reveals the intuitive process as much as the purely rational process. Both processes are essential.

The artist, on the other hand, deals with life in the raw, life actually existing, life pulsating, not an abstraction of life. The musician is for music, as an art in time, the art of molding time. While the music is on, people are living, breathing, and feeling. It is a creative process. It is not only a creation in the abstraction; it is not only something that can be nailed down or looked at. I do not belittle painting, which is also a reflective process, the process of the painter assimilating his impressions and living them and expressing them. Painting can be as moving as music, but music is specifically an art of living in time. You have to live with the music you are hearing from the first note to the last; it reflects the essential creative urge of mankind.

I believe that we must all feel the need to exist as entities in our own unique expressive ways. The evolution of life has been in the direction of greater expression for the individual and greater responsibility. For instance, if we take the spawning of fish—I am not speaking of whales and dolphins but of endless millions, billions of eggs—there the individual counts for very little, and it is largely a matter of chance which of the eggs will flourish. The individuals themselves, the patterns of their lives, are determined by forces beyond their own control and life. One can use the word "evolves," though I am always hesitant about the word "evolution" because people tend to think evolution is a process that happens automatically and goes from good to better. This is not necessarily the case, unless we participate in that effort and make it conscious, unless we are committed to a certain direction, a direction from darkness to light, like the tree that grows from earth toward the sun. There is, I believe, a magnet ahead of us drawing us into the light, just as there is a source that is maybe in the dark.

MORAES: Are you yourself interested in the actual physical processes of bringing all this about?

MENUHIN: Well, I see life as a balanced form of living awareness that partakes of everything that exists. The human being is a synthesis of every force, of every mineral, every element in the universe. He is light and darkness; he is electricity; he is mechanics; he is chemistry. Even the trace elements are recognized today as being essential. There isn't anything of which man does not partake. I see him, therefore, obligated to remain in some sort of balance with nature. He must recognize that he is subservient to the time cycles, to life and death, and that he is subservient to the laws that maintain him in harmony and balance with laws of nature. This is his only protection. He cannot willfully deny these powers in favor of a one-track development, be it for greater industrial production, greater commerce, greater education, greater literacy, any one single development on which he sets his heart— even for greater liberty.

Life is so complex that if we take any single element, however valuable and important it is, it appears that if we cultivate and pursue it to the exclusion of a balanced development, it will turn sour. Our liberties in the free countries are turning sour because they have been divorced from these responsibilities; order turns sour when it is divorced from compassion and a respect for the dignity of life. There isn't any road, any path, to which man is committed in this fanatical one-track-minded way that does not inevitably turn sour, if he excludes all other elements from his obsession. I cannot bear dogmatic movements and fanatics for these reasons. I am concerned with the food that people eat, the music they hear, the company they keep, the thoughts they have, because I feel we are more and more responsible for what goes on in our minds and hearts. Civilization, in fact, consists in replacing automatic reactions with reactions that are somewhat delayed and considered.

We all know of the development of nuclear physics and the mammoth commercial and industrial development of technological forces. These have grown out of proportion to the individual. The individual today can no longer feel as important, as unique, as essential to a civilization, if he can no longer meet another man face to face and hold his own. The discrepancy, the desperate discrepancy, between a single man and the bureaucracy, between a single man and the police, between a single man and the institutionalization of the various elements in society, or between a single man and the city of today are all out of proportion, beyond being coped with by a single human being. I am afraid that a natural process takes place when millions of people become too passive and are no longer able to assert their uniqueness, their discovery of themselves as individuals, as groups, as families, as tribes, as regional entities. The larger the group that is helpless or passive, the more powerful and dominant the few become. Those who control the machinery of the institutions we have referred to naturally have always been in a position of power, but for a time there was a good balance whereby the individual could hold his own against these institutionalized or organized powers. Today, more than ever, it is essential to recognize that if people are to remain what we would like to think of as human beings, rather than become an insect race, like the ants, where only collectivity seems to determine their actions, then we must make of each human life something of enormous value and do this from its inception, or almost before its inception.

MORAES: You are now talking about selectivity.

MENUHIN: Yes, this is another dynamic process of biological evolution that seems at the moment to meet an inverse process, an opposite process of social and technological evolution. The biological evolution has been from, shall we say, the fish we were speaking about, born in millions, to the human being who raises a family with only a few children. This collision of processes leads to a terrible situation: very cheap and inadequate food, standardized, and made to last, is available today, indefinitely, on the shelves of grocery stores or in shipyards. These foods are made not to rot but to be, as it were, rotten—junk from the start.

So far, the availability of the resources accumulated, the resources of the ages, are being exploited in one, two, or three generations. This is not to mention the fertility of the earth. Through our chemical fertilizers it is made to increase its potential for a few decades, but again at the expense of the future and at the expense of the accumulated work of the past. We know that the soils that have been treated with fertilizer become dry as dust. They can contain very little fluid, very little liquid, and are no longer rich soil, which was the case before they were exploited. These developments have created a mass of human beings, surviving in numbers that have never existed before and, in fact, degrading the logical process that aimed at a higher and higher quality of life and greater responsibility for people. The commercial world creates the urge to buy and to spend, to produce, to distribute, to waste, to discard. The result of these urges is to degrade the human being who was, in fact, on the verge of very high qualitative development. I don't exactly know when one could say selective development reached its highest point, but one of the points of decline would certainly be the Industrial Revolution, when things like white flour and sugar become readily available. Now almost everything—degrading literature, degrading movies, and music that is either too loud and deafening or stealthily subliminal—is easily available.

Some indulgent simian side of man's nature seems to urge him on to an ever greater wish to satisfy cravings that normally would be the final fruit of a prolonged effort, whether in hunting, cultivation, in the disciplines of the various arts or the sciences, or in exploration. In Sicily, for example, traditional courtship lasted three years. Once effort and time were required for the satisfaction of all ambitions, cravings, dreams, visions. Now commerce and industry have attempted to create a world in which desires are immediately gratified. Everything requires money: Happiness is equated with money; power is equated with money. That is one of the curses of free countries, which actually owe a great debt to money, to free exchange, to its anonymous democratic quality. Unfortunately, commerce and industry have also come to regard money as an end in itself, instead of merely as a convenience and means. These have created a world in which the individual has lost a sense of the proportion of effort to reward, not that people do not suffer as much as they ever have.

MORAES: Don't you think today they suffer *more* in certain areas of the world?

MENUHIN: Certainly, they suffer more in many ways. There are the old traditional sufferings of heartbreak, diseases, abandonment, famine. On top of that there are the sufferings caused by wars, which are more cruel than ever before. In all the wars of the past there were always pockets of land that were fairly untouched. There were little hordes of people going about with pitchforks and little guns, who did plenty of damage, sacking towns and so on, which was ghastly enough. But there was at least a slightly closer relationship between man and man, even in fighting, than there is between a missile and the town that is destroyed. People are also suffering more mentally. Physical sufferings have always been with us—the anguish of families separated and of individuals lost or kidnapped or killed. But man's own hope for an ultimate future has never ebbed so low as it has today, because of the very fact that he holds so much in his hand. So long as he did not achieve the abundance and fulfillment that science, art, and literature promised him, his hope was high that through science, through literacy, through learning, through many things that were considered valuable and worthwhile, he would attain a better life. Now we have the evidence of great countries that have achieved a high level of this kind of civilization, that have organization, literacy, initiative, independence, where people have a voice in their future. But somehow or other nature or fate has contrived to bring us to a point of despondency equal to that which existed in past civilizations far less equipped than we are with the goods of the world, without the speed of communications that we have. So we are beginning to doubt whether we can really live up to our present responsibilities and powers.

MORAES: Is it not also true that because technology has created what is popularly called the population explosion, people can now live to be older, which is causing one of the most terrible problems, in fact, the most terrible problem the world has ever faced?

MENUHIN: Of course, the statistics show that a greater number of people are reaching old age. Up to a point it is true, but it isn't quite as true as the statistics make out, because average age is automatically raised enormously by the fall in the death and birth rates and in the rate of infant mortality. I think that you will find, if the statistics are pursued, that after a certain age the expectancy is not much greater than it was. In other words, the average is much higher—the average age of death used to be twenty or thirty, and now it is sixty or seventy—but those people who did reach the age of fifty in the past could look forward to almost as many years, if not as many years, as those who reach the age of fifty today. That should be made clear, because I know that it is always said that people live longer today. It is only partially true.

That is a minor point. The fact is, of course, that population is piling up. What is one to do to counteract this? One asks oneself what is it that would make it important to people to make the most of individuals and not to make the most number of individuals. The kind of population to develop is a qualitative rather than a quantitative one. It is one in which the joys of expression, of creating, of living one's own potential to the full, would find innumerable outlets and opportunities, where from the beginning life would be considered infinitely interesting, challenging, adventurous. We must not say blindly and simply that it is good to give any amount of condensed milk to children and feed them with anything that keeps them alive, if it is quality we are speaking of. Naturally, once a child is alive we have to do the best by it, but it is important to remember that just feeding is not what will keep something alive: It is much better to have fewer people with better food.

MORAES: How do you think this is going to be brought about?

MENUHIN: I think it can be brought about in three ways: First, it can be brought about by autocratic dictatorship, which is the most horrible way; in other words, countries submitting to a form of sterilization, to free abortion and all the rest.

Second, it can come about through the growing awareness of the population, through the search for quality and the encouragement of that search for quality: For example, if in this city of New York people were shown that every street could be improved with beautiful gardens, with levels built on top of streets where pedestrians could walk in green areas, with cars, taxis, and other forms of transport plying underground or on the present street level, if they could walk through buildings with the lower floors taken right out so that they could walk under them, with very, very high ceilings and catwalks between high buildings on high levels, where people could shop from 100 feet, so they would have good air to breathe, that would fire the imagination, give people a kind of joy. These kinds of joys would make the city renew its value to people. Instead of having dead office buildings, half of the buildings could be for living quarters, so people could live near their work. All this could happen through a democratic process, although various vested interests would have to be overcome.

The third method consists of nature's everlasting automatic brakes and processes. It is estimated that a large percentage of the people who walk on the streets of New York have some mental disorder, depression at least, or some graver mental disorder. People who are mentally disordered, or starved in certain vitamins may still remain alive. We know that schizophrenia, for instance, is a direct result of too low an intake of vitamin B_3 or, in many cases, the result of the body's transforming its own adrenalin into adrenachrome, so that it continuously poisons itself, a process that can be arrested very often by nicotinamine, which is a vitamin, in large quantities. Eventually, however, these people will go mad or will die as a result of existing conditions. Countries may go to war with each other, wars that will decimate the population. There are many possibilities that nature eventually will bring about simply through our own inaction. It cannot be otherwise. It will happen sooner or later; we cannot indefinitely stave off the retribution of natural forces, let alone the retribution of the animals who are made to suffer innocently, with a device here or a device there, a shipment here or a shipment there, a chemical here or a chemical there, a town here or a town there. I am not saying that the whales will rise up and attack the humans, but that the humans are going to suffer from the absence of the whales they are exterminating. No life can exist today at the expense of other species, of other lives.

But I do not think it is necessary to throw aside all past values. I believe throughout human history the great people—Buddha, Christ, philosophers like Spinoza—have pointed the way, and there are many good people who have raised healthy families, despite the evolution of today. There is so much that is sane still, and good, and wholesome, that it can be built on. We don't have to throw anything aside.

Many of the values are somewhat distorted and twisted today: Freedom has been twisted. The opportunity for young people is wonderful, but the respect they should owe the past has been forgotten, an example has been lost. We learn from different books and teachers all the time, but the old tradition of those who remember and those who see has been lost in favor of those who read and who have no memory. Still, I would not like to take a pessimistic view of our prospects. I cannot do that as long as there is any life in the world at all. As long as there is life, there is an element of self-determination. We have it in our powers to destroy life altogether, but as long as I can have my family around me, as long as I have my violin to play, I cannot feel despair.

G. MICHAEL SCOTT

G. MICHAEL SCOTT, Anglican priest, Diocese of Chicester, was born in 1907 in England. In 1947 he appealed to the United Nations on behalf of two tribes of South West African Mandated Territory, raising a question that was eventually referred to the International Court of Justice. He was banned from South Africa in 1960. Later, after heading the Nagaland peace mission, he was also banned from India. His books are: *Shadow over Africa* (1950), *Attitude to Africa* (1951), *African Episode* (1954), *Orphan's Heritage* (1958), *A Time To Speak* (1958), *The Nagas in Search of Peace* (1966).

When the great Greek philosopher was being pressed, on pain of death, to proclaim his belief in the gods, he persisted in expressing his doubts about their existence. When his followers implored him to give them a definite opinion on which they could base their plea for a stay of execution, he said he was inclined to agree more with his enemies than with his friends. A lifetime, he maintained, was too short for a man to dispel all his doubts about the existence of the gods. The universe was very great and space and time very far and wide in comparison with the life span of a single man. Whatever they said or did, for him it remained true that the gods may exist or they may not. He would continue to weigh the problem, but if they should decide to cut short his life because of his unbelief they would not thereby decide anything but their own ability to shorten his life. For him the question would thus remain open.

Two and a half thousand years later another great philosopher in England tried to arouse the conscience of mankind to the imminent danger of life's extinction from the new discovery of the power of atomic fission and fusion and the access to hitherto unknown destructive or creative energy. Bertrand Russell felt that the more conventional democratic procedures of dialogue, franchise, and litigation were too slow to be effective in face of the ever-accelerating speed of human history. Despite the increasing scope of the media of communication, these were themselves becoming so effectively controlled by private interests on the one hand, and state ownership on the other, that more drastic and dramatic methods were required if the common people of the developed world were to be alerted and mobilized for action.

At first he considered the possibility of the nation that had first discovered the secret of atomic power, and used it to bring about the destruction of Hiroshima and Nagasaki, being persuaded to use it or enforce the acceptance of a federal system of world government. There were, however, other chemical methods of mass destruction, and when the use of atomic force to compel agreement proved unfeasible, if only because the secret was soon discovered by other powers, he decided, as Gandhi had done before him, to resort to mass civil disobedience. Since the writer had used this method against the color bar in South Africa, Russell suggested a joint manifesto calling for civil disobedience to be organized in Britain and other countries. This manifesto, entitled "Act or Perish," was printed and distributed as a public pamphlet. It resulted in civil disobedience in London's Parliament Square, to which, after a demonstration by about twenty thousand in Trafalgar Square, we marched down Whitehall with a procession. In defiance of police orders about five thousand sat down outside the Ministry of Defense. When we went to attach a notice to the door, the fire brigade that had been ordered by the government to use its hoses on us refused, and the notice was attached by Russell not à la Martin Luther with hammer and nail but with a piece of cellophane tape to avoid damaging the door.*

Inevitably, there was government reaction. For five thousand people to assemble and deliberately disobey the law within the

* See Bertrand Russell, *The Autobiography of Bertrand Russell*, Vol. 3 (London: George Allen and Unwin, Ltd., 1969), 112, 137–39.

precincts of Parliament and attach a challenge to the door of the
Ministry of Defense produced official retaliation of a kind difficult to contend with but all too often successful throughout history. It was not met straightforwardly by imprisoning everybody
who had courted imprisonment. It was a mixture of ridicule and
denigration instigated by the counterinsurgency of security services. These make the operations of freedom-loving individuals
and movements increasingly difficult with all the technical aids
available in modern times, as the Watergate and other bugging
scandals in America have revealed. Other countries have their
Watergates that seldom come to light, for if they do they become
counterproductive and stimulate the very forces they are intended
to counteract.

Toward the end of his life Russell was made very aware of these
methods and of the way in which such activities are aided by the
actions of eccentric activists. These, while espousing good causes,
are sometimes unable to subordinate their "ego trips" to the often
delicate requirements of strategy and tactics in the perpetual struggle against forces armed with superior military might and intelligence. It may be this that has prompted a recent remark by Professor Lewis Mumford: "I think the Dark Age is already here,
only we don't know it." Do nations, and does humanity, always or
ever get the leaders they deserve? There is usually more selfless-
ness and sacrifice in the cause of truth and justice among scientists
and research workers than among many professional politicians.
Does power necessarily corrupt and absolute power, as Lord Ac-
ton put it, corrupt absolutely? The record of the rise of Nazism
and Fascism within the most developed countries of the world in
our own generation could be matched by the growth of dictatorships among some newly independent states, unless positive action
is organized to prevent it.

There is an urgent need today for exact knowledge of the methods and means used by governments and the media to achieve the
ends they serve, whether these are legitimate ends such as those
fostered by many pressure groups for their own economic advantage or the more illegitimate aims of states to get the better of one
another. "War," said Clausewitz, "is an extension of policy." If

civilization is to survive, and if mankind is ever to emerge into a new era of enlightenment, there is the necessity to reverse the process of which that could be said. Whether deterrent or détente is the keynote of diplomacy, there must be the possibility of a rule of reason and understanding, one wherein states are not in a perpetual state of confrontation, in which all the worst features of this social system face one another. This inevitably brings out the worst opposite traits in their adversaries. Ways must be found of enabling the positive features and creative attributes of man to be brought into play in the coming struggle of human civilization to survive. The myths and bigotries that still play so large a part in international and social relationships must be brought into the light of day and shown to be what they are, for what men believe to be true can be more powerful than the truth.

Myths and faiths

Of the great myths that menace modern society, even more than the medieval notions of "the millennia" (so ably researched by Professor Norman Cohn), some of the most potent exist in the realm of theology and politics. These, for reasons I shall try to show, religious institutions have been powerless to resist. But perhaps one of the most menacing, and least discernible, exists in the realm of mathematics, of business, and of finance. Here the geniuses who operate the financial system to their own advantage are all the more cleverly concealed by the seeming absurdity of their description—"Gnomes of Zurich." The banking and currency system should be subjected to the same intensive and systematic scrutiny as that which went into the space program and alone made possible the actual realization of myth, the landing of a man on the moon.

The golden cow

The role of gold in the world's financial system, which necessarily includes both West and East, has been described by an economist as a myth. A comparatively rare and imperishable commodity that has acquired the centrifugal position in the financial scheme of things, the metal has taken on a mythical value that, for want of any other, financiers have attributed to it. Gold, however, has a reality of increasing value for the gold-mining companies who, with the aid of cheap migrant labor, have recovered many times over their capital invested in gold production. They have developed a fantastic system whereby millions of tons of conglomerate ore are brought from six thousand feet below the earth's surface and pulverized into a powder in order to extract from it a precious ounce or two of gold. The object of the operation is to stabilize a not noticeably stable currency system. The system has another kind of reality for African miners, drawn from their improverished lands hundreds of miles away to work underground at a wage of less than twenty pounds per month, while gold prices and profits have rocketed.

Describing this system, in which the central role of gold is still sustained, a scientist who tried to investigate its workings called it "The Great Confidence Trick" of all time. Since the Napoleonic wars, it has enabled the financiers to exert a decisive influence over the destiny of nations through the banks and their control over currency and credit. The political and financial system must similarly be subjected to an intensive scrutiny as thorough as that which went into the space program. This system alone made possible landings on the moon and penetrations into the mysteries of space and time, impossible to any era that has preceded ours.

The growth of the power of the banks traces back to the creation by private enterprise, at the time of William III in 1694, of the Bank of England, founded upon gold as the universally acceptable scarce commodity. This saw the beginning of inflation and of the trade cycle. Since then, every war has meant a vast increase in bank-created money and has been followed by a depression and a financial crisis.

The twisters

The world of finance is not the only sphere on earth that is subject to the phenomena called a twister by Americans. This is a spiraling vortex of air that can assume enormous destructive power. It sweeps on irresistibly gathering up everything movable in its seemingly arbitrary path.

The process of distortion is still more evident in the sphere of ideas and ideals where its potential for destruction and havoc in the affairs of men must be understood and revealed to the peoples of the world, if the power of the people is to become a force for life rather than the death of our civilization.

The religious nation state

Some myths that have exercised a disastrous influence on the peoples and nations of the world belong to the spheres of theology, nationalism, and, ironically, the politics of liberation. It is impossible to estimate the conflict and human misery that have been caused down to our own time by the concepts of a "chosen people" and a "promised land" and the doctrine of racial superiority that resulted in the holocaust for 6 million Jews. Such concepts deprived whole peoples of their lands and rights and became the doctrinal sanction on which whole state systems of law have been erected, such as apartheid in South Africa and even, ironically, in Israel. The aim, it is argued, is security for one people against the supposed threat, which consequentially may become real, from others.

All the computers in the world could not calculate the human misery caused to the colored people of the world by this mistaken notion and to Arabs and Jews alike in Palestine today. "Voices for life" of the common people of the world must answer the demagogues who use these notions to usurp the reins of power and establish "security systems" to make safe the continuance of their tyrannies in one state after another in our own time. In a world where the population will have doubled itself by the end of the century, the logic of such notions is as fatal as the doctrine of the escalating deterrent.

It will not be by force alone that these tyrannies will be destroyed. Though force may have to be used in the last resort to overcome tyranny, as it was to overcome Hitler, it is to be hoped that it will never again be used on such a scale, for that would almost inevitably precipitate a nuclear war. In every country now a new spirit has to be born in contradiction of these false concepts. The long and arduously acquired human virtues such as generosity, understanding, and positive appreciation of the varieties of human nature and life can be cultivated. They will bear fruit, and no matter what cynics may say, will be recognized in the socioeconomic systems of the future. They are far from recognized as having value in our "every man for himself and devil take the hindmost" societies. On this subject voices must speak courageously in the context of their own nation's problems and possibilities. One can only speak from within one's own country's condition. Britain once ruled a great Empire but may still have something of value she can contribute to the reconstruction of the world of tomorrow. This will be for the generation that now knows its own growing pains. The younger generation is living through an ever-accelerating process of history such as no generation before it has ever known. And adaptation to it is correspondingly more difficult and painful, if less dramatic, than the world wars of previous generations.

Alternate to fascism and counterinsurgency

In face of the power of the modern state the young have come to know that the forms of protest and demonstration used from the time of the Chartists to the Aldermarston marchers are not very effective. While some in their desperation have resorted to hijacking and kidnapping, these methods are seen to be sometimes counterproductive and to be used as pretexts for widespread repression of organized labor and trade union movements and even coups d'état by the military.

In Britain, on the other hand, the security forces are also increasingly bewildered and desperate. In relation to the problems of Ireland they find their activities widening to include protection of the civil population. Mediation by a third force might even yet succeed where an occupation army becomes mistrusted by both sides. Problems similar to those inherited by Britain from her past relations with Ireland exist in other countries of the world where mediation is resisted as "interference in our domestic affairs." The United Nations is inhibited at present by Article 2, paragraph 7, of the Charter. But to conclude with the problems of Britain, in the United Kingdom today, caught up in the great battle of ideas that heralds, we hope, a more expansive era, and the conflicts of religious and national bigotries that have come down to us from the past, the policeman's lot is not a happy one.

The task of the security forces is made more difficult by the swift transition from great empires to a multiplicity of sovereign states that have followed in the wake of liberation movements and the winds of change. Subject peoples sometimes tend to take over the security systems they had known and inherited from the past and use them for their own purpose.

Yet the need remains for a framework of law and justice that will make possible a maximum of freedom to exchange ideas and to promote beliefs and change. An aspect of this, vital to the security in the future, is security itself. A commission of enquiry is needed into the effect on the life and work of organizations and individuals of their use by the Special Branch and other secret services in what used to be called psychological warfare. This has now developed into a permanent political counterpart and is the field of action, not only of the secret services but of pressure groups with commercial or departmental interests.

Voluntary organizations are necessary and play a vital role in a healthy democracy. But now they are becoming dependent either on charitable foundations or corporations with commercial interests. They are also being squeezed by taxation and inflation of their assets as well as being dependent on the press and media, which have their own problems of promotion.

All this tends to lay them open to infiltration by those who have other duties or interests than the objectives of the organization that employs them.

Having been associated with several nongovernmental organizations aiming to do imperative tasks for justice and freedom in the West, I have seen much of their work damaged and some of it destroyed by such abuses as infiltration and by the suspicions engendered by allegations regarding their sources of finance.

In other parts of the world the winds of change have been gathering momentum until they have reached the velocity and destructive power of twisters, leaving not only physical but moral and spiritual disintegration in their wake. In Britain life is quieter, but organizations have become so much a part of the Establishment, and so dependent on their endowments, that the voice of prophecy and change is dangerously muted. Sometimes to foreigners it almost appears as a conspiracy of silence. But before cynicism and despair make the work of the Special Branch even harder than it is, may we not have a parliamentary enquiry into the working and financing of nongovernmental organizations in such essential fields as those I have mentioned? People and Parliament perhaps need to be reminded of the late Poet Laureate's, John Masefield's, words:

> It is the logic of our times,
> No subject for immortal verse
> That we who lived by honest dreams
> Defend the bad against the worse.

An interfaith religious leadership is needed now.

FRANK HERCULES

FRANK HERCULES, writer and lecturer, born in Trinidad, is now living in New York City. His most recent book, *American Society and Black Revolution* is a political and social history, but he is currently at work on a new novel and book of essays to be published in German in Germany. His other novels are: *Where the Hummingbird Flies* (1961), *I Want a Black Doll* (1967).

I was born and reared to early manhood in a British colonial society in the West Indies. To locate the place of my birth with more precision: Port-of-Spain, Trinidad; and to define the time of my birth in its relationship to the colonial circumstances I have indicated: during the reign of His Britannic Majesty, King George V.

These facts, barely stated as they are, can nevertheless construct a historical context that embraces a more or less typical segment of the colonial experience. I do not mean that as a black British subject in the West Indies, bereft by law and custom of the vested rights of an Englishman, my experience corresponded in exact detail with that of an Indian, African, Malaysian, Palestinian, or Hong Kong Chinese, in their respective countries. It is true that we were all subjects of the Crown, our corporate affairs administered and our individual lives determined in accordance with policies handed down from on high by the Colonial Office in London. But these policies differed from one subject country to another, depending on the particular degree of development attained in the view of the Colonial Office, the economic value of the territory from the standpoint of its natural resources, or its strategic potential in military terms. Another criterion also was employed by the Colonial Office in assessing the capacity of the overseas territories of the Crown for self-government. This was the criterion of race. The white races inhabiting Canada, Australia, and New Zealand, for example, were conceded the ability to govern themselves a good deal sooner than was the case with the colored races. These latter were, in fact, the "lesser breed without the law," as they had been classified in Rudyard Kipling's poetics of race.

The Crown Colony of Trinidad and Tobago was an instance of the political theory of colonialism that manhood suffrage cannot logically be extended to people who are regarded as "children" and therefore unable to govern themselves. During much of the reign of George V, the population of Trinidad and Tobago numbered around half a million people. Not only were they considered children at their stage of civilized development but backward too. Trinidad and Tobago was therefore administered as a Crown colony. This meant in political practice that they had little or no voice in their own affairs. The right of suffrage was severely restricted. The legislature that theoretically represented their interest was the creature of the executive whose will, incarnated in the person of the British governor, was paramount. The governor was, in fact, invested with a residual power of veto over all legislation.

So at the age of twenty or thereabouts, I lived subject to a political despotism in the sham benevolent guise of Crown Colony government. It was easy to run afoul of the Sedition Ordinances, and one had to be careful about one's political utterances.

I was still a child when my father was sent into permanent exile from the colony. The burden of his offense was his opposition to the absolutist character of the Crown Colony system of government, whatever the velvet glove in which it might be ensheathed. My father was a left-wing intellectual imbued with the romantic tendencies of nineteenth-century English liberalism. Despite his nationalist fervor and his attachment to the cause of black equality, he had little notion of *Realpolitik*. For him, the ideal of impartial justice and the spirit of fair play were inherent in the British tradition. They had only to be invoked with splendid eloquence and brilliant learning in order to transform the squalid actualities of the colonial situation. With these attributes of learning and eloquence, he was superbly endowed. He had excelled as a student at the local Queens Royal College and afterwards at the University of London. He was employed at one time in the Trinidad civil service and then as Vice-Principal of Naparima College in the south of Trinidad. During a period of acute labor unrest after World War I, his public utterances in the course of a series of lectures delivered in various parts of the West Indies were deemed incitements to disorder. On his return to Trinidad he was forbidden to land. The official ground of his exclusion was the fact that he had been born in Venezuela, South America, and was therefore not a British subject. The truth of the matter was that both of his parents were British subjects; he had been brought to Trinidad while still an infant; and he had spent almost the whole of his life on the island. The colonial authorities had, however, come to the conclusion that he was a "dangerous" person. His permanent exile followed.

The incident scarred my childhood and made my formative years difficult. With the casual cruelty of children, the companions of my early years insistently reminded me that "they [meaning the colonial authorities] deported your father." As a result, I have always associated formal learning with cruelty. School became a nightmare for me. I sought refuge in solitude and grew increasingly withdrawn. I did not understand what had happened to my father, why he was no longer at home, and why my mother walked up and down the house sobbing in the dead of night. The muted sound of my mother's grief has haunted me all my life. When at length I understood what had taken place, an inseparable connection was formed in my mind between British colonialism and the blighted lives of distraught women; between British colonialism and the broken lives of banished men.

A colonial society, such as Trinidad between World Wars I and II, is a case history of political disfranchisement, economic exploitation, and social imbalances engendered by a racist caste structure reinforced by class hostilities. Whiteness was the key to status and the good things of life. The whiter one was, the better off one tended to be. The blacker one was, the worse off one tended to be. There were exceptions, of course, to this rule.

Whiteness, though arbitrary in its determination of the possibilities of life, could at times be circumvented. People who were not white, who even were black, were occasionally brilliant of intellect, clever in business, or conspicuous for their spotless respectability. In general, however, the iron law of colonial circumstances dictated that for your own good you had better be white or as nearly white as a prudent choice of parents could make you. Brothers and sisters by the same mother and father would have very different social destinies and enjoy vastly dissimilar levels of economic opportunities according to the degree one looked white, the other not so white, and the next a shade too dark. The first would have access to a clerkship in a commercial bank, the second little difficulty entering the civil service, while the last might have to be contented with becoming a teacher at an elementary school or something relatively undistinguished in the scheme of colonial careers. They would also keep different company, their social lives being stratified on different levels of the color caste system, and they might even ignore one another in public. On the whole, in a colonial society such as Trinidad, one did not mix socially with people darker than oneself except at the risk of incurring disfavor with people as light-skinned as oneself or lighter. Again, however, the exceptions to this rule must be stressed. Such exceptions, when they occurred, were almost invariably made because the individual concerned was uncommonly successful in a profession or some other acceptable pursuit and might also be described as a "black gentleman" or a "black lady." If one was white or sufficiently near-white, the categories "gentleman" and "lady" were superfluous. Purely by reason of one's approved skin color, one had transcended the need for such saving epithets of social redemption.

The psychological havoc wrought by this system of color caste is indescribable. Black women of excellent cultural attainments and, indeed, of alluring physical charm found it difficult to secure suitable husbands and either did not marry or were obliged to marry beneath them. The English, Scots, Irish, or Welsh businessmen and bureaucrats were at the apex of the social pyramid, with the French Creoles (somewhat tainted by miscegenation) directly below them. Theirs was the Kingdom of Heaven. I had long since left the island and was residing in the United States after several years in England when the first black man was commissioned an officer in the police force in Trinidad. Until then no black could rise above a noncommissioned rank. Up to World War II, black Trinidadians in the middle ranks of the civil service, which was as far as they were permitted to go, having worked for forty years, would be earning a salary of less than fifty dollars a week. But this was princely by comparison with the wages of a laborer in the sugar-cane fields who earned, on the average, less than two dollars each week, working six days a week, twelve hours a day.

The immigrant laborers from India were, in the main, the toilers in the sugar-cane fields. Around the time that I was born, one of every three inhabitants of Trinidad was an Indian. I grew up with Indians. They were the people whom, as a homogeneous group, I knew best and with whom, as a whole, I had the closest personal ties. My best friends in my youth were Indians. I ate the food of the Indians, lived side by side with them, attended their festivals, spent endless hours at play with them. They were my constant companions. It has always seemed curious to me that alone among my youthful associates, my Indian friends never taunted me with the fact of my father's exile. For many years now, Trinidad has been replaced by the United States as the country of my allegiance. Yet the sound of Indian voices in conversation, whether speaking English or Hindi (but especially the former) arouses nostalgia in me, and I grow suddenly homesick for Trinidad. There were other elements in the diverse ethnic composition of the people of Trinidad—Chinese, Portuguese, Assyrians among them. But with none were my relations so congenial as with the Indians. My interest in philosophy was first stimulated by an Indian who subscribed to the theory of metempsychosis. Altogether, the Indians dominated the cultural life of the little town of San Fernando in which I grew up in the south of Trinidad.

At twenty years of age I was in the psychological throes of an inward quest for my father. I was also impelled outwards by a consuming urge to come to grips with the imperialistic usages of colonialism. I read insatiably and planned, in silence, to avenge my father. For I had achieved by then a faint understanding of the political trap that had been set to ensnare him. My mother

was the youngest daughter in a family of landed proprietors long
settled in the south of Trinidad. She was very beautiful, with a
loveliness of spirit that made the idea of revenge deeply repugnant
to her. Yet I was not actuated solely by a desire for vengeance.
The entire complex of colonial circumstances nauseated me: the
arrogant white racism, the color caste structure of society, the
pervasive mass poverty, the decay of gifted individuals and the
defeat that shriveled their lives, forcing them to trim their beliefs, trade their principles, bend, stoop, cringe, crawl, hammered
to their knees by colonialism. It was not only my father's an-
guished outcry or my mother's solitary wandering in her grief in
the wilderness of night; it was also the economic misery, the social
cruelty, and the political constraints counterpointed by epidemic
violence and the manic relief afforded each year by Carnival. I
could bear it no longer. I left for England, there to study law
and thereafter, as I secretly resolved, to devote my life to the
overthrow of colonialism. For it was clear to me that this form of
Imperial oppression was a political evil of the first magnitude. Its
effect upon the so-called subject peoples—"the niggers (who)
begin at Calais"—was intolerable.

At this time of my life my religious leanings were aesthetic
rather than supernatural. I believed in truth, goodness, and beauty.
I conceived it possible, granted only fair play on the part of the
major world powers, for the general standard of human existence
to be raised to decent levels protective of the ideal of universal
freedom and dignity. I believed that human beings were fully human only when existing within inviolate safeguards of their inherent right to be free under just laws and to be sacrosanct in
their persons under enlightened customs. Colonialism in practice,
despite its vaunted theory of a "civilizing mission," was a cynical
denial of this belief. I still was convinced, however, that in the
metropolitan country, at any rate, Tennyson's vision of "freedom
broadening down from precedent to precedent" into a "parliament
of man, a federation of the world" was not an empty dream. My
illusions did not survive two English winters. By then I savored
with bitter relish the smugness and complacency of the celebrated
poet's mid-Victorian liberalism.

At this stage the quality of life seemed to me to be a question of values. If you subscribed to the right values and believed, as I did, in the true, the good, and the beautiful, then action to translate them into concrete circumstances need not be precipitate. I loathed colonialism and all its works. Yet gradualness was the armor I put on. The revolution I envisioned was a revolution of aesthetic values. In its train would follow the gradual reconstruction of the world on surer foundations of universal freedom and dignity.

The London of my student days was a place of extraordinary intellectual ferment. Bertrand Russell and J. B. S. Haldane, Bernard Shaw and H. G. Wells, Harold Laski and John Maynard Keynes, Sidney and Beatrice Webb, Julian and Aldous Huxley— these were some among the luminous stars in a galaxy of uncommon brilliance. I found J. B. S. Haldane especially illuminating. After World War II he went to live in India and became an Indian citizen.

When I began my studies for admission to the English bar, I soon realized that if my purpose to avenge my father was to be fulfilled, then my chosen weapon of the profession of law would have to be discarded. It became plain to me that membership of the English bar carried with it an inherent necessity to play the Imperial game and to play it by those very rules that, in their psychological effect, were methods of recruitment to the ranks of the ruling class, whether in England or the colonies. For it was not simply a matter of acquiring a body of professional learning and mastering techniques of courtroom advocacy. In the process a certain type of mentality was created. A black, trained in England, practicing in the British colonies his profession as a barrister-at-law tended to be a caricature of his white counterpart at work in the metropolitan country. To begin with, a black man wearing a seventeenth-century wig in a hot climate cuts a figure that calls up the notion of a masquerade, whatever the seriousness of the business he may be engaged upon. Imitation of the metropolitan power is the cultural essence of colonialism. In the next place, a black man as a member of the English bar carrying on his profession in the colonies acquires a class ethos essentially hostile to the interests of the oppressed. As a colonial barrister-at-law he becomes in numerous instances an agent of the Imperial oppressor, thus, by necessary extension, an enemy of human freedom. Whatever the nineteenth-century romanticism of his political outlook, my father had never faltered in his view of human freedom and dignity as the sovereign goals of society. It was increasingly clear to me that by becoming a colonial barrister-at-law, I should be a traitor to my father rather than his avenger.

This realization involved me in profound conflict with myself. The question whether to continue or abandon my studies obsessed me to the exclusion of the studies themselves. The issue was resolved by my leaving England and taking up residence in the United States. But during my residence in England I had discovered that white racism and other inequities permeated a good deal of English life; if the former was less blatant in England than in the West Indies, it was only because the metropolitan power in its domestic usages adopted guises more dissembling than those it assumed in the colonies. From a racial standpoint the quality of life in England was not better; it was merely different. By this time the naïve idealism that had accompanied me from Trinidad to England lay dying. It was given the coup de grâce on contact with white racism in the United States, where I conducted its final obsequies.

The changes I had envisioned in the quality of life as a result of my experience of colonialism seemed nowhere more possible of realization yet nowhere less hopeful in this prospect than in the United States of America. At the time of my arrival here, more than 6 million people were unemployed. That statistic, grim as it is, conveys no more than a hint of the widespread misery and suffering, the massive dislocation, the festering political conflict within the society. Starvation menaced the poor. Civil strife stalked the land. Abroad, Europe was at war. Solely from a domestic angle, however, the salient feature of the social landscape was racial prejudice. Negroes were lower than dirt. So case-hardened had the United States grown in its cultural biases that it did less than it might have done to save the tormented Jews from the clutches of the Nazi terror. So long and so shamefully had it mistreated its black citizens that it could turn not a deaf but a callous

ear to the terrible plight of the Jews. Where racial prejudice had
existed in the British colonies and the metropolitan country as a
matter of unwritten convention, here in the United States over a
large section of the country it was a part of the statute law. Also,
as in the West Indies, it was deeply entrenched in social custom,
but with this difference: Here in the United States it was shorn
of subtlety and bestrode the country in all its terrifying nakedness.
One was either white or nonwhite. If the former, then one belonged to a higher social caste; if the latter, then to a lower social
caste. The blacks (or Negroes, as they were called) occupied the
lowest caste position of all.

Observing the constitution of things in the United States and,
from this vantage point, looking out on the world beyond, my
Weltanschauung became tinctured with despair. I revered truth,
goodness, and beauty no less, but I believed in them no more.
Privately, I prostrated myself before them, but publicly I ceased
to proclaim them. I gave them a hiding place in my heart, for I
had come to see that they were fragile. No longer did I regard
reason and the arts of persuasion as the touchstones of constructive and harmonious developments in human affairs. Instead, the
conviction grew in me that solutions to human problems must be
sought, not in the abstractions of philosophical idealism, but in
the gross facts of human biology and the shadowy underworld of
psychology. I dismissed as fanciful the possibility that the meek
would inherit the earth, and I accorded recognition to the fact that
the mighty were in complete command. I had once dreamed of a
world transfigured by gentleness. As a boy, I used to be reluctant to walk on grass lest, unknown to me, the blades were capable of feeling. Now it was plain to me that where human beings in
the mass were concerned, force was likely to accomplish a great
deal more than reason. The quality of life was sorely in need of
elevation for most of mankind. It would be, above all, however,
a problem of the intelligent and unsentimental application of precisely calculated degrees of force to secure enlightened ends.

Meanwhile poverty, racism, and war polluted the lives of people
everywhere. The highly industrialized West consumed a disproportionate quantity of the world's resources. I attributed to this

fact that maldistribution of goods and services which, in its imperialistic design, was a principal function of colonialism. To justify this inequity, imperialism resorted to unscientific theories of race and spurious professions of missionary ideals. I reasoned that war was a necessary outcome of the failure to distribute the world's resources on an equitable, cooperative basis. There were other causes of war, but this was one of the most direct. Unrestrained rivalry for monopolistic control of raw materials was another of the immediate causes of war. I saw in this trinity of poverty, racism, and war a remorseless wheel to which mankind was bound because of the, as yet, low level of evolution of the human species. A more intelligent species than man would have recognized eons ago the abysmal folly of internecine war and risen above it to enlightened systems of cooperation for the sake of the common weal. In my view, the great obstacle to human well-being was not theological sin or scriptural wickedness but congenital stupidity. This was the conclusion to which I had been drawn by my experience of life under colonialism in the former British West Indies, in the domestic circumstances of the metropolitan country, Great Britain, and afterwards up to the present time in the racist context of the United States. Reinforcing it is the voluminous testimony of recorded history. I had awakened from a dream of human greatness and splendor to a reality of squalid men— kings, presidents, prime ministers, and other potentates. They had no vision of the oneness of mankind but were inveterately self-seeking. They conceived of human destiny as a thing of lesser account than their personal ambitions whose accomplishment they pursued, cunning, ruthless, and unprincipled, through nationalism, racism, and war.

It is fatuous to adduce visits to the moon and other triumphs of technology as conclusive evidence of an ascent in the quality of life. By the simple test of the collective happiness of mankind any such demonstration must, inevitably, fail. Mankind now as a whole is no happier, its moral quality no higher, its social intelligence no greater, than at any point during the past two thousand years. Within the last decade millions of people have been exterminated in Southeast Asia by the most barbarous methods of modern technology employed by a Christian power in one of the most shameful wars ever waged. I shall quote briefly from *The Manchester Guardian* of March 2, 1974:

> In a devastating indictment of the American use of chemical herbicides during the Vietnam war, the National Academy of Sciences has forecast that the harmful effects on the Vietnamese ecology will last for at least a century. It has also indicated that evidence showed that the chemicals resulted in the deaths of Vietnamese children.

There were more frightful horrors still in the course of that war, but this is not the place to disclose them. Barely more than a generation ago scores of millions of people, combatants and civilians alike, were slaughtered during an episode called World War II. Scarcely more than a generation before that, scores of millions of people were slaughtered in another seizure known as World War I. There is little in the human record for mankind to preen itself upon: a few extraordinary individuals, most of them either hounded into martyrdom or, if they are fortunate, maliciously ignored; a few half-hearted attempts to regulate the affairs of mankind by means of a universal organization; some halting steps in the direction of compassionate attitudes toward the weak, the old, the sick; more equalitarian behavior toward women; more enlightened treatment of children. Much of the time, however, rudimentary advances have been made at such inordinate social cost as to raise serious questions if the struggle has perhaps been costlier than the objective.

As the prospects of mankind unfold, the control of world population is canvassed with mounting concern. There already exists ample warrant for the probable correctness of the Malthusian thesis. But side by side with this there is the spectacle of vast areas of the United States, Canada, and Australia that are still relatively uninhabited while Latin Americans, Asians, Africans, and other poor, nonwhite peoples are being exhorted by every imaginable device of propaganda to reduce their population growth to zero.

This state of affairs does not impair the case for the limitation and control of world population, but it does cast a disquieting light on certain facets of racism and exclusionist immigration policy. While huge and habitable areas of the earth still remain unpopulated, it is misleading to talk as though the world were already bursting at the seams with people. At the same time it would be unrealistic to deny that this will soon be the case if the present rate of increase continues unchecked. Rapidly multiplying numbers of people are exerting dangerous pressure on the available means of subsistence. Epidemic famine in India exacts a gruesome toll. So does starvation in Africa. The Nobel Laureate Norman Borlaug said recently: "Only a handful of people are aware of just how close we were to having 50 to 60 million people die this year [of famine] in developing countries."

Solutions to the problems of mankind have often been sought in the creation of institutions. For lack of a workable alternative, the search must continue along these lines. Yet institutions do not possess an independent life of their own. Their animation derives from the human beings who create them. It is, pre-eminently, these human beings—and not their creature institutions—who must provide the solutions. To speak of the quality of life is to speak of the quality of the human species. Institutions, as such, are incapable of elevating the quality of life. Only human beings can do so. For human beings to elevate the quality of life is, however, to elevate themselves in the scale of evolution. Is this within their capacity?

The record of the human species up to this time suggests a grave deficiency in social intelligence. Yet it is precisely this attribute, above all, that must be brought into play if the human species is to enhance its evolutionary position by improving the quality of life. The problem is, therefore, primarily genetic and only secondarily institutional. More effective institutions will require more intelligent human beings first to devise and then to operate them. Forms of government, whether local or universal, partake of the nature of institutions. Their efficacy in any circumstances depends on the quality of their human administration. Means and ends are not formulated and pursued by institutions but by human beings. The emphasis cannot be shifted: Responsibility for the quality of life does not inhere in institutions but devolves on human beings. Closer attention will have to be given to eugenic considerations than has hitherto been thought consistent with humanistic ideals. The quality of life—human life—is inseparable from the quality of human beings. A way must be found to produce higher types of human beings on a scale commensurate with the vast range of human problems and at a rate faster than the ordinary processes of social development or the probabilities of casual reproduction would allow. It must be noted however that, so far, genetic engineering is scarcely more respectable as a biological concept than genocide.

On the economic plane, traditional confusion between the standard of living and the quality of life needs to be dispelled. People are not necessarily happier because their per capita income is higher. The gross national product is not an index of gross national contentedness. It may supply evidence of material prosperity or indicate the absence of it; it may be a symbol of the level of industrial advancement, but it does not make a definitive statement about human well-being. Nor does its calculation of goods and services proclaim its respect for the environment or its concern for the less fortunate members of the society: the poor, the criminal, the afflicted. It enunciates a single value, namely, material wealth. We deal in the hollowest of phrases when we discuss the quality of life without including in that concept an unfaltering adherence to civilized codes of conduct in all circumstances. The recurrent crises of mankind—and the contemporary instance is especially cogent—require for their successful management a high order of intelligence and will, as well as the moral resolution to be just. If it is reasonable for the United States, the major supplier of grain, to raise the price of wheat by 300 per cent, then is it unreasonable for the oil-producing countries to raise the price of oil by a similar factor? Cheap bread would seem to be more essential to human survival than cheap oil. The greatest contribution that the industrialized West can make to the rest of the world is to cease to regard itself as the axis on which all mankind revolves. The solipsism of the West has been one of the most intractable hindrances to the forward march of world civilization. No segment of mankind has proclaimed devotion to the great human verities with such zeal and subverted them with such ingenuity. The West must resolve to serve mankind instead of manipulating the latter ruth-

lessly for the sake of its own nationalistic objectives. Analysis of
the world situation from the standpoint of natural resources makes
it plain that economic growth, like population growth, must be
controlled. This, however, is repugnant to the West, to whom unrestrained economic growth has long been cherished as the outward and visible sign of racial superiority. The Club of Rome in
one of its studies, *Frontiers of Growth,* concluded that zero
growth in economics and world population was indispensable to
the survival of mankind. More recently, after a conference at Salz-
burg, the club declared that "economic growth should be selective
and aimed at fundamental human requirements." This slight modi-
fication of its previous attitude still conveys its conviction of the
necessity to subject economic growth to more discriminating restraints than have hitherto been contemplated by the industrialized
West. It is not simply a matter of redressing the grievances of the
so-called Third World or of reducing the gap between rich and
poor, the haves and the have-nots, the West and the rest. Much
more than this, it is an urgent task of ensuring the very survival
of mankind. Ecological balances will have to command much
greater respect than now is the case. The environment as a whole
must be regarded as a matrix of existence whose integrity is a
sacred trust confided to the utmost care of human beings. The
happiness of mankind must replace the material prosperity of
particular groups as a test of civilized achievement. Work and
leisure, education, security from want, equal protection under
just laws, freedom from torture, freedom from arbitrary imprisonment and from oppression, must all be accorded place in a universal charter of the rights of man ratified by all the countries of
the world. The outlawry of war, the discarding of nationalism, the
abandonment of racism will be proof that we no longer quantify
human progress, but on the enlightened basis of the supersover-
eignty of a plenipotent world organization we measure it by the
quality of life.

Twenty years ago, McCarthyism in the United States had driven
the large majority of professed liberals in this country into prudent
silence and craven hiding. Today, however, in the face of a consti-
tutional crisis of grave peril and complexity, attended by Mc-
Carthy-like attempts to stifle adverse criticism, people of varied

political allegiances, including the liberals, appear to be less fearful of the consequences of speaking out. If this is indeed the case, then it must be regarded as a distinct improvement in the quality of life. Further evidence of such an improvement is to be noted. For example, women have now taken their destinies into their own hands and are asserting their equality with men in every area of the national existence. This is true not only of the United States but of many other countries. Anti-Jewishness and racial prejudice against blacks and other nonwhites are being combated with unabating vigor and perhaps greater success than ever before. A Jew now occupies the post of Secretary of State of the United States, and blacks have won elections as mayors of major American cities. The first step toward a guaranteed income for all citizens of the United States has been taken in the form of legislation enacted by the Congress. Less than a decade ago this would have been denounced as "galloping socialism." The physical environment has become the object of national concern, and its pollution is no longer tolerated simply as a matter of course. If a harmless substitute can be found for heroin, and if work can be made available to all, regardless of race, on a remunerative and otherwise self-respecting basis, if this can be buttressed by decent housing and adequate education, I may yet be able to resume my former habit of walking about my beloved New York any time and any place I choose. I may even be able to go at midnight to the Apollo Theatre in Harlem, where I reside, to hear the divine Aretha Franklin sing. Freedom from muggers—what an enhancement of the quality of life that would be! Why, it would be just like old times—less than a generation ago.

GLORIA STEINEM

GLORIA STEINEM, writer and editor, born 1934 in the United States, an editor and founder of *Ms.* magazine and a convenor of the National Women's Political Caucus, is one of the best-known feminists in America. She has been a free-lance writer for publications in the United States and Europe since 1962.

Yes, there is a feminist view of what is now referred to as "the population problem." And most of the solutions practiced or proposed so far—especially those advocated by the almost totally male councils of religions, national governments, and some international organizations—seem doomed to substantial failure precisely because they ignore that view or simply don't know that it exists.

How can a powerful, decisive female presence be excluded from any representative council? Or from any group, with or without democratic pretensions, discussing a process that takes place largely in the bodies of women? If our cultures, East or West, were less patriarchal, this exclusion would seem foolish—and self-defeating to men as well. As it is, even our small understanding of racism surpasses our consciousness of sexism and the political uses of sex-as-caste. It may now seem immoral, or at least impractical, for a white, Europeanized minority of the world to make decisions for a nonwhite Third World majority, for instance, but it still seems moral, practical, and even "natural" for men of every race to make decisions for the half of the world that is women.

So natural, in fact, that many people, some women as well as men, are sure that females in power would either duplicate the male population planners' ideas exactly (though perhaps with less skill, since we have fewer "experts" among us), or express our natural differentness and purpose by disastrous, uncontrolled production of children.

But both these predictions are based on male-supremacist values: In the first, male culture is seen as the model or even the only choice; in the second, women's primary impulse and value is assumed to be breeding. The truth is that, whenever we have been allowed the ability to enforce it, women have turned out to have an effective and culturally distinct solution to "the population problem." Its essentials are as old as the women of ancient Greece and pre-Christian Rome, or even the gynocracies of prehistory, if mythology and archaeology are any guide. Its current extensions sound similar, whether the feminists advocating them are in India or France or the United States.

Of course, modern patriarchal governments and religions won't like this solution very much, for it requires free and powerful women. Population planners will mistrust it for the same reason, as well as for its vesting of decision-making power in nonexperts, men as well as women, without a centralized control. But in modern dress, the prescription would go like this:

1. *Establish reproductive freedom as a fundamental human right, never to be denied by government or by other individuals.* This means, for instance, no forced sterilization—of men or women. It also means an end to forced motherhood—no restriction, whether by husband or state, of a woman's right to abortion, contraception, and the control of her own body.

2. *Make the provision of free and safe contraception and abortion a major responsibility of government.* Easy access to information and to a full range of contraceptive methods, with research on improvements for men as well as for women, should be close in priority to the provision of food and shelter.

3. *Allow women and men equal political power, human value, and opportunity to develop as individuals.* This not only gives women—and men—choices of rewards other than parenthood, but it will eventually remove a patriarchal motive for overpopu-

lation: the need to continue procreating until there are one or many sons. Social equality also leads to equal responsibility for children, an emphasis on parenthood rather than motherhood, which increases men's stake in family planning.

4. *Advocate free choice, not impossible and oppressive conformity.* Even phrases like "population control" betray their elitist origins and tend to make the least powerful groups fearful that they will be restricted the most. "Reproductive freedom," both as phrase and reality, does not. "Two or Three Children Are Enough," for instance, has been an unsuccessful slogan, whether used by Plato or the modern planners of India. It manages simultaneously to alienate the person who wants four, five, or six children and to suggest that someone who doesn't want to be a parent at all is abnormal. "Children Are a Choice" accommodates both —and the average number of births is the same.

Of course, these conditions are goals and directions, not states that can be perfectly achieved. And they leave gray areas that will always have to be carefully thought out according to the morality and compassion of each situation. Should a government be allowed to give gifts to those who agree to be sterilized, for instance, as cruelly overpopulated India has done? If a plummeting birth rate threatens the economy, then is any state justified in offering economic incentives for maternity leave and for families with children? But perhaps the point at which incentive becomes coercion is crucial, and so is an individual's understanding of the consequences of her or his act.

But incentive and education must be the limits of control, so that a choice remains humanly possible. Our power over our own bodies—our right to reproductive freedom—must be inalienable, and governments forcibly usurping that right should face condemnation through international tribunals, media, and economic sanctions, just as they should for the practice of torture, purposeful starvation, or genocide.

Since most existing solutions to the population problem call for a stronger central authority, not increased personal freedom, this feminist-humanist solution has an uphill battle to reach acceptance. Much more than groups proposing familiar, authoritarian programs, we will have to answer the question: "But can it work?"

It can. It already has. True, there are not many situations that approximate true equality for women, but what does come across even from imperfect examples is this: Increasing women's right to control our reproductive lives is a far more reliable way of lowering the birth rate than is the increasing of literacy, industrialization, per capita income, urbanization, or other factors that experts tend to consider more important. Furthermore, this right and the ability to exercise it is not just a function of technology, literacy, and the like, as many analysts assume—a kind of luxury or frill that only rich countries can afford. It has existed, past and present, independent of them all.

In ancient Greece, for instance, the culture was basically patriarchal, but some values of the gynocratic past survived. Most important, contraception and abortion—developed and handed down among women—was legal and widely practiced. (One of the few restrictions was Aristotle's mild advice that abortion be done "before the fetus receives life," probably before the sixth month.) Athenian law gave women the right to own and control their own property and to divorce without penalty by simply repudiating the marriage. In Sparta and Crete women had even more political power and sexual freedom. The result seems to have been that, when Plato wrote in the *Laws* that women should have at least two children, he was expressing the need for sustaining, not reducing, the population. Left to themselves, women's own considerations of physical health and time to use other of their human talents had meant that they did not choose uncontrolled breeding at all.

Now, when the low birth rates of industrialized countries are analyzed, they are said to be the result of "modern" (and, by implication, male-developed) birth control technology—and the higher status of women is said, in turn, to be a function of that lowered birth rate. But mightn't the truth be just the other way around? After all, women seem to have passed down the rudiments of contraception and abortion techniques whenever they have been allowed to do so. (Witches and gypsies were among the freedom fighters in this regard, practicing medicine for women in times when it had been forbidden and forgotten. The Margaret Sangers of the world continued this tradition.) In fact, the problem has more often been the suppression of these techniques by men. So the sequence would more logically go like this: a high status for women, the power to use contraception by those most motivated to do so, and a less excessive, more realistic birth rate as a result.

In Gabon, for instance, the birth rate is one of the lowest in the world and impossible for the experts to explain through the traditional causes of technology, education, and the like. In this poor and agricultural country on the west coast of Africa, women hunt, harvest crops, run small market businesses, and make most of the important decisions, while their men concentrate on ceremony and religion. One World Health Organization expert explained the low birth rate as a possible result of male impotency or infertility brought about by the use of alcohol or drugs. Perhaps so (though low birth rates in the West are rarely attributed to alcohol, no matter how widespread its use). But the patriarchal assumptions of the same expert are more clear in his second hypothesis: Women's unnatural strength and productivity may be producing psychological impotence on the part of the men. (See Dom Moraes's *A Matter of People,* 1974.) It seems to be a rule of patriarchy that, whether it's rape or impotence, the fault originates with women.

In fact, women may be so naturally motivated to avoid excessive pregnancies that, even with limited power and few alternatives, they will do so if given any chance. In modern Japan, for instance, where the position of women is still far from equal and pronatalist cultural pressures are strong, the birth rate plummeted as soon as the government made contraception and abortion legal and available. In the communist countries of the Soviet Union and East Europe, governments often mistrust or have not perfected such newer methods as antiovulents and intrauterine devices, and even the older, mechanical methods are in short supply. This leaves abortion, usually considered the method of last resort, as the only cheap and easily available means. Still, women use it so heavily that many of these governments are now seriously concerned about a diminishing labor supply.

Even areas within the same country, with the same access to contraception, may reflect a substantial difference in its use. In South India, for instance, there are areas in which contraception is somewhat better accepted than in comparable areas to the north. The reason is said to be a higher literacy rate, and that is certainly important. But this southernmost part of the subcontinent was also the one area where matriarchy developed, and some of its forms and influences linger on. Shouldn't that factor at least be assessed?

All these examples of limited population growth as an apparent function of a raised social status for women—or even women's minimal access to choice—need more analysis, one that takes into account many more variables than has been done here. There are obviously contrary influences at work, too: women who have found most of their recognition and sense of value through childbirth and child-rearing cannot easily change that conditioning, even when the means are at hand.

But the evidence of women's desire for choice and self-control is impressive. In the cities of newly independent Africa, many women seek out contraception and abortion, even in defiance of their own male political leaders who often condemn "population control" as yet another racist plot to limit African power.

In the African interior, women may walk miles to find a family-planning worker, even though fear of their husbands' wrath —husbands who believe that wives not constantly threatened by pregnancy may be unfaithful—causes them to give false names, thereby denying themselves the safety of any medical follow-up.

In Brazil and many other countries of Catholic Latin America, where contraception other than the rhythm method is outlawed, and even that is rarely taught, desperate women regularly risk their lives in unsafe abortions. Indeed, illegal abortion is a major cause of maternal mortality throughout Latin America. Even the few women who can get medical help after such butchered abortions are so numerous that in Columbia and Chile they take about a third of all hospital beds.

In the United States women in large numbers have chosen the known risks of antiovulents and intrauterine devices (though not without pleas for more careful research and for the development of male contraceptives) and fought hard to win the right to safe,

legal abortion. Even Catholic women, who face the most opposition, use birth control in ever-growing numbers. Those who
still are less educated in contraception because of its religious
proscription may defy the church even more when they find
themselves pregnant: One New York State survey found for instance that Catholic women had abortions in greater proportion
than their population in the state.

Yet in each of these instances, women's desire for self-control
is flouted in some degree. The African leader does not consider
that the female half of his own population might rightly and
democratically have veto power over the cost and efficacy of trying to outbreed the opposition. The family planning clinics of
African and other countries, no matter how great their concern
about the world population crisis, may still assume that a husband
has a right to decide for his wife and turn back the woman no
matter how heart-rending her pleas. (It is still a common practice,
for instance, even among the most population-conscious doctors,
to assume that a wife needs her husband's permission for a sterilization procedure but not the reverse.) It's no accident that the
Catholic Church, in Latin America as elsewhere, has chosen to
ban all the means that might put the woman in control, and to
accept the rhythm method, a form of birth control that is not
only the least effective but also depends on male cooperation and
therefore keeps the woman constantly vulnerable to the male
decision. As for the United States, contraception is still only
selectively available, and abortion is virtually the only instance
in which the courts and legislatures usurp the physician's right
to decide when a life is viable. Even this limited right to abortion
remains one of the country's most controversial and polarizing
issues. (It may also be the only area in which the government
will even go against its own clear financial interest: Both state
and federal legislators continue to try, sometimes with success,
to forbid the use of government funds, whether in the form of
foreign aid or domestic welfare payments, for contraception and
abortion—even though the resulting children will probably have
to be supported by the government at infinitely greater cost.)

Why is there such fundamental resistance to the reproductive
freedom of women? Why may even the most conscientious of

population experts ignore or deny the possibility that women are indeed population's most natural and effective controllers?

The answer is deeply emotional and political, a pure issue of power. If men give up or are forced to relinquish the ability to coerce women into bearing or not bearing children, they have lost society's most fundamental political power: the control of the means of production.

That control and the cultural constructs to justify it are the definition of patriarchy, the power structure that underlies virtually every current form of government to varying degrees, whether socialist or capitalist, industrial or agricultural. From pre-Christian nomads to the postatomic, corporate multinationals, there are shared assumptions based on this power. Without it, men of every race would no longer be deemed superior at birth. Without it, men would no longer be able solely to dictate the perpetuation of themselves.

It goes very deep, this culture of control. Indeed, some anthropologists and mythologists believe that the only time of complete freedom for women was in prehistory, before paternity had been discovered, before there was any motive for such control. It was thought then that women, like trees, simply bore fruit when they were ripe, a mysterious gift that was proof of their superiority. In religious ceremonies men worshiped and imitated the act of childbirth. A variety of cultures may have prevailed, but all of them were gynocratic. The gods were female gods.

Once conception was understood, once the fact of paternity became clear, a slow but drastic change began. Men's relationship to children became more clear. Women began to be restricted in their freedom at least enough to determine paternity, a restriction from which various systems of marriage evolved. Controlled in this way women began to be viewed as possessions and to be given the less honored and desired tasks to perform, until femaleness itself became a mark of secondary or inferior status.

The reversal of the social order was slow, complete, and often cruel. "The very strictness of the patriarchal system," wrote the Swiss scholar J. J. Bachofen in *Myth, Religion and Mother Right,* "points to an earlier system that had to be combatted and suppressed."

But women became simply the perpetuators of dynastic chains of command, the anonymous producers of patronymic children. By controlling this means of production one group or tribe or nation could simply outbreed another or produce more and more children to populate and control more and more land. Wombs produced the society's basic wealth or workers and soldiers, and the control of these factories was crucial.

The only question became the degree of male power, how enlightened or benevolent it might choose to be, but never its existence. In a Rome that had once had many gods and some limits to its assumption of male superiority, for instance, Christianity and one God brought a more strict and uniform morality. Women became possessions, pure and simple, and could not belong to more than one man; there was no divorce and no reproductive controls that they might exercise without their master. The first Christian emperor made abortion illegal. By the eleventh century A.D. the liberal abortion policy suggested by Aristotle had changed to one that made even an involuntary miscarriage a crime punishable by burning. In many parts of Asia and Africa, polygamy allowed one man to accumulate more wealth in the form of children and wives. In expanding countries, even though monogamous, the unending pressure to have a baby nearly every year often produced the necessity of more than one wife. In frontier America, for instance, the average man married at least twice: When the first woman had died from exhaustion, frequently in the act of childbirth itself, a second was brought in to care for her predecessor's children and to produce more of her own. (And we must remember that contraception—especially pessaries and condoms—have been known in some form since time immemorial.)

The assumption of power over women became the one shared characteristic of male leaders: Kings and despots might exercise it more cruelly, but libertarians still didn't have female liberty in mind. Orthodox Jews and Muslims and Catholics, even such polar opposites of history as Adolf Hitler and Mahatma Gandhi, all assumed the naturalness of male control. The difference in their tactics was drastic. Hitler forcibly sterilized both Jewish women and men, while carrying on programs of forced insemination for those women considered sufficiently Aryan. Gandhi simply opposed the introduction of contraception and abortion in India as unnatural, putting an end to many such programs instituted by the Indian supporters of Margaret Sanger. But the result for most women was the same: They were not sovereign over their own bodies. Even for the women of a dominant group, this meant a constant vulnerability—whether through rape, love and desire, or nationalistic loyalty—to nine months of involuntary pregnancy (still somewhat more dangerous than a legal abortion, much less any form of contraception) and probably to many years of child care as well.

Now we are living in an era of enormous, doom-struck concern about our multiplying population. India and other populous countries have instituted national, centrally controlled programs of family planning. The women of more industrialized, less crowded countries are being socially encouraged toward small families. In some tragic instances women of groups not considered racially or socially desirable are being literally forced *not* to produce. (In the United States, for instance, there have been a few cases of poor women—a disproportionate number of them from the country's black minority—being sterilized against their will, without full knowledge of the consequences, or as an illegal precondition to receiving government aid for themselves and their families.)

The general effect of antipopulation pressure has been to accelerate women's entry into the work force outside the home and therefore to strengthen women's struggle for social equality. As one American feminist put it, "The baby factory is closed down, and the women are looking for jobs."

But we cannot be misled into believing that the current crisis will bring permanent support for our self-determination. Indeed, with the dark side of our minds, we wonder if increased population pressure might not cause us to be dealt with in an even more authoritarian way: forced sterilization after two or three children, for instance, or, if we are from a socially despised group, sterilization before any children at all. (The first alternative is already being seriously discussed in some population councils.

The second is a not altogether paranoid fear among many of the world's poor.) The major reason such measures have not been widespread so far is probably neither respect for females as equal beings nor fear of our political power. No, the real reason is more likely that men of each national or racial group simply don't want such forced limitation to happen to *their* women—to the enemy's women, okay, that might even be desirable, as the few horrific examples of forced sterilization have proved, but not to their own.

In a way women in our powerlessness have this national or tribal or ethnic group pride to thank. It has caused men to protect particular groups of females, their own personal means of production. But as long as our individual right to reproductive freedom is usurped by any government, no matter how benevolent, women will continue to be possessions manipulated according to current need. And population will continue to be a function of racism, nationalism, and the like, a function of competition among groups.

Examples are all around us. When Japan's policy of increased access to contraception and abortion caused the population to drop too far, the government restricted that freedom—without regard to the larger population crisis of the world. Its concern was more parochial: to maintain a labor force and therefore Japan's position as a top manufacturing power. East European countries have gone through the same authoritarian cycle of de-control and then control again, in spite of the protests of official women's groups. In 1974 Hungary abolished a policy of abortion on demand that had been in effect since 1956 and replaced it with a far more restrictive policy. A declining rate of population growth (with more than twice as many abortions as live births) had alarmed officials, again without regard for the world at large—or for the welfare of women. In 1973, for instance, the Committee of Bulgarian Women warned, "You have no idea what sort of social problems you will create if you try to force women to have unwanted children." But they lost. Bulgaria returned to its restric- tive abortion policy just the same.

In the Soviet Union the concern is less nationalistic than racist. The birth rate of its Central Asian republics has gone up, while that of the Slavic areas has declined. The ruling group, faced with the possibility of becoming a minority in what they regard as "their" country, is alarmed and trying to remedy the situation with centralized policy. It is probably the most sensitive political issue in the country.

This nationalist or ethnic concern is historically illogical. Quantity has rarely ruled over groups that have been able to develop individual quality. More often, it has been the other way around. As one woman family planning advisor in India tries, often vainly, to convince her people, "Better to have one leopard than ten jackals." (See Dom Moraes's *A Matter of People*.)

But nationalism and ethnicity as divisive forces are not going to disappear. The only answer is to fortify the rights of the individual—especially the female individual—against them. Women's concern for our own health and status, wherever it was set free, has been a force strong and self-interested enough to counter aggressive breeding in the past. It can do so again.

It is logical. It is the only limiting force to population growth that does not require authoritarianism. As such, it is in men's interest, in the interest of humankind, in many ways.

Without this principle of individual reproductive freedom, some powerless or less powerful men will always be in danger of extinction, too—through their own forced sterilization, as well as that of their women. Nazi Germany is not the only example: About 2 per cent of those being forcibly sterilized today in the United States are males. And with the development of chemical contraception there has come the specter of substances put in the water supply and other means of forced limitation.

With this principle of reproductive freedom, a group or government desire for increased population will have no alternative but to prolong and strengthen the lives already here—and the valuable few to be expected in the future. That desire for group power might just be an incentive for better health care, more useful lives for older people, more concern for the individual, and less callousness to deaths by wars or natural disasters. Lives in short supply might not be held so cheaply anymore. And without the one control that patriarchy requires, power structures would be forced toward democracy at last, toward an equal value for individuals regardless of sex or race.

Large groups of people don't share their power voluntarily —and those dependent on patriarchal assumptions make a very large group indeed. Sharing it with women means giving us a kind of personal and global veto power. But the population crisis is clearly a threat big enough to start some thinking. We've had gynocracy. We've tried patriarchy. The only way out of this delemma is personal freedom and humanism.

Will the population planners and the decision-makers of the world ever agree—or be forced—to see women as powerful equals? As the group whose freedom holds the answer for us all? No one knows. At the moment women can't even get into the meetings.

R. BUCKMINSTER FULLER

R. BUCKMINSTER FULLER, engineer and designer, born in 1895 in Massachusetts, is the inventor-discoverer of energetic-synergetic geometry and tensegrity structures, and his geodesic domes have been used for everything from World's Fair pavilions to backyard playhouses. Some of his books are: *Nine Chains to the Moon* (1938), *No More Secondhand God, and Other Writings* (1963), *Ideas and Integrities, A Spontaneous Autobiographical Disclosure* (1963), *Operating Manual for Spaceship Earth* (1969), *I Seem To Be a Verb* (1970), *Intuition* (1972), *Earth, Inc.* (1973).

COMPREHENSIVELY ANTICIPATORY DESIGN SCIENCE'S UNIVERSAL REQUIREMENTS FOR REALIZING OMNI-HUMANITY-ADVANTAGING LOCAL ENVIRONMENT CONTROLS THAT ARE OMNICONSIDERATE OF BOTH COSMIC EVOLUTION POTENTIALS AND TERRESTRIAL ECOLOGY INTEGRITIES*

Working assumptions:

Universe is an eternally regenerative entropically vs. syntropically pulsative system.

The stars are all entropic, giving off energies in ever more expansive and disorderly ways.

* First inscribed 1927. Revised 1930 and pubilshed in Fuller's *Shelter Magazine* in 1931. Revised 1938 and published in Fuller's first book *Nine Chains to the Moon*. This version was revised in 1949 and published with minor additions in *Architectural Design*, March 1960. Revised and published in *The Buckminster Fuller Reader*, 1970. Revised again in 1974 for this publication. Written and copyrighted 1974 by Buckminster Fuller.

Planet Earth is a syntropic center converting random energy
    receipts into orderly systems.
The vegetation through photosynthesis converts the random re-
    ceipts into orderly chemical molecules.
Hydrocarbons in turn are assembled into beautifully orderly bio-
    logical species—
The postdeath residues of which are stored ever more deeply
    within the Earth's crust as fossil energy resources.

Human mind operates terrestrially as a local cosmic monitor.
Humans mind's syntropic effectiveness
As compared to that of any other species' biological functioning
Is as the speed of light is to the speed of sound,
Which is 1 millionfold more effective.
Minus their minds human organisms function only entropically.

The design scientist's function
Is to solve problems
Only through introducing new artifacts
Into the environment
The availability of which will induce
Their spontaneous employment by humans
Thus coincidentally discontinuing and rendering obsolete
The previous problem producing human behaviors and devices.

Universe to each must be
All that is, including me
Environment in turn must be
All that is, excepting me.

Me the observer, Me the awareness.
Life is awareness.
No otherness, no awareness.
Environment is all the otherness
Of which the we-me life
Becomes progressively aware
And must progressively complement.

"All the Otherness"
Is a scenario of nonsimultaneous

And only partially overlapping sets
Of physically and metaphysically
Transforming events
Of and by which we-me
Becomes progressively and cumulatively aware
And teleologically inspired
In a succession of sleep and attention-spaced
Special case frames
Each integrating a plurality
Of differentially sensed info-concepts
Recallably stored in the senses' coordinating brain
As a consequence of whose cumulative totality stimulus
Human mind from time to time
Spontaneously intuits conscious awareness
Of the presence
Of an only mathematically stateable
Exponentially variable relationship
Always existing between certain classes
Of special case entities—
Which relationships are not identifiable with,
Or predicted by, any of the special cases describing
Dimensions, weights, chemistries, behaviors, or
Any integral constituents or qualities
Of any of the special case entities
When each is considered
Only by itself.

Such, for instance, is the principle of gravity,
Which is the variable interattractiveness of
Nonmagnetic bodies,
Which interattractiveness varies
At a second-power rate, inversely proportional
To the relative distances intervening the masses,
As those distances vary
Only at an arithmetical rate of change.

So far as all our human experience informs us
Human mind and only human mind

Is capable of discovering
These eternally operative,
Exclusively mathematical, exponential interrelationships
Existing only *between* and never *in*
Any of the components
Of complex aggregates of physical entities.

And only human mind can employ the
exponentially augmentative principles
To participate in nature's
Thus ever inexorably transforming
Evolutionary events,
Thereby to ever advantage
Both the survival and comprehension of humanity.

Number one consideration
on the part of the design scientists
is the question:
What can and May the individual human do
on behalf of other humans
that will not trespass on any humans
nor frustrate any of the regenerative integrity of the omni-ecology?
What do I have the right to do
that is going to affect other people?

When I can see, but you don't,
that something is going to fall on your head
and I jump to pull you out of the way
just as the thing crashes to the floor,
I don't think I am trespassing on you.
You might say:
"Well, I wanted to die."
And I reply:
"That has to be your option.
You didn't know that there was such an option;
I did, and had no time to tell you of it.
If you want to jump out the window that's your option."
The point is that if I see something

that is going to be fatal or damaging to you—
or on the other hand might be of great advantage to you if acted
     upon in time—
of which your experience has not made you aware,
then as a design scientist I have the cosmic responsibility
to prevent those debilitating conditions
and to realize on your behalf the advantageous potential
that could no longer have been realized
when you too learned that there had been such a potential.

There are many advantages for you
I or others can secure on your behalf
that you don't know about.

I must always be sure
I am increasing your elective freedoms.
Your life can be capitalized as the number of hours you will
     probably live.
How many of those hours are really free?
You will find that a great many hours are engaged
in the fact that you and I are a process;
there are a great many involvements because of this
and relatively few of them that we can actually direct.
So I must—as a design scientist—
increase the proportion of your total life
that is at your disposal.
I must reduce the restraints.
I must reduce the number of negative restraints
set upon you by circumstances
and increase the number of your favorable electives.
For instance,
if you would like to speak with someone at a great distance away,
if I design and install a telephone where you may be,
you now have the option to communicate
without spending much time
in getting from here to there.
You don't have to use the telephone,
but if you want, it's there.
I will make available, then,

artifacts that make it possible
for you to do what you want or need to do
and try continually to increase the magnitude of your effectiveness
while always reducing the restraints upon you and saving you
hours.

All environmental controls deal with the locally convergent events
of Universe,
which impinge upon you from outside you,
and all the events that impinge upon you from inside.
There are all kinds of magnitudes and frequencies.
The biggest ones are least frequent
and the lesser ones more frequent.
They are on a quantum-wave basis of absolute regularities.
I want to be able to provide what you want
when you want it.

I don't try to insulate;
I provide automatic means of intercepting
and shunting angularly into holding patterns
for further usability.
The intercepted energy or materials
to be valved by you into your presence
in the magnitudes and frequencies most favorable to you
while being effectively considerate
of all the ecological-sustaining contingencies.
Environment-controlling artifacts consist essentially of
structures and *machinery.*
Mechanical advantaging environmental controls
consist of lever complexes.
Gear trains and turbines are lever complexes.

There are optimally efficient structural strategies for providing
the most advantageous environmental control.
We must be able to let whatever we want *in* from *any* direction.
I must think of our controls as omnidirectional.
We must be able to get in and out in any direction with least effort.
We must be free to go in any direction we want.
We need an omnidirectional shutterable sieve

where we can increase or reduce the magnitudes of our omnidirectional environment valve openings.

Since we wish to be able to see in any direction,
and likewise to be able to obscure in any direction,
We recognize that it is difficult to make an opaque wall transparent
But it is very easy to opaque a transparent wall
by curtaining and shuttering.

Our structures must be considerate
of all human requirements
from those of the newly born child to those of the most aged.

Structures are always complex interactions
of associative and disassociative forces.
Structures are self-stabilizing, even complexes,
which complexes are always triangular.
Triangles *are* structures—
structures are triangles.
There are no self-stabilizing polygons.
Systems divide all of the universe of events
into all of universal events transpiring outside the system
and all the events occurring within the system
and the events that comprise the system
and separate the withinness
from the withoutness.
The tetrahedron is the minimum polyhedronal event complex
having insideness and outsideness.
Tetrahedra are the minimum systems of universe,
being also omnitriangulated.
Tetrahedra are then the minimum
and prime structural systems of universe.
Our design science structuring
is omnitetrahedronally formulated.
Crystalline or triple-bonded tetrahedronal complexes
provide the highest tensile coherence of systems—
while double-bonded tetrahedra
act as liquids and provide

the most powerful noncompressible compressional agents,
while single-bonded tetracomplexes
produce pneumatic aggregates
whose high compressibility
affords the most effective shock-impact diffusions
for all structures.

Teleologic Schedule

Check list of the
Universal Design Requirements
of a Scientific Local Environment Controlling Facility—
as a component function
of a new world-encompassing, service industry—
predesigned,

Rather than haphazardly evolved—
and thus avoiding
a succession of short-circuited
and overloaded burnouts
of premature and incompetent
attempts to exploit the ultimate
and most important phase of industrialization,
to wit,
the direct application of highest potential of scientific advantage
toward advancement of world living standards—
to be accomplished by inauguration of a
comprehensive anticipatory technology
scientifically informed of the
probable variables and possible randoms—
the new volition to succeed
the era of "survival"—
that is *survival-despite*—
despite preponderant submission to ignorance—
ignorance of future probabilities
and general behavior of nature—
which heretofore "survival," tolerated lethal opportunism,
wherein the progressive deteriorations bred emergencies

which called upon scientific ability
to perform last-minute miracles but
only as a curative dispensation
of morbid inertia.

The Universal Design Requirements of a Scientific Environment Controlling Facility are that it accomplish comprehensive advantage for man over all primitive factors of energetic nature. The factors may be broadly classified in four parts as follows:

I. Essentially *Random* and *Subjective* Phenomena
  A. *Exterior* variables—factors of destructive useful potential; of nakedly intolerable magnitudes, inescapably impinging
  B. *Interior* variables—factors of destructive or useful potential; of nakedly intolerable magnitudes, inescapably impinging
  C. Exterior *constants* of relative inertia forgotten through persistent obviosity and randomly re-encountered

II. Essentially *Routine* and *Subjective* Phenomena—*Internal to Dwelling—Predictably Periodic, Rhythmic*
  A. Inescapable functions of the organic processes, internal to dwelling and external to man
  B. Inescapable function of the organic processes, internal to dwelling and internal to man
  C. Interior constants of relative inertia forgotten through persistent obviosity, and regularly rediscovered, *e.g.,* furniture to be lifted with each housekeeping

III. Essentially *Random* and *Objective* Phenomena—*Internal to Dwelling—Initiative, Spontaneously Intermittent—Teleologic*
  A. Investment of earned increments of lifetime for free will regeneration of the advantage of life over *a priori* environment. *Realization* of man's potentials as an *individual*
  B. Implemented and insulated spontaneity of feedback *acceleration-continuity* of the self-amplifying individual

IV. Essentially *Incisive and Routine Objective* Phenomena—

External to Dwelling—Initiating a Sustainable Complex Continuity-Design Realization of All Humanity's Joint Potential—*Teleologic*

A. Investment of earned increments of technical advantage of the science-industry complex in *design realization* of the *complex dwelling facility service*

B. Implementation and insulation of synergetic feedback of higher order accruing to spontaneous group realizations of newly evolving potential

Note: That I and II above are *subjective* and *defensive* and *exclusive* and that III and IV are *objective* and *offensive* and *inclusive*.

Note: That I defines the outer ramparts and II the inner defenses while III represents the inner initiative-taking and IV the full-grown outer offensive—conquest—contact.

Note: That this arrangement is geometrically telegraphic, *i.e.*, omnidirectionally convergent-divergent—propogative.

Expanded Expression of Four Broad Classifications of Universal Design Requirements for a Dwelling Facility. Original topic of broad classification not repeated and referred to only by number.

I. A. *Structural, Mechanical, or Chemical Interception and Control of Externally Impinging Factors*, either by *Rejection, Reflection, Deflection*

Through shunting, channeling, impounding, modulating, and/or retiming of volumetric flows of variable external factors of nakedly intolerable magnitudes

1. Immunization against aperiodic, energetic interferences—externally impinging at intolerable magnitudes and heretofore classified as *"cataclysmic"*—because exceeding the practical stress abilities of as yet available technology—*However* (new era essence): Since accomplishment of higher physiochemical stress abilities in, for instance, supersonic flight and snorkel submarine, the stress abilities of technology in general now far exceed the predictable stresses of the hitherto cataclysmic structural inter-

ferences—the 180 m.p.h. velocity of Antarctic hurricanes or Pacific typhoons is now a relatively minor aeronautical velocity-of-interaction of designed structures. External impingements are classified in the order of frequency of probable occurrence and *relative magnitudes*.

a. *"Cataclysmic"* *

Improbably annual, possibly "never," and *least frequent*, but of *highest stress when occurring*

(1) earthquake   (8) bombardment
(2) tornado   (9) forest fire
(3) hurricane   (10) tidal wave
(4) typhoon   (11) plague
(5) avalanche   (12) radio activity
(6) landslide   (13) lethal gases
(7) volcanic   (14) B.W. (bacteriological
    eruption   warfare)

* We do not include Astro-Novae as no human control capabilities of such phenomena are at present conceivable.

b. *"Dangerous"*

Probably annual, of borderline "disaster" magnitudes

(1) gale
(2) local fire
(3) flood
(4) pestilence
(5) lightning
(6) selfishness (self-preoccupation pursued until self loses its way and self-generates fear and spontaneous random surging, *i.e.,* panic, the plural of which is mob outburst in unpremeditated wave synchronizations of the individually random components)

(a) vandals   (e) fanaticism
(b) marauders   (f) commercialism
(c) meddlers   (g) materialism
(d) politics

c. *"Inclement"*
Of high seasonal frequency and of low orders of
stress or of naked intolerability

(1)	fumes	(8)	heat
(2)	hail	(9)	cold
(3)	rain	(10)	epidemic
(4)	snow	(11)	vermin
(5)	dust	(12)	insects
(6)	electrolysis	(13)	fungi
(7)	oxidation	(14)	minor random missiles

2. *Rejection,* or *deflection* for delayed or immediate use as
   a. energy, admitted into direct work as, for instance, radiation or electronic reaction, or indirectly into work as, for instance, impounded wind (aeronautical) or water (hydraulic) power
      (1) piped—for direct use
      (2) wired—for direct use
      (3) valved—for direct or delayed use
      (4) stored—in cistern, tank, or battery for delayed use
      (5) stored—in thermal bank or compost bins, etc.

I. B. *Dynamic Control of Internally Impinging Factors*
  1. Interception of and dispellment of the momentum trends of ignorance—through incorporation of experience informing natural design replacements, realized in physical principles
  2. Interception and neutralization of bacteria by isolation of—or by direct elimination
  3. Elimination of physical fatigue
    a. human robotism and drudgery by provision of adequate mechanics of technical advantage
  4. Elimination of psychological fatigue (repression) by
    a. removal of accident hazard through mechanical adequacy (don't proofing)
    b. removal of arbitrary cellular limitations to permit free interaction of living functions

      c. provision for selective privacy by push-button sound, sight, and smell barriers surrounding any interior space

    5. The elimination of emotional fatigue

      a. factors stimulating nerve reactions to be automatically controlled in "neutral" until voluntarily brought into play by the occupant through:

    6. Provision of mechanics for wide range in selection of means and degrees of sensible realization of the prosaic or harmonic phenomena

      a. visual

      b. aural

      c. tactile

      d. olfactoral, *i.e.,* taste and smell

I. C. *Control by Anticipatory Design over Exterior Constants of Inertia Forgotten Through Persistent Obviosity and Only Randomly Re-encountered*

    1. Constants of environment, *i.e.,* the mud forgotten between rains, odorous winds from remote sources, snowdrifting

    2. Control devices installed for seasonal duration only requiring inordinate time investments

    3. Chemical accumulations (oxides, sludges, fumes)

    4. Biological accumulations

      a. vegetation, composts, weed

      b. insect, animal residues, nestings, general growth changes

    5. Surprise emergencies of environmental complex unique to locality, *i.e.,* possible water, oil, gas springs and seepage

II. A. *Provision* for (Unselfconscious) (Spontaneous) *Mechanical Performance of Inevitable Organic Routines* of the Dwelling and Its Occupants with Minimum of Invested Attention or Effort

    1. Fueling of

      a. house

      b. occupant (eating) (metabolism)

2. Realignment of house or occupants in sleep by allowed muscular, nerve and cellular realignment accomplished by designed elimination of known restrictive factors
3. Refusing of house or occupants
    a. internal, *i.e.,* intestinal, etc.
    b. external, *i.e.,* bathing or pore cleansing
    c. mental, *i.e.,* elimination by empirical dynamics
    d. circulatory: external—atmospheric control; internal—as respiratory functions

II. B. Control by Anticipatory Design over Interior Constants of Relative Inertia Forgotten by Fatigue Closure of Feedback Sensibilities and Routinely Re-encountered (Such as Heavy Furniture to be Moved about Daily for Cleanliness Operations, Storages to be Overhauled to Obtain the Tentatively Retained Devices of Possible or Infrequent Use)
1. By *provision* of adequate occupational-speciality storage means
2. By home employment of travel equipment
3. By dimensional reduction (*e.g.,* of collections of large data to microfilm)

III. A. Provision of Ready Mechanical Means, Complementing or Implementing All Development Requirements of the Individual's Potential Growth Phenomena—Allowing the Facile, Scientifically Efficient, No-Energy-or-Time-Loss Spontaneous Development of Self-Disciplined Education by Means of
1. *Conning, i.e.,* selectively stimulated awareness of the momentary interactions of universal progressions accomplished by means of facile reference to vital data on
    a. history
    b. news
    c. forecasts
       calls for a conning facility combining book and periodical library, radio, television facilities, systematically arranged incoming reports on

    (1) current supply and demand conditions

    (2) current dynamic conditions—weather—earthquakes—latest scientific research findings

    (3) social dynamics-surfacing of commonweal problems of comprehensive readjustment to new potentials and concomitant obsolescence factors

    (4) latest technical reference in

        (a) texts

        (b) movie documentation

        (c) television university (soon evolving to increasing importance and reliability as the Autonomous Dwelling Facility becomes widely available)

2. *Adequate mechanics of personal articulation* (prosaic or harmonic) for the spontaneous investment of the imagination-gestating intellectual-increments of experience—(teleology) which trend ever to satisfy the evolving needs—prosaic or harmonic—routine or plus. This category of *original articulations* also includes the necessity or crystallization of universal progress

a. instruments and tools of communication

    (1) direct

    (2) indirect

    (3) aural

    (4) visual

    (5) tactile

        (a) music, writing, drawing, measuring instruments

        (b) wood, metal, and chemical working tools

        (c) typewriter

        (d) wire-tape-and-disc all-purpose recorder-radio-phonograph

        (e) easel

(f) photographic equipment—taking, developing, printing, projection

3. *Recreation*—appropriate equipment to full physical development

4. *Procreation*

III. B. Insulation, or Isolation, of the Instrumented Initiatives

III. C. Means of Displaying, Exposing, Experimenting, and Measuring for Progressive Improvement of "Target" or "Trend to Target" or "Trend Following" Assumptions-of-Realization-Initiative-and-Articulation, *i.e.,* "Vital navigation" or "teleology," *i.e., personal* and *social* and *cosmic* feedback control. The comprehensive "frame"—relative to which *display, exposure, experiments, measurement,* and *progressive dynamic trend assumptions* may be referenced is FOURFOLD.

A. "Objective Aspect"	B. "Subjective Aspect"	C. "Consolidate Intellectual Advantage, or '*Aids*'"
1. *Subvisible* Microcosmic	nuclear particles atoms molecules cells, genes	atomic charts, periodic, etc. spectographic charts molecular models biological slides
2. *Geovisible* Geographical (*Visible, near*) Earth	crystallographic biologic subsurface surface envelope	globes, maps, geological stratification maps world and local physiological data spectrum charts
3. *Astrovisible* Macrocosmic (Visible, remote)	comets asteroids planets stars nebula	star globes star charts
4. *Supravisible* Comprehensive Omnipermeative	abstracted principles gravity radiation number sets group behavior phenomena probability transformations independent of dimensions infinity	energetic geometry devices (vectorial, formative, transformative, number)

IV. Realization by Design

A priori Design Realization Assumptions

Asking not
why, whither, nor whence
human-life?
But assuming
the accumulated experience evidences
that biological phenomena
in general
and human life
in particular
function in universe
as the syntropic (*i.e.,* anti-entropic)—
the antirandom—the simple and complex *organic*—
the systematically convergent phases
of the comprehensive cycling
of omni-energy transformations
and in consequence that *industrialization*
constitutes the comprehensive—transformative expansion
of the human-life function in universe—
and therefore the realization that human-life's extension
into cosmic measurement-taking ability
already billionsfold
the sensory limits of integral faculties and
presages a further successful amplification
of the human-life function in universe
and therefore
that the regenerative ability of intellect
in extension, acceleration, and expansion
of the extracorporeal cosmic-functioning-stature
of the human-life in universe
is realizable
in comprehensive design initiative
amplifying relayed through industrialization
and therefore the function of comprehensive design
is most naturally and effectively
preoccupied with omni-abetment

of the realization in full
of the potentials of the "individual" complex—
an organic nebula
identified superficially as human—
human potential includes
regeneratively improving potentials
of sequential derivative orders
of increasing advantage of the organic
over the (random-entropic) chaos growths,
"Individual" man's highest potential
may be realized in terms of full interaction
of all men's potentials—
ergo man's universal function trends
to amplify first the full potential of the individual—
but inherently multiplicative human-life.
Therefore
on first priority
in design consideration
is the full realization
of individual potential
in order to reach the second derivative—
full realization for all individuals.
Keys to design realization
are the anthropological measurements,
of the limiting factors
of corporeal man,
beyond which extracorporeal articulation
of the integral faculties
may be accomplished by extension in principle
through atomic-complex trains,
and energetic transformations
to cosmic stature advantage.
Universal Conditions of Design Realization
commence with the static and dynamic
dimensions of humans
and their basic behavior involvements
of which there exists a wealth of data.

	Typical	Limited to Slow Change Integrally	Subject to Accelerating Change Latest Extracorporeal
How high can they grow?		8 ft.	1,200 ft.
How high can they jump?		6 ft.	70,000 ft.
How high can they reach?		9 ft.	750,000 ft.
How far can they see?		100 million mi.	$186,000 \times 60 \times 60 \times 24 \times 365 \times 1$ billion mi.
How far can they hear?		100 mi.	1 billion mi.
How far can they smell?		1 mi.	etc.
How long can they live?		etc.	etc.
Etc., etc., etc.			

All above figures schematic only—for accurate figures see world almanacs.

Critical Path to Ultimate:

IV. *Realization*

The whole program of realization is to be considered in the following order, which breaks into two primary categories or phases: (1) the initial work to be undertaken by the individual prior to his engagement of the aid of associates and (2) original and initial work to be undertaken by the first group of associates. These two phases may be subdivided as follows:

IV. A. Research and Development by Initiating Individual (Prior to Inauguration of Design Action and Development Action Involving Full-time Employment of Others). Inauguration of a General Work Pattern as a Natural Pattern Coinciding with Best Scientific Procedure, to wit:

Preliminary

Initiation of diary and notebook

Initiation of photographic documentation

Initiation of tactical conferences

1. Comprehensive library study of accrued arts *
   a. past
   b. contemporary

* Pertinent arts to be studied by the initiating individual include:

Anthropological data

Energetic geometry, the philosophy of measuration

PHASE I, INDIVIDUAL

and transformation, relative size
Theory of structural exploration
Theory of mechanical exploration
Theory of chemical exploration
Energy as structure
Dwelling process as an "energy exchange"
Dwelling process as an "energy balance sheet"
Theory of structural complex
Theory of service complex
Theory of process complex
Theory of structural and mechanical logistics
Theory of complex resolution
Tensioning by crystalline, pneumatic, hydraulic, magnetic means
Compressioning by crystalline, pneumatic, hydraulic, magnetic means

2. Listing therefrom of authorities available for further information
   a. local, personal contact
   b. remote correspondence
3. Pursuant to information thus gained, calling at suggested local laboratories
   a. university
   b. industry
   c. setting up of informative tests for firsthand knowledge in own laboratory
Theory of design
4. First phase of design assumption
   a. consideration of novel complex interaction unique to project
   b. preferred apparatus from competitive field
   c. design of appropriate flowsheets
5. Flowsheets submitted to
   a. those competitive specialists who have proved helpful in steps b. and c.
   b. industrial producers of similar equipment and assemblies

c. make informative tests for closure of gaps supporting assumed theory

6. Submit specifications and drawings of general assembly and unique component parts for informative bids by manufacturers

   a. second redesign of flowsheet based on available and suggested apparatus, price information, etc.

7. Prepare report consisting of diary of above supported by photographic documentation and collected literature—with trial balance conclusions in indicated economic advantage (which, if positive, will inaugurate Phase II).

IV. B. Design and Development Undertaking—Involving Plural Authorship Phase and Specialization of Full-time Associates, Consideration of Relationship of Prototype to Industrial Complex by Constant Review of Principles of Solution Initially Selected as Appropriate to Assumptions, Adoption of Assumptions for Realization in Design of Pertinent Principles and Latest Technology Afforded

1. Comprehensive survey of whole sequence of operations from original undertaking to consumer synchronization

   Realization strategy #1 by individual (Phase 1)
   Realization strategy #2 by associates (Phase II)

   a. Physical tests in principle of the design assumptions' unique inclusions not evidenced in available data

   b. General assembly drawings (schematic) providing primary assembly drawing schedule reference

   c. General assembly assumption, small scale models and mock-up full size

   d. Primary assembly, subassembly, and parts calculations (stress)

   e. Trial balance of probable parts weights and direct manufacturing costs (approximately three times material costs; includes labor, supervision,

PHASE II, COLLECTIVE

and inspection) and forecast of over-all cost magnitudes, and curve plotting—at various rates of production ratioed to direct costs per part and "all other costs"—*i.e., "overhead," tool and plant "amortization,"* "contingencies," "profit"

f. "Freezing" of general assembly and its reference drawing

g. Drawing for first full-size production prototype commences in general assembly, primary assembly, subassembly, and parts

h. Budget of calculating and drawing time is set with tactical deadlines for each

i. Parts drawing and full-size lofting and offset patterns

j. Prototype parts production on "soft tools" commences

k. Subassembly and primary assemblies replace "mock-up" parts

l. Physical tests of parts and subassemblies with "obvious" corrections and "necessary" replacements (not "improvements" or "desirables," which must be deferred until second prototype is undertaken after all-comprehensive physical tests have been applied)

m. Photography of all parts and assemblies

n. Full assembly completed and inspected—cost appraised with estimates of possible "improvement" savings to be effected

o. Static load tests

p. Operation tests

q. Assembly and disassembly tests

r. Photography of all phases

s. Packaging and shipping tests

t. Estimates of savings to be effected by special powered field tools

u. Opinion testing

v. *Final* production *"clean-up" prototype* placed in

formal calculation and drawing with engineering budgeted deadlines

w. Parts cost scheduled by class "A" tools and time

x. Production tool layout fixed

y. Production tools ordered

z. Production dates set

a^1 Lofting and offsets produced of full-size-test "masters" and templates

b^1 Fabrication of special jigs and fixtures

c^1 Production materials ordered

d^1 Production tool-jig-fixture tune-up

e^1 Parts and assembly testing

f^1 Field operation scheduling

g^1 Field tools ordered

h^1 Distribution strategy in terms of initial logic limitations

i^1 Field tests with special tools

j^1 Field tools ordered or placed in special design and fabrication

k^1 Test target area selected for first production

l^1 Production commences

m^1 First field assemblies with power tools

n^1 Maintenance service instituted and complaints
  (1) alleviated
  (2) analyzed
  (3) change orders of parts instituted

o^1 Plans for "new" yearly model improvement run through all or previous steps—for original production

p^1 Cycle repeated

2. Production and distribution velocity assumptions

3. Plotting the assumed progressive mass-production curbs to determine basic velocities of new industry

4. Consideration of manufacturer's basic production forms—relative to proposed design components for determination of minimum steps, minimum tools, and minimum waste in realization

5. Establishment of priority hierarchies of effort

6. Time-and-energy-and-cost-budgeting
7. Assumption of industry responsibility for field practices, not only in mechanical and structural, but in economic design
10. Designing for specific longevity of design appropriate to anticipated cycles of progressive obsolescence and replacement ability as ascertained from comprehensive economic trend curves
11. Designing with "view to efficient screening of component chemicals for recirculated employment in later designs"
12. Maxima and minima *stated and realized* performance requirements per unit of invested energy and experience and capital advantage of tools and structures employed and devised
13. Logistics assumptions, compacted shipping considerations as original design requirement in
    (a) nesting
    (b) packaging
    (c) compounded package weight
    (d) relationship to carriers of all types
    (e) field delivery
    (f) field assembly
    (g) field service and replacement
14. Consideration of tool techniques
15. Consideration of materials' availability
    (a) at time of design
    (b) in terms of world economic trends
    (c) in terms of world potential
16. Consideration of materials ratio per total design
17. Elimination of special operator technique forming
18. Elimination of novel special soft-tool designing
19. Numbers of
    (a) types
    (b) repeat parts
    (c) subassemblies
    (d) primary assemblies
20. Numbers of forming operations

21. Number of manufacturing tools by types
22. Schedule of forming operations included on parts drawings
23. Decimal fraction man-hours per operation
24. Designed-in over-all one-man-ability at every stage of operation
25. Schedule of design routines and disciplines
26. Establish a "parts" inventory of "active" and "obsolete" drawings—from beginning
27. Establish a "parts" budget of "required" designs of "parts" for assemblies and major assembly and general assembly and molds
28. Drawing dimension standards
29. Establish a numbering system of controlled parts
30. Establish purchasing techniques, jig and fixture, lofting techniques.

IV. C. Public Relations

To run concurrently with all phases of IV. B:

1. Education of public

   Rule I: Never show half-finished work

   a. General magnitude of product, production, distribution. But no particulars that will compromise latitude of scientific design and production philosophy of IV. B.
   b. Publicize the "facts," *i.e.,* the number of steps before "consumer realization"
   c. Understate all advantage
   d. Never seek publicity
   e. Have prepared releases for publisher requests when "facts" ripe

GÜNTER GRASS *

An Interview

GÜNTER GRASS, novelist and playwright, born in 1927 in Danzig, then in Poland, is now a citizen of the Federal Republic of Germany. His most recent book, *Aus dem Tagebuch einer Schnecke* (*From the Diary of a Snail*, 1972) brilliantly illustrates the author's highly idiosyncratic and multilayered use of language to express his amalgam of political and literary concerns. His best-known novels are: *Die Blechtrommel* (*The Tin Drum*, 1959), *Katz und Maus* (*Cat and Mouse*, 1966), *Hundejare* (*Dog Years*, 1963), *Örtlich betäubt* (*Local Anesthetic*, 1969).

MORAES: When you were a child, how did you see the human condition? How did you see the way in which people lived, not only physically but inside themselves as well?

GRASS: When I was a child, I lived in a special situation. I grew up in Danzig. The dominant half of my family was German, but on mother's side it was Kashubian, a Slavic race that lives to the south of Danzig. So, as a child I experienced German-Polish conflicts in the very heart of the family, and at the same time I was stamped with the ideals of a German education that led naturally into National Socialism; an education that lived by high ideals, that saw more in the end than the means, that considered the individual unimportant, the community as the greater goal— at that time it was the people's community of National Socialism. In my childhood there was no alternative, because apart from this party line nothing penetrated—with the exception of a few teachers who allowed themselves a word of criticism in lessons when

* Translated by Jenny Lines

I was thirteen, fourteen, maybe fifteen. But these teachers were not popular. Their opposition role forced them to be skeptical, cynical, or ironic, the kind of behavior that always appears negative to idealistic attitudes, and so we did not heed their warnings. It was in my last school that a teacher was denounced by his pupils and ended up in a concentration camp. These were things that I only grasped later, after the war. At the age of fifteen I was an auxiliary in the Luftwaffe, in uniform, at sixteen I became a soldier, at seventeen I was taken prisoner. At eighteen, after the end of the war—one year after it—I was released. And so an idealistic world finally collapsed.

The lesson I drew from all this is to mistrust every ideological statement, every statement that claims its truth as *the* truth or tries to convince people that its interpretation of reality is *the* interpretation of reality, and in contrast to German history and German development all this actually gave me more of a pragmatic attitude to politics and society. And, of course, it also later determined my political views so that it was only possible for me as a writer, if I was to be involved at all in political work, to work with the Social Democrats who, since the Godesberg Program, since 1959, had thrown overboard the last ideological white elephants of the nineteenth and twentieth centuries and were prepared to allow a variety of interpretations of reality, even within the party.

I have answered your question in a roundabout way because it reminded me of conflicts in my youth, which in turn remind me strongly of conflicts that today's generation is going through again. They make high idealistic statements, this time in mostly Marxist, or even Stalinist, terms, where the goal is everything and man is unimportant, with a lot of promises of freedom and liberty. As we can see, if we're prepared to learn from history, the results and side effects can be terrible. It's a sorry tale.

If we start from the principle that all ideologies—and I'm including religion here, let's take Christianity since we're in Europe —with their promises of happiness and their pledges of liberation, have in the end only created new forms of oppression, then we must conclude that in spite of enlightenment, technical progress, and our belief in education, nothing remains for us but to recognize that man is a misconstruction, although a misconstruction of genius. He is well equipped, he has brains, he has talent, and all these can and should be shaped and developed by education. But there is plenty of proof that the practice of terrorism is on the increase, in that intelligent people are practicing it and thereby making it more perfect. And of course that calls into fundamental question some of the hopes and expectations of the European Enlightenment, which I still share.

In addition to all this, I believe that if we are looking for a guiding principle—and that must be the point of this conversation —we would have to start by recognizing that all our inherited ideologies have failed, because reality conflicts with their claim to absolute truth, and that this basic recognition is really essential for people's awareness of each other before the foreseeable catastrophes come upon us—catastrophes for which none of the ideologies has an answer. I even fear the attempt that has often been made to develop the superman, the Christian, the socialist; all these aims demand too much of the individual, make him small and insignificant, and result in the rule of terror. I believe much more that we must accept this misconstruction as something we have to live with; we must develop—or perhaps I should say suggest—a style of living that will make allowances for the misconstruction, which has after all something magnificent about it, so that man doesn't have to live under the pressure of having too many demands made on him, and so that he can, even in his broken state, find himself.

It is quite possible that with the help of scientific progress we will succeed in thirty years, or it may take as long as a hundred, in performing genetic operations, in other words in subduing the inborn and acquired aggressive urges in man. But that too will be only a new form of terror, since the decision to use such means presupposes an elite that will continue as the ruling class. Such things have often been described in science fiction novels, which all have something fanciful about them, but they are certainly conceivable. But they're not alternatives to our existence, however difficult it may be.

MORAES: Do you think the kind of ruling class we have had should change, in the sense that in the Middle Ages scientists, for example, were to some extent persecuted by the church for their views, which was very deplorable, but at the same time shows that the ruling class was taking *some* notice of the scientists, whereas nowadays in the Western world the scientists are more or less ignored. They predicted the energy crisis, they predicted the population crisis many years ago, and they were completely ignored by the governments. Now, do you think a new kind of government into which scientists were brought would be a more successful type of government?

GRASS: I don't believe that scientists are better people. Whether it was in the Middle Ages, or Galileo in the Renaissance, or the atomic physicists in our time, they've made their discoveries and had their pleasure in discovery, but they didn't exactly strain their intelligence when it came to calculating the consequences of their discoveries. They placed these discoveries at the disposal of whoever was in power at the time. Scientists in both great power areas in our world still do that today. Of course, there are other scientists who, as you so rightly say, predicted the coming of certain crises—the energy crisis, the population explosion—like the Club of Rome and other organizations, but in fact neither scientists nor politicians are prepared to see the consequences, especially since some of the people working in the Club of Rome were not only scientists but politicians, too. Such a tightly constructed world is evidently so interdependent that governments of industrialized nations, for example here in Europe, sail straight into these catastrophes, with their eyes open, with analyses in their hands, with every bit of knowledge they can accumulate; they know what they're doing, they even say so, behind their hands in an undertone, and yet we still have traditional national conflicts like that between England and France or the one between China and the Soviet Union, which has nothing to do with communism but goes back to the time of the Mongols. These traditional structures are stronger, more dominant, and more penetrating than the power of reason, which remains an abstraction.

I was in New York when Willy Brandt gave his speech [at the United Nations] a few weeks after the military coup in Chile, and Brandt said, in so many words, that of course you can use force of arms to change something that does not fit into a power scheme. You *can* do it that way, but you don't have to. He was referring to the fact that there in an explosively charged continent, in South America, an example had begun to develop of how social conflicts can be resolved without sacrificing the substance of democracy. If this example had succeeded, it would have been useful, not only to the people living in South America but also to those who are responsible for this misery, the people in industrialized nations. And yet it was destroyed through shortsighted interests, not just copper interests—even the Soviet Union saw no reason to intervene because to their shortsighted interests the development of democratic socialism was equally inconvenient. It was suppressed in Czechoslovakia, and if something like that had succeeded in Chile it would have been proof that socialism can develop democratically, too. I believe that to add to our experience of repeated periods of terror, we have here a clear example of how intelligence, diligent research, scientific results, and insight into man's development are of no use whatsoever if the so-called vital interests are affected, whether those of capitalism or the supremacy of the Soviet Union within its own bloc.

MORAES: Which of the old values, the old religious values, the old traditions of behavior do you feel are valid today? Do you feel none of them are valid and that we should evolve a completely new system of values and of thinking?

GRASS: One of the oldest values, for me—and I am too much of a European now to be able to leave Europe out of it—is the development of democracy in Greece and also to a certain extent among other groups in very early Europe. It was thrown overboard in the Middle Ages but rose to the surface again and again. In more recent times, during the period of the European Enlightenment, it was the feeling for social justice, one of the mainsprings of socialism. But it was not the only discovery of the European Enlightenment; the concept of toleration has never been more precisely formulated than in Voltaire's time. And I still consider these concepts and practical models of democratic behavior—toleration, the protection of minorities, and the social goals of a democracy (where again toleration is an essential element)—to be a possibility for society. Such concepts are very difficult to put into practice, because this path has no final goals; it preaches no teachings of salvation, no deliverance of mankind. It does not strive for *one* justice but tries rather to achieve *more* justice, simply *more* justice. A path like this, which is not simply political, creates—and I think this is good—no great enthusiasm; it requires sober reason. Those are the values to which I will always be committed, although I know all too well how endangered they are and how quickly they are discarded as soon as an ideology—called one thing today, another tomorrow—takes an unconditional stand.

MORAES: So far you have been talking mainly about the development of ideologies and abstraction by and large, but we surely ought to be able to look at the physical welfare of the people in the world now with the population crisis, the food shortage. They say that next year the world supply of wheat, at one point in June, will come down to three weeks' world supply; the population is going to double by the year 2000. With all this going on, do you feel that there is any possibility of people extending their mental fields before being able to overcome their physical disadvantages, and do you think that there is a possibility that these physical hurdles will be cleared?

GRASS: The individual, in his small world, hears about it but pushes the thought away, or he feels compassion and tries, as a Christian or a socialist, to make his contribution, large or small. Those are all drops in the ocean. As we can see today, they are even dangerous, because they pretty the problem up. If you ask me what's to be done, I can really only roughly suggest a utopia, the kind of development that I know cannot be realized: that is to say, a world government and tax, a worldwide tax measured to the gross national product, which would of course primarily affect all the industrialized nations. The distribution of aid to developing countries should be controlled centrally, for example by the United Nations, so that it would be removed from the national influence, the ideological influence of the blocs. But of course it's almost laughable to put forward this idea because, as you, coming from the United Nations, know quite well, neither the industrialized countries and the two big power blocs, nor the developing countries, would consent to a world government set above them to distribute these resources. I think that both sides would resist it because a good part of the developing states are going through a phase today that I would call national, even nationalistic. It would be arrogant on the part of the Europeans to say: Please don't make the same mistakes we made in the nineteenth and twentieth centuries. I've heard the answer often enough: That's our problem; it's our right to make our own mistakes, even if they are duplications of European mistakes. These irrationalities are, of course, in direct opposition to the views I hold. But I can't think of any other way than to initiate worldwide aid with the economic and financial resources that are, after all, concentrated in the industrialized nations and the two bloc systems. That's my answer.

MORAES: Is this again to do with your view of the fallibility of human nature, the fact that man is a misconstruction? Is it because of human nature that you think this is likely not to happen or is it because of national interests? Or simply because men are like they are?

GRASS: Man's mind wears boots a size too big for his body—at least the one he has now. We can see it in individual people. Take a painter like Picasso, who with his vision of the world showed us new perspectives in his paintings; in his private life he would not recognize his own children and behaved like a petit bourgeois. Here you have a streak going right through the middle of a man of genius. That's only one example, a very common one, but it is an illustration of human greatness and human mediocrity. And I can only repeat, the one thing that can help is if we erase all ideals concerning the image of man, cancel them out completely, and accept the broken image as it is and as something that we ourselves have a stake in. We can only aim at what is possible, something that doesn't demand too much of us. Excessive demands on the individual, as on a group, simply fail, and failure in its turn stores up aggressions, because in the competition for a larger image no one will admit to failure. Just how these aggressions then explode in history we know all too well. That's reflected right back into family cells and the individual, for that matter, with the urge for self-destruction and the desire for annihilation, which in Germany is especially strongly marked.

MORAES: Everything you write is basically about the human condition, but, as a writer, do you feel that writers should be committed to solving particular problems about the human condition, or should they pursue these through their own work in their own individual way and not propound solutions?

GRASS: I have often been asked that question, but I don't really understand it. Every writer and every artist is necessarily a product of his times, and—to go back to the writer—a product of his language. This language is spoken in a country and in the context of a history, and so he's involved in a number of national, regional, historical, and, therefore, social problems. I have sometimes wondered where I would have got to in the literary or artistic world with my talents as a writer and designer if I had been born in another country, in Sweden, say. I would have had to take over a quite different set of difficulties. Whereas in my case, with my very artistic, very playful, and often overplayful talent, my duty became clear all at once, at the point when I approached the reality of seeing myself in relation to a German past. I mean the past of this century, which after 1945 had become inaccessible and was already being seen as ideological or demoniacal, in that National Socialism and Hitler were presented as a natural phenomenon, as divine Providence or as a crime of Satan. And yet it all happened in broad daylight and could have been foreseen and even looked up in the history books before it happened. It took place within society, and certain classes, the petite bourgeoisie, the big industrialists, the church, all had a share in Fascism, made it possible, or tolerated it.

I stood face to face with this theme, and I couldn't have avoided it even if I'd wanted to. If I had only used my talent to play with form—one of the things I really like doing—I would soon have been played out. The freedom to do it simply didn't exist. Whenever I started to play I very soon came across superimposed layers that had to be peeled off, one after the other. That's the kind of resistance against which I developed and without which I wouldn't be conceivable. And perhaps there's something else to it, too, something especially German. But things must have been much the same for other writers of my generation in other countries. Anyone who went through the war knows that he is lucky to be alive, and I never forget in my writing, nor in the subsequent successes, that there were certainly a great number of talents, perhaps greater than mine, that today lie buried under a mound of earth in Africa, in the polar sea, or the tundra. War is counterselective, if it is, in fact, selective at all.

These are the problems that challenge this profession, which still, thank God, has and should always hold onto the potential for play. These are the problems that make it complex and contradictory. It is from this contradiction, the formal, artistic play instinct on the one hand and on the other the demands from outside, the demands of social and other realities, that what we generally and broadly call art is or can be generated.

MORAES: Do you feel that the talents of a writer should be devoted to social questions, or would his talent then fail?

GRASS: That is difficult to answer. The writer has his own talent, and those of the scientist, journalist, politician, or priest cannot replace it. He can, for example, tell a story, a quality that has no competition but is very much there. The need people feel to tell a story is elementary, the need to have a story told is also elementary. The writer must make the most of this talent; he must not put whatever the world brings him by way of demands and problems into disciplined systems. The political leader or scientific treatise may be more effective at the time, but the writer must stick to his talent, to his potential, and that means to present, in a narrative form, the contradictions of reality. During the ten years since I became politically active, I have always made a distinction between what I do professionally as a writer, narrator, and poet, and the demands that everyday political life make on me, for example, election speeches and personal daily engagements. I've made the distinction in the sense that I have carried out the political work primarily as a citizen who happens to be a writer by profession. But what I've tried to do, someone in a different job could also have done as a citizen; after all, many others worked with me. The thing I am against is, to quote Trotsky, making literature the handmaiden of the Revolution. Then it becomes literature of confirmation or what is broadly termed agitprop literature. It does not question the writer or the reader but simply confirms the current or future party line. It is of an apologetic nature, and that contradicts its very being. Art questions, art can undermine; in the midst of a world and a reality that puts on a positive face, art can signify a fantastically resounding "No." But wherever it simply confirms, it becomes just an ornament or decoration.

MORAES: You are a Renaissance man in a way: You are a sculptor, you do etchings, you write poetry, write novels, you are engaged in politics and so forth.

GRASS: And I am a good cook!

MORAES: Oh, you are? Well, apart from all this, do you think if people occupied themselves with more things they would be happier? Do you think that because a man starts to work as a clerk in an office and remains a clerk all his life that is a very bad thing for him? Do you think he should diversify his activities?

GRASS: Yes, that's an important dream and desire, and I am conscious of the fact that, for all the difficulties of my profession —especially in the initial stages when there were economic difficulties too—I am a privileged person. I have far greater opportunities to realize myself, to live a full and productive life, than most people, and yet I believe that the potential invested in the artist can also be found in the individual. The individual, however, is not given the opportunities—and he himself does not create the opportunities—to live a diverse life, to provide an outlet for his hidden reality, which lies in his fantasy and in his imagination. On the contrary, he sets up moral laws for himself, of a puritan kind, which allow him without reason to become sober and lock him out of these areas of reality. I really do believe that the ready aggression in man would be reduced—it wouldn't disappear, but it would be reduced—and humanized if there were more playgrounds, not just for children but for adults, too. Of course, they would look different from children's playgrounds, but they would include the whole creative area, the opportunity to enjoy life to the full with all your fears, desires, and needs, however perverse they may be from the moral point of view. You don't have to do it physically at all. If you have the opportunity to do it creatively, then there's more to it than just an outlet—you actually get pleasure out of it, you acquire obsessions that give you a different set of values. You don't have to act aggressively toward others, you don't have to pay high psychiatrists' fees. This area is undiscovered or, as always, only accessible to the privileged. But what I'm describing now—and it occurs to me while I'm saying it—is the understanding that comes from the later phase of a civilization that, in the midst of a prosperous society, is weary of growth and yet aware that growth must go on far into the future, because if it did not, other duties —for instance, the obligation to the Third World—would be pushed to one side. Apart from economic considerations, I would really only like to reduce growth for this reason, that in individual countries and individual peoples, man's play instinct falls short.

MORAES: You said earlier that people should not consider that they have failed in confronting all these catastrophes and so on. But in view of these catastrophes that are on our horizon now, do you feel a sensation of fear and apprehension of what may come in the next few years? For example, your little daughter, do you feel afraid about what life may be like for her when she has grown up?

GRASS: I certainly do, and I speak to my children openly about it. Of course, they get their idealistic injections all the time in this country and in these times, through their education at school and wherever else. I try to isolate the antidote and make my children familiar with realities as they are. I try to talk them out of believing the harmful antithesis of beautiful and ugly because I don't believe in the antithesis. I try to dissuade them from black-and-white thinking and to show them, not only artistically, that we have a rich scale of gray tones. And at the same time I try to show them that on the one hand there's no reason to go around proving your courage, but that on the other hand you shouldn't be afraid, because fear smells of fear, and when you show fear you invite heroics, and would-be heroes will smell you out.

INDEX